100 DAYS *of* REAL FOOD

ONE DOZEN
EGGS
REFRIGERATED

100 DAYS of REAL FOOD

HOW WE DID IT, WHAT WE LEARNED, AND
100 EASY, WHOLESOME RECIPES
YOUR FAMILY WILL LOVE

LISA LEAKE

wm
WILLIAM MORROW
An Imprint of HarperCollinsPublishers

The author is not a trained dietitian, nutritionist, chef, or medical professional. The information in this book is based on facts, research, and personal experiences. This information is not intended to diagnose, prevent, treat, or cure any disease. Never dismiss any advice your health physician gives. The author and the publisher will in no event be held liable for any loss or other damages including but not limited to special, incidental, consequential, or any other damages.

The advice in this book is intended for otherwise healthy individuals and should not take priority over advice from a doctor. Please remember though that not all doctors are created equal, so when in doubt get a second opinion.

The author's reference to various brands does not equal endorsement or sponsorship.

HarperCollins books may be purchased for educational, business, or sales promotional use. For information please e-mail the Special Markets Department at SPsales@harpercollins.com.

FIRST EDITION

Designed by Kris Tobiassen of Matchbook Digital
Food photography by Carrie Vitt
Lifestyle photography by Kelly Trimble
Photograph on page 247 by Heidi Darwish
Nutrients in Wheat Flour chart on page 17 courtesy of Oldways Preservation Trust and the Whole Grains Council, www.wholegrainscouncil.org
Whole Grain Stamps on page 18 are a trademark of Oldways Preservation Trust and the Whole Grains Council, www.wholegrainscouncil.org

Library of Congress Cataloging-in-Publication Data has been applied for.

ISBN 978-0-06-225255-5

14 15 16 17 18 ID/QG 10 9 8 7 6 5 4 3 2 1

To my amazing husband and daughters,

who have wholeheartedly supported me throughout this journey. You are the light of my life.

CONTENTS

Introduction: How It All Began

I was a child of the eighties raised in Tennessee by Midwestern parents who, like millions of others, didn't think too much about where their food came from. We were a fairly ordinary family who shopped at our local supermarket chain, ate boxed cereal (Golden Grahams and Honey Nut Cheerios were my favorites), made our sandwiches on white bread, went out for Chinese food, occasionally ordered pizza, and even celebrated my birthday with a party at McDonald's (pictured). A favorite family snack was Doritos topped with melted cheese.

That's not to say my parents didn't cook. My dad was actually the head chef of the house and frequently made risotto (with white rice) and homemade pasta (from white flour). I even remember him feeding us kids veal at a very young age. My mom wasn't as fond of cooking, so she was more likely to fall prey to convenience foods like cans of cream of mushroom soup, packets of seasoning mixes, and even the occasional frozen dinner. And while my parents served vegetables at our house, I clearly remember my brother making a point to never eat anything green (he made an exception for cupcake icing). His resistance became a family joke, and, while our parents often served vegetables with dinner, they never really insisted that eating them was a requirement.

While I was happily consuming the Standard American Diet at home in Tennessee, my husband, Jason, spent his first several years of life on his family's hippie commune in Oregon. It's hard to imagine anything more opposite to my childhood. If Jason's parents needed milk they got it from their cow; if they needed eggs they got them from their chickens; if they needed flour they ground it themselves; if they needed honey they'd get it from their beehive; if they needed clothes they went to the thrift store or fashioned their own; and if they needed a new barn they built it themselves (occasionally even naked!). After several years in Oregon my husband's family started moving around the country and ended up in South Carolina. Removed from their life in Oregon, they started consuming more "industrial" food, but they didn't totally forget their years of living off the land. My husband was the kid in the cafeteria with the "boring" whole-wheat sandwiches and no Little Debbie snacks. (Not being a huge vegetable or salad person myself, I once asked my mother-in-law if she really liked eating so many vegetables or if she just did it for her health.)

As a young adult I was one of the "lucky" ones who could eat whatever I wanted and easily get away with it. So I did. I've always had a very big sweet tooth—and still do—but in the old days I wouldn't hesitate to satisfy it with Nutty Bars, Swiss Rolls, Snickers bars, homemade chocolate chip cookies, and—even as a new mom—handfuls of brightly colored Skittles.

I wasn't a total junk food junkie, though. I was adamant that our two daughters eat at least one type of fruit (conventionally grown, of course) at both breakfast and lunch and at least one vegetable with dinner. I did feed them Kraft macaroni and cheese mixed with cut-up highly processed hot dogs (just as when I was a kid), but my rule was *no more than once a week*. Looking back I honestly don't know why I had such a rule. I certainly wouldn't have been able to explain it, but something about giving them too much Easy Mac just didn't feel right. I also had my limits on fast food restaurants and long ago voluntarily gave up on some of the more notorious ones like McDonald's and Taco Bell.

While I enjoyed cooking and had the inclination and desire to feed my family healthy foods, in reality, I was only buying foods that were "healthy" by food industry standards. I had never before read an ingredient label, never been to a farmers' market, never eaten an entire piece of whole-wheat bread, never shopped at a "health food" store, and never purchased anything that was organic (at least not on purpose). I could never have explained to you what it meant for something to be organic and why it mattered. And I certainly didn't understand all those "tree hugger" types who cared so much about it.

Meanwhile, my husband would routinely decline my "homemade" Aunt Jemima pancakes topped with highly processed pancake "syrup," request a separate loaf of bread so he could have his own whole-wheat sandwiches, and ask why I was buying junk food for the kids when I purchased something like Go-Gurt (it was just yogurt, right?). He likes to give me a hard time by saying he'd been trying to tell me for years to change my ways—especially since I do the meal planning and food shopping for our family. But I never really believed him until one day I also heard it on *Oprah*. Yep, *Oprah*.

I was just minding my own business one evening when an Oprah show came on entitled

"Food 101 with Michael Pollan." The day's topic—"Where Our Food Comes From"—was alarming because I suddenly realized I had no clue. And even though it was tempting to just continue living in the dark, I turned on the show and simply could not look away, nor could I "unlearn" the shocking information I was hearing. I was so intrigued by Michael Pollan's common sense about highly processed foods and why they should be avoided that I went out and grabbed the only book of his that was available at our library at the time, *In Defense of Food*. My husband followed suit, and together we also watched the documentary *Food, Inc.*

What I continued to learn was shocking and frankly kept me up at night. Pollan was calling the packaged foods that I thought were healthy "food-like substances." He explained that these "foods" were specifically designed never to rot, causing a disturbing increase in diet-related illnesses, and were nowhere near resembling the wholesome foods our ancestors had survived on for centuries before us.

I was overwhelmed just looking at our pantry. How could the Goldfish and pretzels I was feeding my kids basically be refined junk food with very little nutritional value? What in the world would they eat as a snack if those were no longer options? How could the "strawberry" syrup I was using to flavor their milk not even have "strawberries" as an ingredient? And how could I switch to whole-grain bread and pasta if I hated the taste?

My husband assured me that we didn't have to change our eating habits overnight, but I was on a mission. Now that I knew better, how could I spend even one more day feeding my precious children produce that was sprayed with chemicals, meat from unhealthy feedlot animals, and factory-made "fruit" snacks with no real fruit in them?

I dragged my husband (who was a step ahead of me in knowledge) and two young children to every supermarket in the area. I'd go down every single aisle and say, "Okay, what can we eat in this section?" These outings were painful at times, but I had to start reading ingredient labels to figure out what crackers we could buy, what cereals were okay, where we could purchase acceptable meat, and what breads we should avoid. I had to completely relearn how to food shop and cook for my family now that we were trying to avoid white flour, white sugar, conventional produce, factory farmed meats, and packaged foods with more than five ingredients, and I'm not going to lie . . . it wasn't exactly a good time.

I was obsessed with telling friends and family members about our new mission and even convinced my parents to read *In Defense of Food*. Like many of our friends, they thought I sounded a little crazy all of a sudden, but luckily they didn't write me off just yet. I felt certain that if others were informed they'd also want to make dramatic changes to their eating habits. And if I could share everything I'd learned they wouldn't have to go through the same difficult transition we did to figure out how to find the real food in this processed-food world.

So in 2010 I decided to devise a plan to help me get the word out to as many people as possible. I convinced my husband and daughters that we should take a 100 Days of Real Food pledge, for which we would follow strict food rules (no matter if we were home, traveling, eating out, or at a friend's house) and blog about it. (If you want to take a look, it's still available at 100daysofrealfood.com.) The idea was to draw attention to how much our society has come to depend on highly processed food. We wanted to prove that a typical family in the suburbs of Charlotte—not exactly a real-food mecca—could in fact survive and thrive without processed food.

I remember a good friend saying to me, "What's your plan? How are you guys really going to do this?" I honestly didn't have a grand plan, and we hesitantly dove right into our first week by hosting a neighborhood barbecue at our house (featuring local, grass-fed burgers on specially ordered 100 percent whole-grain five-ingredient buns), having our first real-food lunch at a restaurant (after asking loads of questions, of course), and sending my husband off on a business trip (with a bag full of "emergency" snacks in tow). And with that, my food blogging career and life-changing experiment truly began.

Each time we ran into a roadblock on our 100 Days of Real Food journey, like our daughter's dramatic meltdown over a forbidden doughnut or having to spend hours figuring out how to pack enough "approved" food to simply leave our house, I had serious doubts. Maybe this little experiment of ours was a bit crazy and over the top after all. Maybe involving—and restricting—our two young daughters wasn't exactly the right thing to do. But, about a month into our 100 Days of Real Food pledge, my feelings took a sharp turn. On day 33 of our pledge, my older daughter, who was five at the time, and I found ourselves waiting in line for a cup of water at a concession stand. Just as we were staring at all the display cases full of candy bars and flavored potato chips and hot items being served such as chicken nuggets, fries, and hot dogs, she of course announced that she was hungry (shocker!). So I said, "We can't have any of this right now, but I promise I will give you something as soon as we get home." Then a few minutes later my daughter proudly said, "Look, Mom, they have a basket of bananas over there on the counter. Can I have one of those?" Right then and there I realized I was not only teaching my child to spot, but also to want, the one and only whole food in sight.

I was finally starting to appreciate how far we'd come. I could see a clear picture of all we'd gained—what a positive impact this experience was having on our health and the lives of our children. We almost immediately witnessed an improvement in our daughter's constipation, a decrease in her episodes of wheezing, an increase in my energy level, some pounds lost by both my husband and me, and a dramatic improvement in my good cholesterol; it was hard not to wonder what other underlying changes were taking place.

I didn't expect that our pledge would have such a big impact on me personally. When I was prepping for the 100 Days pledge, I moved a big bag of candy and highly processed treats into our guest room closet to save for when our pledge was over. But much to my surprise, about halfway through, I got out that big bag of candy and chucked the whole thing into the garbage. If we were just fine without it for that long, what was the point of bringing it back into our kitchen again?

When I started the 100 Days of Real Food pledge, I imagined us making our point, hopefully having an impact on some other unsuspecting families, and then going along on our merry way. I could have never anticipated that our little project would attract millions of readers from all over the world and that years later I would still have so much to say about it. As it turns out, this is much more about a necessary lifestyle change—one that so many others are waking up to each day—than it is about a three-month experiment. If you'd told me a few years ago that I'd be writing a book—about eating right, no less—I would have thought you were absolutely and utterly crazy. And my husband would have agreed.

I'm not sure exactly why, but from the beginning I've always felt extremely passionate about spreading this important message. From the very start I felt compelled to share my extensive research, newly adapted recipes, and findings with others. And one thing I've learned throughout this journey is that a deep passion like this can take you to some pretty amazing—and unexpected—places. So with that, it's time to let your own real-food journey begin.

WHAT'S IN THIS BOOK

The goal of this book is to convince you that cutting out highly processed food is the right thing to do and, more important, that it can be done. Whether you work full time, have multiple kids, adhere to a tight budget, don't live near a farmers' market, are a single parent, or take classes in the evenings, with some guidance and preplanning you *can* make some pretty dramatic changes that will eventually become your new normal. With this book as your companion and guide, you can transition to real food while leaving your sanity very much intact.

This first half of the book is a guide that will lead you through your own real-food transformation (and a reference that you can refer back to as needed). If you don't remember everything there is to know about real food the first time you hear it, you're not alone! The book details the differences between real food and processed food, how to read ingredient labels, where to begin in your own kitchen, and how to shop for real food (even if you're on a budget). It includes tips on making your transition a smooth one—and on convincing your reluctant spouse and picky kids to join you. And the second half of the book features more than 100 tasty, easy, family-friendly real-food recipes that will even make the newest home cooks look like stars in the kitchen. We're talking makeovers of recipes your family already loves (like tacos, mac and cheese, pancakes, and barbecued ribs), using ingredients you're familiar with and probably even own already.

If you want more inspiration as you dive into *100 Days of Real Food*—the book and the mission!—I highly recommend reading *In Defense of Food* by Michael Pollan and seeing the documentary *Food, Inc.* And be sure to check out my blog (100daysofrealfood.com) and Facebook page (facebook.com/100daysofrealfood) for continued support, updates, and even more recipes. The blog is a true real-food community made up of millions of readers from all over the world, and we'd love for you to be a part of it as you begin your own real-food adventure!

PART ONE
THE PLAN

Information on Ingredense

if You went or are going to go to The Store to get dessert. But Stop right There Look at those ingredince. do you cook with hignogemated oilo? "No" well then would You like to eat it" "No" well then Why are you aboteto buy it if You Have know Idea What it is. So then Just make →

Page:

Your own if You do not want it. ok? "ok" good.

P.S. for a cake respea log on to 100 days of real food.com!

Second-grade assignment by Sydney Leake.

1. What Is Real Food?

Real-Food Tip: To find out if a packaged food is "real," you must read the ingredients.

It's tempting to dive right in and start cleaning out our pantries, but first there's a very important question we must address: What is "real" food, anyway?

When I first felt motivated to cut out processed food, I immediately started searching the Internet for things like "list of processed food" and "define: processed food." I was still learning about terminology; I even called a grain company to inquire if their flours and grains were "processed." The owner seemed confused by my question, and no wonder: unless you're eating wheat berries right off the stalk, there has to be some processing involved. The word I was looking for was "refined." Even cooking is technically a form of processing or changing your food. To say we avoid all "processed" foods would actually mean we're on a strict raw-food diet, which our family is not. So to more accurately describe eating real food we should probably say we avoid all "highly" processed food. And just to be clear, my definition of real food has evolved over time, so check the sidebar on page 10 to see the exact rules we followed during our 100 Days pledge.

REAL FOOD IS . . .

- **Whole food** that typically has only one ingredient, like "brown rice," or no ingredient label at all, as with fruits and vegetables!
- Packaged foods made with **no more than five unrefined ingredients**
- **Dairy products** like whole milk, unsweetened yogurt, eggs, and cheese

- Breads and crackers that are **100 percent whole grain**
- **Wild-caught seafood**
- Locally and humanely raised **pastured meat products** like chicken, pork, beef, and lamb
- **Dried fruits, nuts, and seeds**
- Naturally made sweeteners including **honey and maple syrup**
- More a **product of nature** than a "product of industry"[1]

REAL FOOD IS NOT . . .

- Labeled as **"low-fat"** or **"low-carb"** or **"low-calorie"** (in most cases)
- Made with **refined sweeteners** like white sugar, brown sugar, organic sugar, cane juice, or corn syrup **or artificial sweeteners** like aspartame or sucralose (brand names: Equal and Splenda)
- **Deep fried in refined oils** like canola oil
- 100-calorie packs or any foods **made from refined grains** like white rice or white flour, which is often labeled as "wheat flour" without the word "whole"
- In packages with **loads of ingredients**, some of which you cannot pronounce, and, therefore, are most likely unwanted, refined additives and you would not cook with in your own kitchen

100 DAYS OF REAL FOOD PLEDGE RULES

The more I've learned, the more my diet has evolved. These are the exact rules we followed during our 2010 pledge:

- No refined grains; only 100% whole grain
- No refined or artificial sweeteners; only honey and pure maple syrup
- Nothing out of a package that contains more than five ingredients
- No factory-farmed meat; only locally raised meat products
- No deep-fried foods
- No fast food
- Beverages only to include water, milk, occasional all-natural juices, naturally sweetened coffee and tea, and (to help the adults keep their sanity) wine and beer in moderation!

- **Highly processed foods that are labeled as organic** (like organic Cheddar crackers, organic cookies, or organic candy)
- Meat from **factory-farmed animals**
- Most anything from a **drive-through window or gas station**

Before I started my 100 Days of Real Food pledge, I was confused about what foods were healthy—and I wasn't alone. Why? Well, what do you see when you walk up and down the aisles

"I think junk food is bad because it's like filling a new car with mud, but real food is like filling it with gas."—SYDNEY, AGE 9

of the supermarket? Thousands upon thousands of packaged foods labeled and advertised by the food industry to help you "lose weight," "lower your cholesterol," or "reduce your chances of heart disease." It's no wonder shoppers are inclined to choose processed food products adorned with all these appealing health claims.

Our society has become so dependent on packaged, processed foods that many of us have lost sight of the whole foods our ancestors survived on for centuries before us. In 2010, when our family decided to take the 100 Days pledge and strictly avoided all highly processed food and refined ingredients, the stunned reaction from friends and family said it all. People imagined that we would starve if we followed our rules, but once we stopped eating all those packaged foods loaded with refined oils, sugar, and salt, we truly started to appreciate and prefer the taste of fresh, seasonal, simple, whole foods. We actually felt as if we were getting spoiled by wholesome, filling meals that tasted exceptionally good and fresh.

Meanwhile, ask five people on the street what it means to eat "healthy" and you'll get ten different answers. Today's popular diets often require you to eat fake, nasty-tasting, low-fat "health" foods, which regrettably have given "eating right" a pretty bad rap. Millions of people have good intentions but waste their time counting calories, eating manufactured "low-fat" foods, adding up points, tracking protein intake, avoiding gluten (without a true allergy or sensitivity), or eating organic junk food. Before taking our real-food pledge we were just as guilty as the next family of feeling as if we were making "healthy" food choices when in fact those choices were actually highly processed and not healthy at all. And even worse, they threatened to strip away the joy of eating.

WHY AVOID HIGHLY PROCESSED FOOD?

You don't have to look very far these days to find both scary and sobering statistics about the declining health of our nation. Farmers' markets and organic food sales may be on the rise, but so are the number of food-related diseases like obesity, type 2 diabetes, heart disease, and even certain types of cancer. According to the Centers for Disease Control and Prevention, obesity in children "has more than tripled in the past thirty years."[2] In fact, as chef and healthy-eating advocate Jamie Oliver has stated, this is the first time in history that "our children have the destiny of a shorter life span than their own parents."[3] Think about that for a moment.

Our family felt compelled to dramatically change our diets because we thought it was the right thing to do. Here are the most compelling reasons behind our decision:

1. Processed foods are an illusion, often **appearing to be healthy** (with claims like low-fat, low-carb, vitamin-fortified, no trans fat, contains omega-3s, and so on) when these foods are in fact the very thing making a lot of Americans unhealthy, sick, and fat.

2. **Coronary heart disease, diabetes, stroke, and cancer**—four of the top ten chronic diseases that kill most of us—"can be traced directly to the industrialization of our food,"[4] according to Michael Pollan.

3. Making smarter—and sometimes more expensive—food choices *now* may **reduce your healthcare costs** later in life.

4. Why would one want to eat a processed food-like substance that has been scientifically **designed never to rot**? Shelf life is high priority in the food industry, but it's about profit, not health.

5. The food industry adds **way too much salt, sugar, and/or oil** to almost everything it makes—far more than you'd allow if you were cooking it yourself.

6. When we eat white bread and other foods made with white flour, a highly processed version of wheat, we're basically consuming **empty calories** with far less nutrition than the whole-wheat or whole-grain alternatives provide.

7. It's estimated that up to **90 percent of processed foods in the supermarket contain either a corn or soy ingredient**[5] in the form of an additive under an array of different names. Since the majority of corn and soy in our country have been genetically modified, this puts you at a high risk of eating GMOs (see page 28 for more info).

8. Cutting out processed foods could lead you to experience a variety of **health benefits** such as having more energy, losing weight, improving cholesterol levels, helping with regularity, reducing sicknesses and ailments, or just feeling healthier overall.

9. Rather than counting calories, watching fat grams, or reducing carbs for "healthy eating," simply eat whole foods that are more a product of nature than "of industry." It certainly is **less complicated**.

10. It just makes plain old sense to **fully understand the foods you're eating**, to be able to pronounce everything on the list of ingredients (if there is a list), and to know exactly where that food comes from . . . don't you think?

REAL-FOOD IMPACT ON OUR HEALTH

We created our real-food pledge to help draw attention to how dependent our society has become on processed food. But I didn't expect how big an impact this experience would have on me personally, and how many unexpected—and positive—changes would be made to our health, including the following:

- **Constipation reversed:** Our younger daughter's constipation completely went away within five days of cutting out all highly processed food. And other family members have experienced improved GI symptoms as well . . . let's just say we all seem to be pretty regular in that department.

- **Improvement in asthma:** Our younger daughter also suffers from mild asthma, and her episodes of wheezing suddenly reduced from approximately five per year (in 2009) to less than one per year.

- **Reduction in sicknesses:** This same daughter was no stranger to illness. In 2009, between bronchitis, croup, ear infections, fevers, and asthma, she seemed to be sick as often as she was healthy. Since switching to real food, her health has improved dramatically, and even when someone does get sick around here—we of course aren't invincible—it seems to be less severe and somewhat short-lived.

- **Better cholesterol levels:** In my 2009 annual physical my HDL level (aka the "good" cholesterol that you want to be a high number) was at 52.9. A little more than a year later, after cutting out highly processed food and not dramatically changing anything else like exercise routines, my HDL level jumped up by almost 50 percent to 79! As my doctor explained it to me, HDL levels greater than 60 are considered to be a "positive risk factor" when it comes to your cardiac health. A positive risk factor can essentially cancel out a negative risk factor, such as smoking cigarettes. So in short, my risk for heart disease when consuming highly processed foods is similar to what it would be eating real food and being a smoker. Shocking, huh?

- **More energy:** Overall I have more energy and need less sleep in order to feel rested. I've also mostly said good-bye to those unpleasant afternoon slumps.

- **Weight loss:** My husband lost about ten pounds during our real-food pledge and I lost a few as well. This was not a goal of ours, but we both did have a small bit of excess we were happy to let go of.

- **Change in palate:** In addition to our health changes, our palates have adjusted to the point where we have much less desire for the junk. Sometimes people will say to me, with pity, "Oh, you *can't* have those packaged cheese crackers or that candy," but what they don't understand is that I no longer even *want* that stuff. I no longer have the desire for highly processed, artificial-tasting junk food. It just does not taste good to me anymore. But what *does* taste exceptionally good is simple, fresh, real, whole foods, including homemade desserts on occasion.

READING INGREDIENT LABELS: THE ONLY WAY TO KNOW WHAT'S REALLY IN YOUR FOOD

The very best place to begin the transition to real food is in your very own pantry, fridge, and freezer. So pull out all the food products you own onto your kitchen counter and see how they stack up against what you learn in this section.

When considering packaged food the best rule of thumb is to **look for products made with five or fewer *whole* ingredients.** When it comes to additives, look for ingredients you are familiar with and would cook with at home—and don't forget that the order of ingredients matters (the ingredient that weighs the most is listed first).

WEIGHT LOSS AND REAL FOOD

Is it possible to lose weight without counting calories or fat grams *and* while eating full-fat dairy? Why, yes, it is possible. The key to maintaining a healthy weight while eating real food is portion control. See page 75 for details.

UNDERSTANDING GRAINS—AND WHY 100 PERCENT WHOLE GRAIN IS BEST

Identifying and understanding whole grains (including wheat, corn, rice, oats, and so on) is one of the biggest challenges for consumers. We see the word "wheat" on bread packages and we might assume it's healthy. When we're offered "white or wheat" toast at a diner, we might go for the "healthier" choice of wheat. But "wheat" isn't the word that matters; both white bread and "wheat" bread are made from the wheat plant.

So, what's the real-food choice here? One hundred percent whole wheat. **Unless you specifically see the word "whole" in front of the word "wheat," you're looking at a highly processed product that won't give you the full benefit of whole grains.**

Let's put this first lesson into practice with an ingredient label for Whitewheat brand sandwich bread from Nature's Own. Take just one look and you'll see there's nothing *whole* wheat about it.

Ingredients: UNBLEACHED ENRICHED WHEAT FLOUR [FLOUR, MALTED BARLEY FLOUR, NIACIN, REDUCED IRON, THIAMIN MONONITRATE (VITAMIN B_1), RIBOFLAVIN (VITAMIN B_2), FOLIC ACID (A B VITAMIN)], WATER, SUGAR, FIBER (SOY FIBER AND/OR COTTONSEED FIBER), WHEAT GLUTEN, YEAST, CONTAINS 2% OR LESS OF EACH OF THE FOLLOWING: CALCIUM SULFATE, CALCIUM CARBONATE, VEGETABLE OIL (SOYBEAN OIL OR CANOLA OIL), SALT, SOY FLOUR, DOUGH CONDITIONERS (SODIUM STEAROYL LACTYLATE, CALCIUM STEAROYL-2-LACTYLATE, MONOGLYCERIDES, CALCIUM IODATE, ETHOXYLATED MONO AND DIGLYCERIDES, CALCIUM PEROXIDE, DATEM, AZO-

"The more ingredients in a packaged food, the more highly processed it probably is."
—MICHAEL POLLAN

DICARBONAMIDE), CULTURED WHEAT FLOUR, GUAR GUM, VINEGAR, FERROUS SULFATE, THIAMIN HYDROCHLORIDE, MONOCALCIUM PHOSPHATE, YEAST FOOD (AMMONIUM SULFATE), SOY LECITHIN, 050710.[6]

I used to be strictly a white-bread girl myself (I was actually a loyal customer of Nature's Own Whitewheat bread). I had certainly tried "whole-wheat" bread, which I of course referred to as "wheat" bread at the time, but to be honest I absolutely despised the taste. I realize now that I didn't care for it because I'd never actually tried *good* whole-wheat bread before. It takes only four or five ingredients to make real whole-wheat sandwich bread, yet factory-made loaves, which have been specifically formulated to hold up on grocery store shelves, have as many as forty ingredients on the label. What is all that other "stuff," anyway? A lot of the additives I can't even pronounce.

Before our switch to real food it never even occurred to me to read the ingredient labels, which is actually the best way to determine how highly processed a food is. If I happened to look at the back of a package, it was to check the nutrition facts panel to somehow magically determine how "nutritious" that food choice was for my family. I even remember comparing the nutrition facts panel on my husband's grocery store whole-wheat bread with my loaf of white bread and determining that my "enriched" bread was more nutritious and therefore "healthier" than his. Talk about misleading!

When the wheat plant is refined and milled into white flour, "most of the grain's nutritional value is lost" during the process,[7] which is why those flours are required to be "enriched." Whole-wheat flour is far more nutritious, so food scientists have to manually add back in the vitamins and nutrients that are now believed to be "missing" from white flour. But how can food scien-

WHY THE 5-INGREDIENT RULE?

We had to draw the line somewhere, and the suggestion of five ingredients (borrowed from Michael Pollan's book *Food Rules*) sounded like a good place to do it. It's important to mention though that this rule does not apply to recipes you cook at home yourself . . . only the packaged factory-made stuff. And there are certainly packaged foods that contain six or seven or even eight whole and therefore "approved" ingredients on the list, like a trail mix made with unsweetened dried fruit and nuts. Then on the flip side there are packaged foods with only three or four ingredients that wouldn't make the cut, like some ice cream varieties. So no matter what—you still have to read the ingredients.

tists truly re-create what nature has given us? Less than a hundred years ago food scientists didn't even know that micronutrients (vitamins) existed, so how can we know what other features found in whole grains (and other real food) aren't yet understood?[8] This is one of the many reasons we choose foods that are as close to their natural and original state as possible.

WHY WHOLE GRAIN REALLY IS BETTER

In 2003 the *American Journal of Clinical Nutrition* published a study that found "a diet rich in whole grains did in fact reduce mortality from all causes." But even after giving subjects refined grains along with the enriched nutrients thought to be missing, they "were not as healthy as the whole-grain eaters."[9]

A Breakdown of the Most Popular Grains

Virtually all grains can be broken down into three parts: the germ, the bran, and the endosperm. **When grains are refined into products like white flour, both the germ and bran are removed, leaving you with just the endosperm,** which Michael Pollan says is "the big packet of starch and [a little] protein in a seed." The endosperm is "nutritionally worthless, or nearly so," which, again, is why refined grains are required to be enriched.[10]

Finding whole-grain products in the supermarket can be tricky for the average consumer. One important thing to understand is that a number of "whole-grain" products, in both supermarkets and restaurants, are not actually 100 percent whole grain. Even breads and crackers containing only 20 percent whole-grain flour along with 80 percent refined-grain flour could technically have a whole-grain claim on the front. Eating some whole grains is certainly better than none, but don't be fooled by misleading claims on the package.

WHOLE GRAIN

Whole grain = Bran, germ, endosperm
Refined grain = Endosperm only

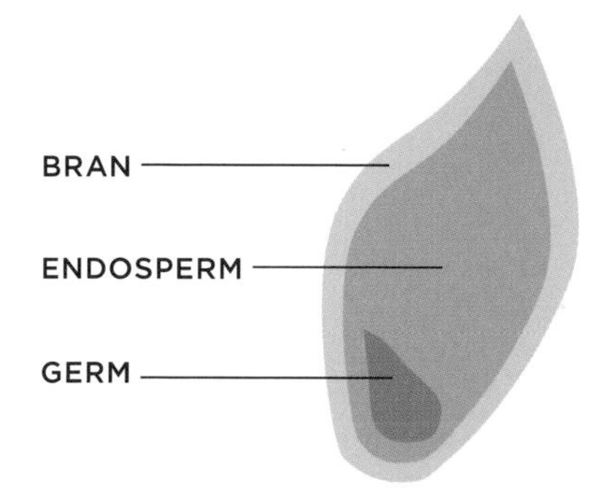

NUTRIENTS IN WHEAT FLOUR: WHOLE, REFINED, AND ENRICHED

Refining wheat flour removes many nutrients, including those listed here. Enriching replaces five nutrients.

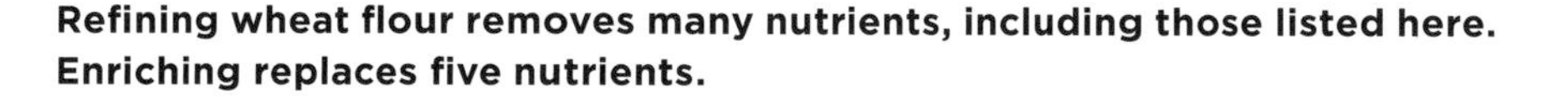

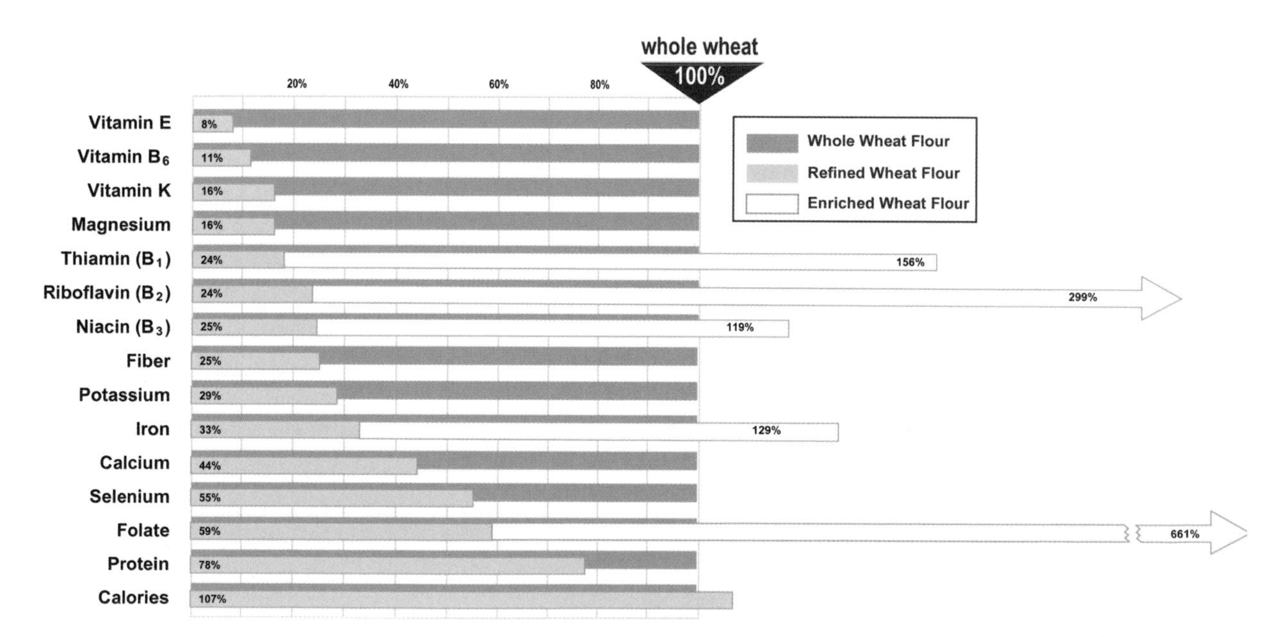

Here's what to look for (and avoid) when reading ingredient labels:

Wheat

- **Whole Grain** = Whole wheat, whole grain wheat, whole durum wheat (*must* say the word "whole" and ideally be 100 percent)
- **Refined** = White flour, wheat, wheat flour, enriched flour, semolina

The Whole Grain Stamp, launched by the Whole Grains Council and currently used on more than seven thousand food packages around the world, comes in both a basic version and a 100 percent version. While I still recommend always reading the ingredient labels, the Whole Grain Stamp can be a helpful resource to confirm if the product you are considering is in fact made with whole grains.

- If a product bears the **100% Stamp**, then *all* its grain ingredients are *whole* grains.
- If a product bears the **Basic Stamp**, a single serving contains at least 8 grams (8g) of whole grain but may also contain some refined grains.[11]

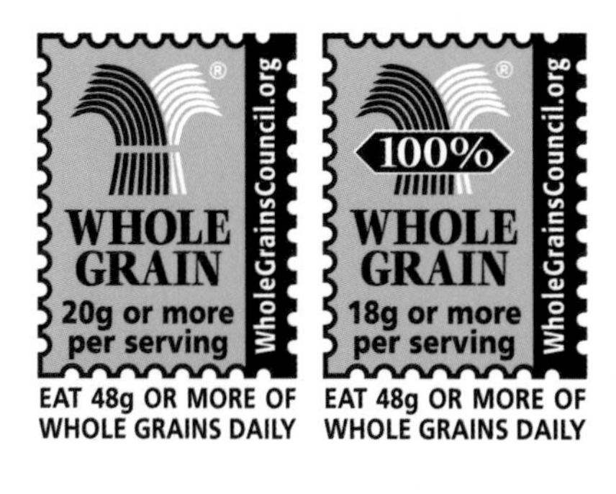

Corn

- **Whole Grain** = Whole-grain corn, whole-grain cornmeal, whole-grain corn flour (also called masa harina), and even popcorn
- **Refined** = Cornmeal, enriched cornmeal, corn flour, degerminated corn, (most) grits, and cornstarch

Rice

- **Whole Grain** = Brown rice and colored rice (like black or purple)
- **Refined** = "Rice" and all white rice (this includes basmati, Arborio, jasmine, short grain, and so on)

Oats

- **Whole Grain** = All oats (rolled, steel-cut, quick-cooking, etc.), whole oat flour
- **Refined** = Oat bran, low bran (aka debranned or extracted) oat flour, refined oat flour

Other grains that are usually only sold unrefined (aka as whole grain) include quinoa, spelt, rye, amaranth, millet, and buckwheat. Note: When it comes to barley, it's a whole grain, but pearl barley is not.

Grain Vocabulary: A Summary

- **Multi-Grain:** Made with more than one grain, which could be either refined or whole. This term alone does not indicate whether any of the grains are whole.

- **Whole-Grain:** Grains that contain all three parts: bran, germ, and endosperm. Products containing more refined grains than whole grains can be labeled as "whole grain," so always check the ingredient list (or look for the "100% Whole Grain" stamp) to determine if the product is actually 100 percent whole grain.
- **Whole-Wheat:** The whole-grain version of wheat; 100 percent whole wheat is your wheat of choice on a real-food pledge.
- **Wheat or Wheat Flour:** The refined version of wheat (aka white flour), which is left with just the endosperm. Unless the word "whole" is clearly stated along with "wheat," then it's refined white flour.
- **Enriched Wheat or Enriched Wheat Flour:** This describes refined wheat (aka white flour) that has been enriched with vitamins. Any time the word "enriched" is used, it's a good indicator the grain has been refined.
- **Rice:** The word "rice" all by itself specifies white—or refined—rice. Whole-grain rice will list a color, such as "brown rice" or "black rice."
- **Semolina:** A variety of wheat that's been refined and commonly used to make pasta. The whole-grain version of semolina is typically listed as "whole durum wheat."
- **Gluten-Free:** Gluten is a protein found in many grains (including wheat, spelt, kamut, farro, durum, bulgur, semolina, barley, rye, and triticale) that some people are allergic or sensitive to, such as those with celiac disease. Similar to the "multi-grain" term, "gluten-free" does not indicate whether any of the grains used are whole. Gluten-free whole grains include amaranth, buckwheat, whole corn, montina (Indian rice grass), oats (only if marked gluten-free), quinoa, brown rice, sorghum, and teff.[12] I don't feel there is any reason to avoid gluten unless you have a specific sensitivity or allergy to it (i.e., feel better not eating it).

Be sure to check out page 32 for some examples of reading labels and Chapter 2 for a list of "real-food approved" whole-grain options.

THE PROBLEM WITH SUGAR

The problem with sugar is honestly not sugar itself, but the quantity in which it's being consumed. Over the last few decades our consumption of sugar has skyrocketed to "nearly 130 pounds of added sugars per person, per year," which is one-third pound (or two-thirds cup) per day![13] That's as much as four times more than the American Heart Association's recommended daily amount of six teaspoons of added sugar for women, nine for men, and three for children.[14] According to chef and author Mark Bittman, "Added sugar . . . is the tobacco of the twenty-first century" and "probably the most dangerous part of our current diet."[15]

A TYPICAL KID'S LUNCH-BOX MEAL

Uncrustable (peanut butter and strawberry jam on white bread)	= 9 grams of sugar
2.25-ounce Go-Gurt yogurt tube	= 10 grams of sugar
8-ounce package honey-flavored Teddy Grahams	= 7 grams of sugar
8-ounce Horizon Organic chocolate milk box	= 22 grams of sugar
TOTAL without including an actual dessert or treat	= 48 grams of sugar*

**As of this writing, there is no way to determine how many grams are "added sugar" versus naturally occurring sugar. The recommended daily allowance of added sugar for children is 3 teaspoons (equivalent to 1 tablespoon or approximately 12 grams).[16]*

One of the biggest concerns is that many people don't realize how much added sugar they're actually consuming. According to the Sugar Association, "Thirty years ago the number of ingredients used to sweeten foods and beverages could be counted on one hand. Today, there are twenty-five ingredients used to replace sugar."[17] You might think you're in the clear if you simply avoid sweets, but added sugar lurks in some pretty unexpected places, including salad dressings, dried fruit, spaghetti sauces, breads, cereals, condiments, flavored yogurts, beverages, and even crackers. And since added sugar is now listed under many different names, it's often tricky to find it on the ingredient label. Some examples of added sugar are words ending in "-ose," such as maltose or sucrose,[18] and others such as high-fructose corn syrup, molasses, cane sugar, corn sweetener, raw sugar, maple syrup, brown rice syrup, agave, cane juice, honey, or fruit juice concentrates.

NATURALLY OCCURRING VERSUS ADDED SUGAR

The best way to determine if a product contains added sugar is to check the list of ingredients. As of this writing, the grams of sugar listed on the nutrition label reflect not only added sugar but also any naturally occurring sugar, which is not a concern and is found in foods like fruit, yogurt, and milk. So while the number of grams is a good indicator of how sweet a product may be, in most cases you unfortunately can't tell how much of it is added (refined) sugar.

Nature does a good job of packaging whole fruit with the right sweetness and also the right amount of fiber, which slows absorption.[19] But watch out for fruit juice; even "natural" single-ingredient fruit juices don't typically contain the whole fruit, and therefore the juice is mainly just the natural sugars from the apple (for example) in concentrated form without the fiber you get from eating a whole

> ## NUTRITION FACTS LABEL VS. INGREDIENT LABEL
> ### (with one sweet exception)
>
> Before our switch to real food I read only the nutrition facts label on food packages, but now I almost exclusively read the ingredient label . . . with one exception. When I see that a product contains some form of added sweetener, I immediately check the nutrition facts label to see how much of it the product contains. This figure does reflect both added and naturally occurring sweeteners, but if the nutrition label says it only has one or two grams of sugar per serving (total), I'm not going to lose sleep over it.

apple. A simple fruit (or vegetable) juice without added sugar is okay on occasion, especially if you water it down a little, but fruit juice is best avoided for daily use unless you're making it yourself in a high-powered blender that uses the whole fruit. With most home juicers, all that good fiber ends up in the garbage or compost heap.

We chose honey and maple syrup as the only approved real-food sweeteners during our 100 Days pledge for a few reasons. First, while they are still both "sugars," they're two of the least-processed sweeteners available, since they're both mostly "processed" in nature. Second, they contain trace nutrients that you won't find in refined sweeteners such as white sugar. Third, and most important, they're less likely to be found in factory-made packaged foods, so by default, if you want something sweet, you're going to have to make it yourself. As a result, you'll eat sweet foods less often and be able to control the quantity of added sweetener when you do.

According to the American Heart Association, "Naturally occurring sugars are found *naturally* in foods such as fruit (fructose) and milk (lactose). Added sugars are sugars and syrups put in foods during preparation or processing, or added at the table."[20] As of this writing, you cannot determine by looking at the nutritional label alone if the grams of sugar are naturally occurring or added (and in most cases refined) sugars. But you can see if a product contains added sugars by looking for them on the ingredient label (under a variety of names).

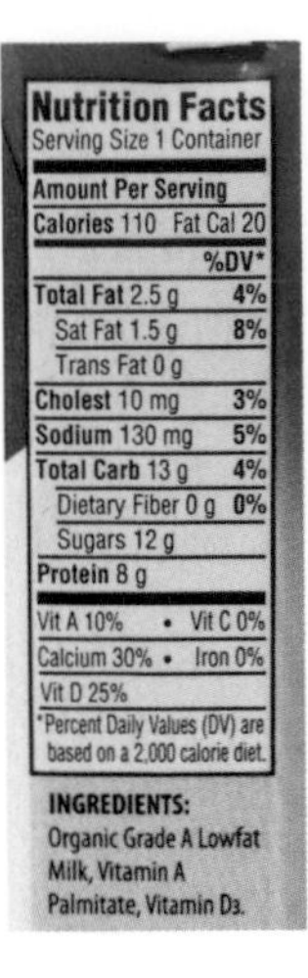

Example 1: An 8-ounce serving of Horizon Organic plain milk contains 12 grams of "sugars" according to the nutrition label, but there are no added sugars listed on the ingredient label, so all 12 grams are naturally occurring.[21]

Example 2: A 6-ounce serving of mixed berry-flavor Yoplait yogurt contains 26 grams of "sugars" according to the nutrition label, but since dairy has naturally occurring sugar and there is also "sugar" listed on the ingredient label, it's impossible to determine exactly how many grams are added (although one could guess by comparing a similar-size container of plain yogurt).[22]

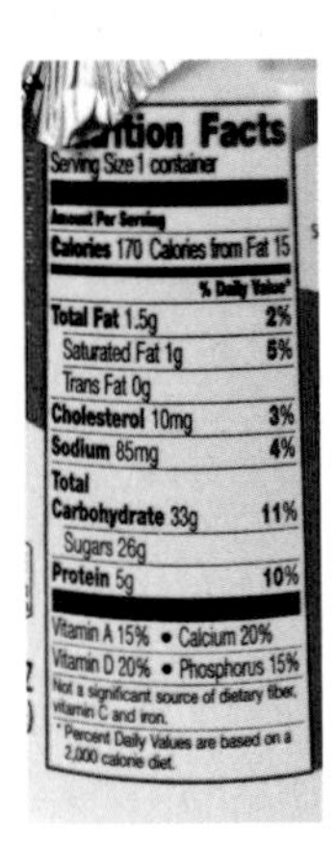

Here's the bottom line:

No matter what sweetener you choose, whether it's more natural or processed, you and your family should consume it in moderation. Just because less processed sweeteners like honey and pure maple syrup may contain trace nutrients that make them a better choice overall, they're still pretty much empty calories.

My two basic rules when it comes to sweeteners

1. Avoid the artificial stuff (see next page).
2. Added sugar is added sugar, no matter what variety you choose.

WHAT'S WRONG WITH ARTIFICIAL INGREDIENTS?

Artificial ingredients are at the top of my personal list of items to avoid. It's not to say it doesn't happen on occasion, but I do my best when it comes to sweeteners such as aspartame, sucralose, and saccharin; food dyes such as FD&C Red No. 40, FD&C Yellow No. 5, and Tartrazine; and artificial flavors such as vanillin (see how tricky they are?).

IDENTIFYING ARTIFICIAL SWEETENERS

Even though we do our best to avoid white (refined) sugar, I'd personally rather eat that (i.e., the real thing) over artificial sweeteners any day. And that's because, in a similar fashion to artificial food dyes, they are chemically manufactured molecules that do not exist in nature—basically the opposite of real, traditional food—and can pose health risks.

When a packaged food is touted as "sugar free," that often means the real sugar has been replaced with an artificial sweetener. So how can

> **LISA'S TIP:** Artificial sweeteners are not included in the sugar gram count on the nutrition label. They may not add calories, but that doesn't mean they're good for you!

you tell what's really in there? Read the ingredient label, of course. And this one is not as easy as it sounds, so here's a little cheat sheet to help you out.

COMMON U.S. ARTIFICIAL SWEETENERS

Brand Name *Usually sold in boxes/packets*	**Generic Brand Name*** *Terms used on ingredient labels*
NutraSweet Equal	Aspartame
Splenda	Sucralose
Sweet 'N Low Sugar Twin Necta Sweet	Saccharin
Sunett Sweet One	Acesulfame K *(also listed as Acesulfame Potassium)*
N/A	Neotame

**These generic versions are currently the five FDA-approved artificial sweeteners on the market.*

WHY I HATE ARTIFICIAL FOOD DYES

- They're made in a lab with chemicals derived from petroleum, a crude-oil non-food product that also happens to be used in gasoline, diesel fuel, asphalt, and tar.[23]
- They've been linked to long-term health problems such as cancer.[24]
- Synthetic food dyes have been shown to cause an increase in hyperactivity in children as well as a negative impact on their ability to learn.[25] As a result, a warning label is required when these dyes are used in the United Kingdom: It reads, "May have an adverse effect on activity and attention in children."[26] They add absolutely no nutritional value to the foods we are eating, while they do introduce serious risks.[27]
- They confuse the senses we rely on to evaluate new foods, just as other artificial additives do, including sweeteners.[28]
- They contribute to the obesity epidemic by attracting children (and adults) to highly processed food, which an increasing number of people are eating instead of fresh whole foods, and in increasing amounts.[29]

WHAT ABOUT SWEETENERS SUCH AS STEVIA, AGAVE NECTAR, AND XYLITOL?

There are a lot of different sweeteners on the market these days and most leave me feeling pretty skeptical. Natural, no-calorie sweeteners that you've never heard of until now should raise a red flag. Products like Truvia are a far cry from their natural source (the stevia leaf), and most agave nectars are unfortunately just as processed as corn syrup. Xylitol is a perfect example a "newer" substance that has to be treated and processed before being added to foods. The moral of the story is, if it sounds too good to be true—it probably is!

WHY LOW-FAT (AND FAT-FREE) PRODUCTS ARE NOT REAL FOOD

When I first learned that the low-fat campaign was pretty much bogus, I was absolutely shocked. For years I was on that bandwagon myself, splurging on everything from low-fat SnackWell's cookies to fat-free flavored yogurt to low-fat sour cream. And as it turns out, according to Mark Bittman, "The low-fat craze caused millions, maybe tens of millions, of Americans actually to gain weight."[30]

It does start to make sense, though, once you look back at how dietary guidelines have changed over time—and how those changes align with declining health in America. In the 1970s, according to Dr. Robert Lustig, a professor of pediatrics at the University of California, San Francisco and author of *Fat Chance: Beating the Odds Against Sugar, Processed Food, Obesity, and Disease*, "a government commission mandated that we lower fat consumption to try and reduce heart disease. . . . And we did. And guess what? Heart disease, metabolic syndrome, diabetes and death are skyrocketing. That's primarily because we replaced a lot of that fat with added sugars. Take the fat out of food, it tastes like cardboard. And the Food Industry knew that. So they replaced it with sugar."[31]

When you strip food of its natural fat content, it's more highly processed by definition. According to Michael Pollan, "To make dairy products low fat, it's not enough to remove the fat. You then have to go to great lengths to preserve the body or creamy texture by working in all kinds of food additives. In the case of low-fat or skim milk, that usually means adding powdered milk. But powdered milk contains oxidized cholesterol, which scientists believe is much worse for your arteries than ordinary cholesterol, so food makers sometimes compensate by adding antioxidants, further complicating what had been a simple one-ingredient whole food."[32]

So you're off the hook. No more blah-tasting "diet" food shall cross your plate again. Let's leave the low-fat craze behind us (including milk and other dairy products!) and move forward by embracing the right portions of whole, real food, and real food only.

WHAT TO LOOK FOR IN DAIRY PRODUCTS

Aren't dairy products processed? As I've mentioned, even cooking is technically a form of processing or changing your food, so when shopping for dairy products, such as milk, cheese, sour cream, yogurt, and cream cheese, you're aiming to avoid all *highly* processed products. This is what to look for:

- **Organic:** This will ensure that the cows producing your dairy products haven't been treated with hormones or antibiotics or consumed feed that's been sprayed with synthetic fertilizers or chemical pesticides (or worse, that's GMO). If you can't find a certified organic option, look for terms like "no hormones administered" and/or "no antibiotics administered."
- **Whole:** In most cases low-fat and fat-free dairy products are more highly processed than whole milk products, since they've been through a process that removes the natural fats.
- **From Grass-Fed (or Pastured) Cows:** Cows are meant to eat grass and they are healthier when they do, which means their dairy and meat products are in turn more nutritious for you.
- **In Block Form (cheese):** Bagged, preshredded cheese usually contains an anticaking agent called cellulose[33] that's sometimes made from wood pulp, and is an extra unnecessary "powdery" additive you won't find in a block of cheese.
- **Pasteurized (milk):** Pasteurization is a heating process that kills bacteria (both harmful and beneficial) and in some states, including our own, is required by law. If possible avoid "ultra-high-temperature" (UHT) pasteurized dairy products, because they're processed at 280°F or higher, and will leave you with even fewer beneficial bacteria. Instead, look for dairy products that are pasteurized at a lower temperature; this sometimes requires simply calling up the company and asking questions.
- **Non-Homogenized (milk):** Homogenization is yet another process that standard milk goes through to suspend fat globules so there's no layer of cream (usually called the "cream line") at the top. The process involves very high pressure and can negatively affect the nutritional benefits and flavor of the milk, so opt for non-homogenized milk when possible. If you can't find it at your local grocer, you can always request that they start carrying it.
- **Plain (milk and yogurt):** When it comes to dairy products like milk and yogurt, it's always best to buy the plain version and flavor it yourself (or just have it plain). The majority of factory-made food contains

far too much added sugar (and salt and oil, for that matter). At home you control the amount and kind of sweetener.

- **Fewest Number of Ingredients:** No matter what type of food you're buying, I *always* recommend reading the ingredient label before making a purchase. Most of the time the least processed equals fewest number of ingredients (as long as those ingredients are "whole," of course).
- **White (cheese):** Cheese is obviously made from milk or cream, which means it is usually some shade of white (not bright orange!). The orange color is typically a harmless, natural color additive, but it is still an unnecessary additive.

HOW TO FIND "REAL" EGGS

It's important to look for "pastured" eggs (not to be confused with "pasteurized"). This means the chickens have spent time on a grassy field. Free-range and cage-free chickens haven't been locked up, but it's possible they were given access to only a tiny plot of dirt. While chickens can easily live solely on grains (unlike cows), they are even healthier if they eat some greens as well and are able to peck around for bugs. And you can see the results in their yolks, which are usually a bright orange if greens have been a part of their diet. I've only been able to find truly "pastured" eggs at our local farmers' market, but if for some reason the market runs out of eggs I feel store-bought organic is the next best bet (although not ideal). See page 40 for more information on egg carton labels.

MEAT AND SEAFOOD FROM A REAL-FOOD PERSPECTIVE

We believe meat is definitely part of a real-food diet (phew!), because real food is basically the traditional foods that our ancestors have survived on for centuries before us, and that includes meat! But our ancestors weren't consuming factory-farmed meat at every single meal (sometimes purchased from a drive-through window). Meat was—and should be—more of a special-occasion food. And it's even more important that the meat products themselves be of high quality—meaning from animals that have been humanely raised and properly fed. After all, according to Michael Pollan, "You are what what you eat eats too"[34] because "the diet of the animals we eat strongly influences the nutritional quality, and healthfulness, of the food we get from them, whether it is meat or milk or eggs."[35]

Since wild animals eat their natural diets in their natural environment, their meat products are an excellent choice when it comes to nutritional value. Same goes with fish; see below.

Consider these basic concepts regarding meat and seafood consumption:

1. **Choose Local, Pastured Meat:** When it comes to industrialized meat, not only does the travel aspect take a toll on our environment, but the resources used to raise, feed, and slaughter the animals do as well. The best way to learn about how the animals have been raised and fed is to ask the farmer yourself, which is pretty easy to do if you're buying directly from the farmer.

2. **Reduce Meat Consumption:** Our society's meat consumption, and particularly the view of what's "normal," is literally out of control. According to Mark Bittman, "Sixty billion animals are raised each year for food—ten animals for every human on earth." He says this rate of industrialized meat production cannot continue because it's causing "enormous damage to the earth, including the significant acceleration of global warming." Secondly, consuming meat at the alarming rate it's being produced is not good for our health. Bittman says that our current rate of meat consumption has "stimulated a fundamental change in our diets that has contributed to our being overweight, even obese, and more susceptible to diabetes, heart disease, stroke, and perhaps even cancer."[36] The moral of the story is that the less meat you eat, the more of something else you'll eat instead, and let's hope it's fresh vegetables and fruit.

3. **Select Wild-Caught Seafood:** Unless you've visited the fish farm yourself and approve of their practices, then wild-caught seafood is the way to go. I also personally look for fish from the United States (or at least my home continent), which I can usually find at our local grocery stores and fish markets. I don't mind if seafood has been previously frozen as long as it hasn't been sitting around for more than a day or two after being defrosted.

IN GENERAL: IS ORGANIC BEST?

I always try to go with the organic version over conventional, but organic food does not always equal real food. First of all, in the simplest terms, "organic" means that a crop has not been treated with synthetic pesticides or fertilizers and that animals have not received synthetic antibiotics or hormones (which is all good stuff!). But there are a lot of products out there that I like to refer to as "organic junk food." An ice cream sandwich may be organic, but it's probably still highly processed.

It's important to note that not all farms can handle the time and expense to become USDA organic certified. Just because a farm is not certified organic though doesn't mean they don't follow organic practices, so it's always best to ask your local farmers questions before making a purchase decision. (See Chapter 2, page 61, for more details on what to ask at the farmers' market.)

ANNIE'S ORGANIC BOXED MACARONI AND CHEESE

Sure, this product is a slightly better choice than conventional boxed macaroni and cheese, because it's made with organic pasta (although not organic cheese) and doesn't contain any artificial ingredients, which is definitely a good thing. But other than that, the product still contains highly refined pasta made from white flour and a conventional powdered cheese product. So unless you buy the one Annie's whole-grain version, which also happens to be fully organic, this would still be considered highly processed (organic) junk food.

WHAT ARE GMOS?

According to the Non-GMO Project, GMOs, or genetically modified organisms, are created from "experimental technology [that] merges DNA from different species, creating unstable combinations of plant, animal, bacterial, and viral genes that cannot occur in nature or in traditional cross-breeding."[37] GMOs were first introduced into the U.S. food supply in 1994 and, according to Robyn O'Brien in a guest post on 100daysofrealfood.com, are currently labeled in more than sixty countries around the world—including all the countries in the European Union, Australia, Japan, the United Kingdom, Russia, China, and India—but not in the United States. Companies such as Monsanto genetically modify crops so they will live through saturation with chemical weed killer or produce their own insecticides, and at this time no long-term, independent studies have been conducted on their safety.[38]

The nonprofit Non-GMO Project, which is leading a voluntary labeling initiative, says the following eight crops are at high risk for being genetically modified (as of December 2011):

1. **Alfalfa**—first planting 2011
2. **Canola**—approximately 90 percent of the U.S. crop
3. **Corn**—approximately 88 percent of the U.S. crop in 2011
4. **Cotton**—approximately 90 percent of the U.S. crop in 2011
5. **Papaya**—most of the Hawaiian crop
6. **Soy**—approximately 94 percent of the U.S. crop in 2011
7. **Sugar beets**—approximately 95 percent of the U.S. crop in 2010
8. **Zucchini and yellow summer squash**—approximately 25,000 acres

The only way to avoid GMOs at this time is to buy organic or look for the "Non-GMO" label (if a product chooses and is approved to have one). But even if you buy only organic whole corn or soy, you're not necessarily in the clear. Both corn and soy are frequently used to make highly refined food additives (listed under a variety of names) that are commonly found in processed foods—so it's important that those be Non-GMO certified or organic as well. According to the Non-GMO Project, these are some **common ingredients derived from GMO risk crops:**

> Amino Acids, Aspartame, Ascorbic Acid, Sodium Ascorbate, Vitamin C, Citric Acid, Sodium Citrate, Ethanol, Flavorings ("Natural" and "Artificial"), High-Fructose Corn Syrup, Hydrolyzed Vegetable Protein, Lactic Acid, Maltodextrins, Molasses, Monosodium Glutamate, Sucrose, Textured Vegetable Protein (TVP), Xanthan Gum, Vitamins, Yeast Products.

So to avoid GMOs, it's best to stay away from these crops and additives, or better yet use this as another reason to just buy organic. Also it's important to know that wheat is commonly mistaken as a GMO crop, but according to the Non-GMO Project it is currently just in the "monitored crop" category and not "high risk" at this time.

A NOTE ON COOKING OILS

We didn't address cooking oils during our original 100 Days of Real Food pledge, mainly because we didn't yet have a full understanding of how the different options would impact our health; but we've since come to our senses and we now try to avoid refined vegetables oils. But even with the information we have today, I still would not have added it to our official list of real-food rules. And that's because the use of refined cooking oils is so widespread that you'd virtually never be able to leave your house and eat out at restaurants, dine at other people's houses, or skip town, which is just not realistic.

When cooking for yourself, however, it's best to avoid all refined or hydrogenated oils (even if they're organic), including:

- Canola oil
- Vegetable oil
- Corn oil
- Grapeseed oil
- Margarine
- Shortening

According to Sally Fallon in her book *Nourishing Traditions*, these refined oils are "cleaned" with chemicals and heated to a very high temperature during processing.[39]

Real-food cooking fats include the following:

- Butter, preferably organic from grass-fed cows
- Ghee, aka clarified butter, which is good for high-temperature cooking (see page 144)
- Olive oil (extra-virgin, cold-pressed, and unfiltered)
- Coconut oil (organic and unrefined)
- Lard (from organic, pastured animals)
- Other unrefined cooking fats: avocado oil, sesame oil, pastured (and/or organic) bacon grease, tallow, flaxseed oil, and red palm oil

BREAKING DOWN THE DIFFERENT TYPES OF FATS IN YOUR FOOD*[40]

HEALTHY		UNHEALTHY	
Saturated Fats	**Monounsaturated**	**Polyunsaturated**	**Trans Fat**
A solid or semisolid fat and mostly found in animal fats (like butter) and tropical oils (like coconut oil).	*Usually in liquid form and found in olive oil, nut oils, and avocado oil.*	*Remains liquid even when refrigerated and is found in vegetable oils like soybean oil, corn oil, canola oil, and safflower oil.*	*Usually in solid form and found in margarine or shortening.*
Saturated fats don't need to be "chemically extracted or molecularly rearranged" and appear to have "little to no correlation with heart disease."[41] While once thought to be the cause of modern diseases, these fats actually play an important role in the body chemistry.	Monounsaturated fats can be found in expeller-pressed oils, such as extra-virgin olive oil. Traditionally these oils are gently extracted under low temperatures, preserving the "integrity of the fatty acids" and natural preservatives in the oil, and therefore are safe to consume.	Commonly used in processed foods, refined vegetable oils are extracted using extremely high heat and then treated with toxic solvents such as hexane.** Just like sugar, the main problem with polyunsaturated fats is the quantity in which they are consumed. Intake of polyunsaturates "should not be much greater than 4 percent of the caloric total," yet in the modern diet intake is typically as much as 30 percent of calories. Excess consumption has been shown to contribute to increased cancer and heart disease among other health issues.	According to the FDA, trans fat, also commonly used in processed foods, is made "when hydrogen is added to vegetable oil"—a polyunsaturated fat—resulting in hydrogenated (or partially hydrogenated) oil.[42] This process turns fats that are normally liquid at room temperature into a solid. Consumption of hydrogenated fats is associated with a host of serious diseases including cancer.

**Most foods contain a combination of the different types of fats. The food examples listed are categorized under the type of fat they predominantly contain.*

***A large majority of the refined vegetable oils on the market today come from GMO crops. See page 28 for details.*

Our ancestors survived on unrefined cooking fats—including saturated fats—for centuries before us. And according to Sally Fallon in her book *Nourishing Traditions*, statistics show that the incidence of "coronary heart disease was rare"[43] in America prior to the 1920s, a time when the industrialization of food—including refined vegetable oils and shortenings—was first on the rise. "Today heart disease causes at least 40 percent of all U.S. deaths," while over the last eighty years the use of traditional animal fats have gone down and dietary vegetable oils—in the form of margarine, shortening, and refined oils—has increased about 400 percent. (In contrast, the consumption of sugar and processed food increased about 60 percent.)

Completely revamping your cooking oils can take some getting used to, but just remember, for high-temperature cooking I recommend coconut oil, ghee, or pastured lard; for low-temperature cooking I use butter and olive oil; and for baking, I stick with melted butter and coconut oil.

HOW TO COOK WITH COCONUT OIL

The melting point of coconut oil is 76°F, which is fairly close to room temperature. That means at our house it's a liquid in the summer and a solid in the winter. I find it's best to melt coconut oil prior to measuring and cooking, although it's not always that simple. If you add melted coconut oil to batter that already contains cold eggs and milk, the oil could turn solid again. I prefer to warm the oil gently along with honey, vanilla, and any other ingredients that can stand to be heated, then add it to the batter at the very end while stirring vigorously.

Note: Coconut oil can go back and forth between the liquid and solid state without spoiling.

More Tips on Reading Labels

Misleading Health and Nutritional Claims

Make a new habit of ignoring the health and nutritional claims on the front (or side or back) of the package and instead rely on the ingredient label! The only way to know what's really in your food is to see what it's made with. Some examples of misleading food packaging claims include:

- "No Trans Fat"—Trans fats are from an ingredient called partially hydrogenated oils. If a product contains 0.5g or less of trans fat per serving,[44] this claim can be used. In 2013 the FDA stated that trans fats are in fact a public health concern and ordered food companies to start phasing them out. This will take time, so for now it's up to us to avoid them.
- "Contains Whole Grains" and "Whole Wheat Blend"—As long as a product contains some whole grains these terms can be used. This does not mean the product is 100 percent whole-grain—and in fact it could well be far less than 100 percent.
- "Lose up to six pounds in two weeks," "heart healthy," "American Heart Association Certified," "low-fat," "excellent source of calcium,"

"no high-fructose corn syrup," "made with real fruit," "baked," and "100 calories or less"—claims like these can still be on products that contain highly processed and refined ingredients. For example, some pancake syrups that say "no high-fructose corn syrup" on the front are actually made from regular corn syrup. So it's more important than ever to look past all of those claims and go right to the ingredient label in order to avoid highly processed additives.

Vitamins and Minerals Listed as Ingredients
You might think it's a good thing for a product to note the addition of vitamins and minerals—but it's misleading. It's the classic sign that a food product was stripped of its natural vitamins and minerals in the first place, and food scientists are attempting to add them back. What does that mean? You're dealing with a highly processed food product. No formula developed in a science lab can truly emulate the "real" thing provided to us by nature.

Ingredient Labels on Ten Popular Packaged Foods

Let's put all of our ingredient label reading tips to the test. First we'll start with ten of the more popular packaged foods on the market:

Packaged Food Product	Ingredient List*	Real-Food Pros	Real-Food Cons
Pepperidge Farm Goldfish Crackers	Unbleached Enriched Wheat Flour [Flour, Niacin, Reduced Iron, Thiamin Mononitrate (Vitamin B_1), Riboflavin (Vitamin B_2), Folic Acid], Cheddar Cheese [(Pasteurized Milk, Cheese Culture, Salt, Enzymes), Water, Salt], Vegetable Oils (Canola, Sunflower And/Or Soybean), Contains 2% Or Less Of: Salt, Yeast, Sugar, Yeast Extract, Leavening (Baking Soda, Monocalcium Phosphate, Ammonium Bicarbonate), Spices, Annatto (Color) And Onion Powder.[45]	No artificial dyes Made with real cheddar cheese Very little added sugar	More than 5 ingredients Made only with refined grains (unbleached enriched wheat flour) Made with refined vegetable oils Some ingredients difficult to prononuce, therefore likely unwanted additives Not organic

** Note: Ingredients on these ten labels (through page 36) were captured June 2012 and can be changed/updated by manufacturers at any time.*

Packaged Food Product	Ingredient List	Real-Food Pros	Real-Food Cons
Aunt Jemima Original Pancake & Waffle Mix	Enriched Bleached Flour (Bleached Wheat Flour, Niacin, Reduced Iron, Thiamin Mononitrate, Riboflavin, Folic Acid), Sugar, Leavening (Sodium Bicarbonate, Sodium Aluminum Phosphate, Monocalcium Phosphate), Salt, Calcium Carbonate.[46]	Technically only 5 ingredients (although none are whole)	Made only with refined grains (enriched bleached flour) Refined sugar is the second ingredient Not organic
Campbell's Healthy Request Tomato Soup	Tomato Puree (Water, Tomato Paste), Water, Wheat Flour, High Fructose Corn Syrup, Contains Less Than 1% Of: Vegetable Oil (Corn, Cottonseed, Canola And/Or Soybean), Lower Sodium Natural Sea Salt, Salt, Natural Flavoring, Flavoring, Citric Acid, Ascorbic Acid (Added To Help Retain Color).[47]	The first ingredient is tomato puree No artificial ingredients	High-fructose corn syrup is used The third ingredient is refined wheat Made with refined vegetable oil Contains vague natural flavor and flavor additives Not organic
Quaker Instant Oatmeal, Strawberries & Cream	Whole Grain Rolled Oats, Sugar, Flavored And Colored Fruit Pieces (Dehydrated Apples [Treated With Sodium Sulfite To Promote Color Retention], Artificial Strawberry Flavor, Citric Acid, Red 40), Creaming Agent (Maltodextrin, Partially Hydrogenated Soybean Oil**, Whey, Sodium Caseinate), Salt, Calcium Carbonate, Guar Gum, Oat Flour, Artificial Flavor, Citric Acid, Niacinamide*, Reduced Iron, Vitamin A Palmitate, Pyridoxine Hydrochloride*, Riboflavin*, Thiamin Mononitrate*, Folic Acid.*[48] **One of the B vitamins* ***Adds a dietarily insignificant amount of trans fat*	Product is 100% whole-grain	This strawberry-flavored product contains no strawberries and instead has dehydrated apples with both artificial strawberry flavor and color Refined sugar is the second ingredient A lot more than 5 ingredients Some ingredients are not items a typical cook would use at home Contains partially hydrogenated oil (i.e., trans fat) Not organic

Packaged Food Product	Ingredient List	Real-Food Pros	Real-Food Cons
Cheerios	Whole Grain Oats (Includes The Oat Bran), Modified Corn Starch, Sugar, Salt, Tripotassium Phosphate, Wheat Starch. Vitamin E (Mixed Tocopherols) Added To Preserve Freshness. Vitamins And Minerals: Calcium Carbonate, Iron And Zinc (Mineral Nutrients), Vitamin C (Sodium Ascorbate), A B Vitamin (Niacinamide), Vitamin B_6 (Pyridoxine Hydrochloride), Vitamin A (Palmitate), Vitamin B_2 (Riboflavin), Vitamin B_1 (Thiamin Mononitrate), A B Vitamin (Folic Acid), Vitamin B_{12}, Vitamin D_3.[49]	The first ingredient is whole-grain oats Even though sugar is the third ingredient, according to the nutrition label it's only 1 gram per serving	Not 100% whole-grain due to the second ingredient (cornstarch) A lot more than 5 ingredients Not organic
Jell-O Sugar-Free Strawberry	Gelatin, Adipic Acid (For Tartness), Disodium Phosphate (Controls Acidity), Maltodextrin (From Corn), Fumaric Acid (For Tartness), Aspartame** (Sweetener), Contains Less Than 2% Of Artificial Flavor, Acesulfame Potassium (Sweetener), Salt, Red 40.** Phenylketonurics: Contains Phenylalanine.[50]	The first ingredient is pure gelatin	This strawberry-flavored product contains no strawberries Artificially sweetened with aspartame Contains artificial flavor and dyes More than 5 ingredients Some ingredients are difficult to pronounce, therefore likely unwanted additives Not organic

Packaged Food Product	Ingredient List	Real-Food Pros	Real-Food Cons
Clif Bar Carrot Cake	Organic Brown Rice Syrup, ClifPro® (Soy Rice Crisps [Soy Protein Isolate, Rice Flour, Rice Starch, Barley Malt Extract], Organic Roasted Soybeans, Organic Soy Flour), Organic Rolled Oats, Organic Cane Syrup, Organic Dried Apples, ClifCrunch® (Apple Fiber, Organic Milled Flaxseed, Inulin [Chicory Extract], Organic Oat Fiber, Psyllium), Soy White Chocolate (Organic Dried Cane Syrup, Cocoa Butter, Soy Flour, Soy Lecithin, Organic Vanilla Extract),Organic Soy Butter (Organic Roasted Soybeans, Organic Soybean Oil, Salt), Dried Carrots, Organic Raisins, Coconut, Sea Salt, Natural Flavors, Spices (Nutmeg, Cinnamon, Cloves).[51]	Contains some whole grains No artificial dyes or flavors Some organic ingredients	The first ingredient is a refined sweetener (organic brown rice syrup), and also contains other sweeteners, including barley malt extract and organic cane syrup A lot more than 5 ingredients
Oreos	Sugar, Enriched Flour (Wheat Flour, Niacin, Reduced Iron, Thiamine Mononitrate [Vitamin B_1], Riboflavin [Vitamin B_2], Folic Acid), High Oleic Canola Oil And/Or Palm Oil And/Or Canola Oil, And/Or Soybean Oil, Cocoa (Processed With Alkali), High Fructose Corn Syrup, Cornstarch, Leavening (Baking Soda And/Or Calcium Phosphate), Salt, Soy Lecithin (Emulsifier), Vanillin—An Artificial Flavor, Chocolate.[52]	No artificial dyes	The first ingredient is refined sugar Also contains high-fructose corn syrup Made only with refined grains (enriched flour and cornstarch) Contains refined oil Contains artificial flavor Not organic

Packaged Food Product	Ingredient List	Real-Food Pros	Real-Food Cons
Powerade Mountain Berry Blast	Water, High Fructose Corn Syrup, Less than 0.5% of: Citric Acid, Salt and Potassium Citrate and Magnesium Chloride and Calcium Chloride and Potassium Phosphate (electrolyte sources), Natural Flavors, Modified Food Starch, Calcium Disodium EDTA (to protect color), Medium Chain Triglycerides (contains coconut oil), Sucrose Acetate Isobutyrate, Vitamin B_3 (niacinamide), Vitamin B_6 (pyridoxine hydrochloride), Vitamin B_{12}, Blue #1.[53]	The first ingredient is water	The second ingredient is high-fructose corn syrup Contains artificial dyes A lot more than 5 ingredients Some ingredients are difficult to pronounce, therefore likely unwanted additives Not organic
Minute Maid Lemonade	Pure Filtered Water, Sweeteners (High Fructose Corn Syrup, Sugar), Lemon Juice from Concentrate, Lemon Pulp, Natural Flavors.[54]	Contains real lemon juice and pulp	Contains a lot of added sweetener (high-fructose corn syrup and sugar)—28 grams per serving, according to the nutrition label Contains vague "natural flavor" additive Not organic

Now let's move on to ten packaged foods that are a little bit more misleading:

Packaged Food Product	Ingredient List*	Real-Food Pros	Real-Food Cons
Special K Cereal	Rice, Wheat Gluten, Sugar, Defatted Wheat Germ, Contains 2% Or Less Of Salt, Whey, Malt Flavoring, Calcium Caseinate. **Vitamins And Minerals:** Vitamin C (Ascorbic Acid), Reduced Iron, Vitamin E (Alpha Tocopherol Acetate), Vitamin B_6 (Pyridoxine Hydrochloride), Vitamin B_1 (Thiamin Hydrochloride), Vitamin A Palmitate, Folic Acid, Vitamin B_2 (Riboflavin), Niacinamide, Vitamin B_{12}.[55]	No artificial flavors or colors	Contains only refined grains (rice, wheat gluten, wheat germ) Refined sugar is in the top 3 ingredients More than 5 ingredients overall Not organic
Earth Balance Original Buttery Spread	Natural Oil Blend (Palm Fruit, Canola, Soybean, Flax And Olive), Filtered Water, Contains Less Than 2% Of Pure Salt, Natural Flavor (Plant Derived From Corn, No Msg, No Alcohol, No Gluten), Pea Protein, Sunflower Lecithin, Lactic Acid (Non-Dairy, Derived From Sugar Beets), And Naturally Extracted Annatto For Color.[56]	No artificial flavors or colors	The first ingredient contains refined oils Contains vague natural flavor additive More than 5 ingredients Some ingredients difficult to pronounce, therefore likely unwanted additives Not organic
Trader Joe's Multigrain Crackers	Enriched Flour (Wheat Flour, Niacin, Reduced Iron, Thiamine Mononitrate, Riboflavin, Folic Acid), Sunflower Oil, Sugar, Scotch Oatmeal, Inulin, Rye Flour, Multigrain Flour Blend (Wheat, Rye, Triticale, Barley, Corn, Millet, Soybean, Sunflower Seeds, Rice, Flax, Durum, Oats), Wheat Germ, Modified Corn Starch, Salt, Invert Syrup, Sodium Bicarbonate, Onion Powder, Malt Flour, Monocalcium Phosphate, Microbial Enzymes.[57]	Contains some whole grains No artificial flavors or colors	The first ingredient is refined wheat flour Contains more sugar (third ingredient) than whole grains Not organic

**Note: Ingredients on pages 37–39 were captured June 2012 and can be changed/updated by manufacturers at any time.*

Packaged Food Product	Ingredient List	Real-Food Pros	Real-Food Cons
Yoplait Light Fat Free Strawberry (Yogurt)	Cultured Pasteurized Grade A Nonfat Milk, High Fructose Corn Syrup, Strawberries, Modified Corn Starch, Whey Protein Concentrate, Kosher Gelatin, Citric Acid, Tricalcium Phosphate, Aspartame, Potassium Sorbate Added to Maintain Freshness, Natural Flavor, Red No. 40, Vitamin A Acetate, Vitamin D_3.[58]	Contains real strawberries	High-fructose corn syrup is the second ingrdient Contains artificial dye (Red No. 40) Contains artificial sweetener (aspartame) Made with nonfat milk Contains vague natural flavor additive More than 5 ingredients Not organic
Snyder's Eatsmart Naturals Garden Veggie Sticks	Potato Flour, Potato Starch, Expeller Pressed Sunflower Oil, Corn Starch, Rice Flour, Tomato Paste, Salt, Potassium Chloride, Spinach Powder, Turmeric.[59]	No artificial flavors or dyes	Deep-fried product (per customer service; not on label) Contains no whole grains Contains more salt than green vegetables Not organic Main ingredients and cooking method resemble French fries or potato chips
Back to Nature Crispy Wheat Crackers	Unbleached Enriched Flour (Wheat Flour, Niacin, Reduced Iron, Thiamine Mononitrate [Vitamin B_1], Riboflavin [Vitamin B_2], Folic Acid), Safflower Oil, Raw Sugar, Defatted Wheat Germ, Cornstarch, Brown Rice Syrup, Sea Salt, Malted Barley Extract, Leavening (Monocalcium Phosphate, Baking Soda), Natural Turmeric Flavor.[60]	No artificial flavors or dyes	Contains no whole grains Refined sugar is the third ingredient, and it contains two other sweeteners (brown rice syrup and malted barley extract) More than 5 ingredients Not organic

Packaged Food Product	Ingredient List	Real-Food Pros	Real-Food Cons
Jif Natural Creamy Peanut Butter Spread	Made From Peanuts, Sugar, Palm Oil, Contains 2% Or Less Of: Salt, Molasses.[61]	Peanuts are the first ingredient	Contains unneccessary additives, including sugars, oil, and salt Not organic
Annie's Classic Macaroni and Cheese	Organic Semolina Pasta Shells From Durum Wheat, Cheddar Cheese (Cultured Pasteurized Milk, Salt, Non-Animal Enzymes), Whey, Buttermilk, Cream, Salt, Natural Sodium Phosphate, Annatto Extract And Beta Carotene For Natural Color.[62]	No artificial flavors or dyes Some organic ingredients (the pasta) Contains real cheddar cheese	Pasta made with refined grains More than 5 ingredients
Annie's Cheddar Bunnies	Organic Wheat Flour, Expeller Pressed Vegetable Oil (Safflower And/Or Sunflower), Salt, Cheddar Cheese (Pasteurized Milk, Cheese Culture, Salt, Enzymes), Yeast Extract, Yeast, Paprika, Annatto Extract For Color, Ground Celery Seed, Onion Powder.[63]	No artificial flavors or dyes Contains real cheddar cheese Some organic ingredients	Contains only refined grains (organic wheat flour) Contains more refined oil than cheese
Pirate's Booty Aged White Cheddar	Corn Meal, Rice, Contains One Or More Of The Following: Rice, Sunflower, Expeller Pressed Canola or Corn Oil, Aged Cheddar Cheese (Cultured Milk, Salt, Enzymes, Whey, Buttermilk).[64]	No artificial flavors or dyes Contains real cheese	Contains refined grains Contains refined oils Not organic (and includes GMOs, according to their website)

Be sure to check Chapter 2 for my sample grocery list with some packaged real-food choices that fully make the cut.

Understanding the Front of the Box

We've already discussed the importance of relying *only* on the ingredient label when making a purchase decision, but I still think there's a lot of value in understanding all the terms and claims that constantly bombard us on the front of food packages.

Term	**Where it's commonly found**	**What it really means**
USDA Organic	A wide range of products including dairy, produce, meat, snacks, and other packaged foods	Per USDA guidelines, chemical pesticides, synthetic fertilizers, and genetically engineered ingredients (GMOs) cannot be used in the production of these products. The USDA organic seal means the product has 95 percent or more organic content. (Note: That is not 100%!) If the label claims that it is made with specified organic ingredients, then only those ingredients are organic. In the case of animals, growth hormones and antibiotics cannot be used, and their feed must be organic.[65]
Natural, All Natural, Made with All Natural Ingredients	A wide range of products including dairy, meat, snacks, and other packaged foods	As required by the USDA, meat, poultry, and egg products labeled as "natural" must be minimally processed and contain no artificial ingredients. However, the "natural" label does not include any standards regarding specific farm practices and applies only to processing of meat and egg products. *There are no standards or regulations for the labeling of natural food products unless they are meat or eggs.*[66] Non-animal products with "natural" claims generally mean no artificial ingredients were used, but not always (for example, Crystal Light Lemonade has a "natural" claim on the front and contains three artificial ingredients!).
Non-GMO	A wide range of packaged foods	GMOs (Genetically Modified Organisms) are man-made ingredients inserted into our foods by chemical companies. They are required to be labeled in most developed countries around the world, but not in the United States as of this writing.[67] Currently the only way to avoid GMOs in the United States is to look for the nonprofit Non-GMO Project label or buy organic. (See page 28 for a list of common GMO crops.)

Term	Where it's commonly found	What it really means
0g Trans Fat, No Trans Fat	A wide range of products made with cooking oils	Per FDA guidelines, this terminology can be used if a product contains 0.5g or less of trans fat per serving.[68] Therefore "No Trans Fat" is not a guarantee that there's absolutely no trans fat in a product. Trans fat is present when partially hydrogenated oils have been used (see page 29 for more explanation).
Fat Free, Low Fat	A wide range of products including dairy, snacks, desserts, and cereals	These labels are used when a product is either naturally low in dietary fat or has been processed to remove or reduce dietary fat. The latter are more "processed" than their full-fat counterparts and often contain added, refined sugars to help improve the taste. Full-fat foods are real foods (see page 24 for more information).
Multigrain	Grain-based products, including breads, crackers, cereals, pastas	There are dozens of readily available grains on the market, including wheat, oats, rice, spelt, barley, and quinoa just to name a few. Products that are multigrain simply contain more than one of these grains, but this term alone does not indicate if any are whole grain (they could still be refined).
Whole-Grain Blend, Contains Whole Grains, Made with Whole Grain	Grain-based products, including breads, crackers, cereals, pastas	The regulations on these claims are loose, so while the product definitely contains some amount of whole grains, the actual amount could be minuscule. For example, a product could contain more refined wheat (aka white) flour and sugar than it does whole grains and still slap this claim on the front.[69] It all goes back to reading the ingredient labels!
Gluten Free	Grain-based products, including breads, crackers, cereals, pastas	This claim identifies products that do not contain gluten—a protein in wheat and related grains such as barley, rye, spelt, kamut, and triticale—but once again it does not mean any of the grains used are whole, and therefore the products could contain refined ingredients.[70] Unless you have an allergy, intolerance, or sensitivity to gluten, I do not believe there are any health benefits to avoiding it.

Term	Where it's commonly found	What it really means
Raw (Milk)	Dairy products	This is literally just the way the milk comes straight out of the cow. It has not been treated, pasteurized (heated to kill pathogens, and, unfortunately, beneficial bacteria along with them), or homogenized (processed to suspend fat globules). Cheese and other dairy products are sometimes made from raw milk. It's currently illegal to purchase raw milk for human consumption in many states, including North Carolina (where we live).
Pasteurized, Pasteurization	Dairy products	This is a process in which milk is heated to kill bacteria (both potentially harmful and beneficial). Milk is pasteurized at a wide range of temperatures from 145°F to 280°F.[71] The lower the temperature of the pasteurization, the more beneficial nutrients are preserved.
UHT (Ultra-High-Temperature), Ultra Pasteurized	Dairy products	A large majority of commercially produced organic milk is ultra-high-temperature pasteurized at 280°F. The product is termed "shelf stable" and often does not need refrigeration until opened, hence the longer-term expiration dates.[72] Once again, pasteurization kills beneficial bacteria, so dairy products processed at the lowest temperature possible are ideal. The best way to find out what temperature is used is to call the company (or farmer) and ask.
Non-Homogenized	Milk	Most milk goes through homogenization in addition to pasteurization. The fat particles of cream are strained through tiny pores under great pressure. This creates a more uniform product; the cream will no longer rise to the top. Non-homogenized milk is sometimes called "cream-on-top" or "cream-line" milk and that's what we buy.[73]
rBGH-free, rBST-free	Dairy products, including milk and cheese	rBGH and rBST are genetically engineered, artificial bovine growth hormones given to cows to increase milk production. These substances are banned for human consumption in all 27 countries of the European Union, New Zealand, Australia, and Canada, but are still currently allowed in the United States (although some manufacturers voluntarily use the "rBGH-free" and "rBST-free" claims on their products).[74]

Term	Where it's commonly found	What it really means
Pasture-raised, Pastured	Animal products, including eggs	Due to the number of variables involved, the USDA has not developed a federal definition for pasture-raised products.[75] Generally speaking, though, "pastured" means the animals had access to a green field (not just any field) and in turn likely provide high-quality, nutritious products. But since this term is not currently regulated, there's no way to know for sure unless you ask the farmer directly (at the market).
Grass-Fed, Grass-Finished, 100% Grass-Fed	Beef products and dairy	As of this writing (2014), the USDA has only a voluntary standard for a grass- (forage-) fed livestock marketing claim.[76] Cows have naturally evolved to eat grass, not grains, but it's common practice to "fatten up" feedlot cattle with grains during their last 3 to 5 months before slaughter. This is known as "grain finishing," and it negatively affects the quality of the meat and dairy products. Unfortunately, "grass-fed" may or may not mean the same thing as "grass-finished." And to make things even more confusing, the "organic" label indicates the animal was fed organic feed, but the feed could very well be grain. Ideally you want "grass-finished" or "100% grass-fed" organic meat, which (should) mean the animal subsisted on organic grass feed from post-weaning to processing. Often the only way to really know what you're buying is to find a local farmer and ask.
No Added Hormones, Raised Without Hormones	Animal products	Federal regulations have never permitted hormones or steroids in poultry, pork, or goat, so this claim, referring to synthetic growth substances, would really be of value only concerning beef or other animal products.[77]
No nitrates or nitrites added	Processed meats, including hot dogs, bacon, and ham	This misleading label only refers to the synthetic—not natural—preservatives nitrate and nitrite. Nitrate and nitrite have been used for centuries to cure meat, but today, conventional meat packers typically use a synthesized version known as sodium nitrite. Organic and natural products—where you'll usually find the "no nitrates or nitrites added" claim—employ celery powder or celery juice, which are both high in nitrate (a bacterial culture is used to convert it to nitrite). So, long story short, your organic bacon and hot dogs still contain nitrates/nitrites, just in a natural form as opposed to synthetic (i.e., artificial, page 22).[78]

Term	Where it's commonly found	What it really means
Free-Range, Free-Roaming	Animal products, including eggs	This label indicates that shelter was provided with unlimited access to food, fresh water, and the outdoors (which may be fenced and/or covered).[79] The label is regulated by the USDA, but there are no specific requirements around the duration or quality of outdoor access. So let's face it: This could simply mean there is an opening to a small, shared dirt yard.
Cage-Free	Animal products, including eggs	This label indicates that the chickens were able to freely roam a building, room, or enclosed area with unlimited access to food and fresh water.[80] Note: Cage-free doesn't mean that time outdoors is provided or that there is a limit to the number of chicken per square feet. I recommend watching the documentary *Food, Inc.* for a window into what the conditions could be like.
Vegetarian-Fed	Animal products, including eggs	These birds are not fed animal by-products, but this label does not indicate anything about the animals' living conditions or what else they are fed.[81]
Wild-Caught	Seafood	"Wild-caught" fish have spent time in their natural environment eating their natural diet. And healthier animals who were raised the way nature intended result in more nutritious foods for us.[82] The label doesn't give you any information on what technique was used to catch the fish.
Farm-Raised	Seafood	These fish are raised in controlled, (sometimes) artificial, and often unnatural conditions. In some cases huge quantities of fish and shrimp are grown in giant nets, cages, and ponds where antibiotics, hormones, and pesticides mingle with disease and waste. Factory farms—both on land and in the sea—can result in lower-quality products.[83] Some fish farms are run responsibly, but unless you pay them a visit yourself there's no way to know for sure.
Made with Real Fruit	Snacks and other packaged products	This claim on products with fruit-based ingredients can be misleading. For example, the only "fruit" in strawberry-flavored Fruit Roll-Ups is pears from concentrate. In addition, products with these claims can also contain potentially harmful ingredients such as partially hydrogenated oils, refined sugars, and artificial dyes (as in the case of Fruit Roll-Ups).[84]

Term	Where it's commonly found	What it really means
No High-Fructose Corn Syrup	A wide range of products, including breads, snacks, desserts, and cereals	This simply means exactly what it says—no high-fructose corn syrup was added during production—but this product could still very well contain other forms of refined sugar, even including regular corn syrup.
Sugar Free	Snacks, desserts, and other packaged products	A claim that may be used on a food that contains less than 0.5g of sugars per serving. Products that contain artificial sweeteners (such as Sucralose/Splenda, Saccharin/Sweet'N Low, Aspartame/Equal) can still be labeled as sugar free. Artificial sweeteners have not been in our food supply for very long (only about thirty or so years) yet have been linked to an increased risk of cancer.[85]
Heart-Check Mark	A wide range of packaged products, including cereals, snacks, and other packaged foods	Regulated by the American Heart Association, there are a variety of requirements including being low in fat, cholesterol, and sodium. Unfortunately a "Heart-Check Mark" gives us no indication if the product is also highly processed (i.e., contains refined ingredients).[86]
Vegan	Snacks and other packaged products	This indicates that no animal products or by-products (such as dairy, honey, or eggs) were used during production.

CLEANING OUT YOUR OWN KITCHEN

Now you may be asking yourself: What should I do with all the processed stuff I just discovered I own? There's no right or wrong answer, but here are some suggestions:

- Give unopened and unexpired items to a local food bank.
- Give unopened and possibly even some opened packages to a willing neighbor or friend.
- Return (or exchange) unopened items at the grocery store where they were purchased.
- Eat through what you have on hand, then replace those items one by one with real-food alternatives.
- Trade in processed-food packages for better alternatives at a health food supermarket that offers such a program.
- Throw them away.

I personally gave the large majority of our processed foods to a neighbor (she wanted them!), and since we're good friends, the whole exchange wasn't awkward. It can feel a little odd, though, giving away food you've deemed is no longer "good enough" for you, so if you fear that may pose a problem, then simply rely on some of the other suggestions to move forward.

ALLERGY-FRIENDLY REAL FOODS

People with food allergies and sensitivities are already used to paying close attention to what they eat. Choosing a real-food lifestyle is a logical next step. Here are some common alternatives to consider:

FOOD ALLERGY VERSUS FOOD SENSITIVITY:

What's the Difference?

My friend Robyn O'Brien is a pioneer and expert in the subjects of allergies and the processed food industry (some call her "the Erin Brockovich of food"). She explains, "A food allergy is an immediate reaction to a certain food. Symptoms can range from hives to runny nose to something life-threatening called anaphylaxis. A food sensitivity is a delayed food-allergic reaction. The symptoms can be everything from a runny nose to behavioral issues to dark circles under the eyes and can appear up to thirty-six hours after the food is ingested."[87]

Common Allergies	Alternatives
Gluten	Lots of foods are naturally gluten-free; some gluten-free whole grains are buckwheat, corn, millet, montina (Indian rice grass), oats labeled gluten-free, quinoa, brown rice, sorghum, teff, and wild rice.
Wheat	If wheat is the only concern—and not the gluten protein found in wheat—all the grains listed above are acceptable, as well as barley, rye, spelt, kamut, and triticale.[88]
Peanuts, Tree Nuts	If peanuts are the only concern, then tree nuts—as long as they aren't processed in a factory that also handles peanuts—are an alternative. Tree nuts include pecans, cashews, almonds, walnuts, pine nuts, brazil nuts, pistachios, and macadamia nuts. For an alternative to peanut butter, consider almond butter, sunflower seed butter (as long as they don't come from a factory with cross contamination), and even cream cheese. If tree nuts must also be avoided, then seeds like pumpkin and sunflower are the best substitutes.
Milk	Whether your concern is a dairy allergy or an intolerance to lactose, consider plain, unsweetened almond milk or coconut milk as an alternative. Rice milk and soy milk are also popular, but soy is one of the top genetically modified crops on the market (see page 28) and is also used in a great deal of highly processed food additives, so it's not at the top of my recommendation list.
Butter	Some people with dairy allergies can still tolerate butter or, even more so, ghee (clarified butter), which has a lower amount of lactose, but check with your doctor first. Other alternatives to butter include coconut oil (both a solid and a liquid; see page 31), olive oil, and pastured lard. I would avoid the factory-made butter alternative spreads because they are typically made from refined oils.

In chapter 2 you'll learn more about shopping for real food and what staples to have on hand.

Silk
Almond Breeze
Almond Breeze
Almond Breeze
Almond Breeze
ORIGINAL
CHOCOLATE
CHOCOLATE
VANILLA
HORIZON
HORIZON
ORGANIC VALLEY
SOY
VANILLA
ORGANIC VALLEY
SOY
VANILLA
ORGANIC VALLEY
SOY
ORIGINAL
ORGANIC VALLEY
SOY
ORGANIC VALLEY
SOY
GOAT MILK
GOAT MILK
GOAT MILK
Silk
Silk
Silk
RICE DREAM
RICE DREAM
3.19

2. Shopping for Real Food

Real-Food Tip: Your new food-shopping routine will eventually become your "new normal."

Now that we've covered the basics on defining real food, let's discuss how, exactly, to find it at supermarkets and farmers' markets (and without breaking the bank, which is covered in chapter 5!). When our family first made the switch to real food, my grocery shopping routine had to change dramatically. I used to shop exclusively at our mainstream food chain—and, believe it or not, I never even set foot in the store. I made all of my selections online—giving zero thought to what produce was in season or where any of the food came from—while taking advantage of store sales and occasionally manufacturer coupons I'd clipped from the newspaper. Then on a set day and time I would drive up to the front of the store, an employee would bring out my groceries, and less than ten minutes later I'd be on my way (without even having to unbuckle the kids!). There's no question it was incredibly convenient, but let's face it; I was headed home in a car filled with highly processed food that was not good for the health of my family.

OUR NEW FOOD SHOPPING ROUTINE

After several months of experiementing I finally figured out (and got used to) my new shopping routine, which now looks something like this:

- **Once a week: Earth Fare (a healthy supermarket)**—The mainstream grocery store I used to frequent isn't too far from home, but I now travel more than double the distance to shop at the Earth Fare store instead. No one ever said real food was more convenient . . . just worth the extra effort! This is where I pick up any produce I couldn't get at the farmers' market, dairy products (including milk), baking ingredients, occasional seafood, bulk items (such as grains, nuts, seeds, and peanut butter), packaged goods (including whole-grain pasta and crackers), and frozen foods (such as berries and peas).

- **Once a week: a nearby growers-only farmers' market**—For in-season organically grown produce, local humanely raised meats (chicken, beef, and pork), pastured eggs, and goat cheese. My favorite market is the Matthews Community Farmers' Market in Matthews, south of Charlotte, North Carolina. (See page 62 for more information on growers-only markets.)
- ***Approximately* once a month: Trader Joe's (a different healthy supermarket)**—This is a budget-friendly choice where I stock up on high-dollar items such as organic coffee, honey, coconut oil, nuts, and wine. I also like their whole-wheat pitas (due to the simple ingredient list) and organic hummus, so I'll often pick those up while I'm there.
- ***Approximately* once a month: Great Harvest (a franchised bread store)**—Sure, I sometimes make my own bread at home, but it's not always realistic, and the bakery that sells decent bread around here happens to be in the same shopping center as Trader Joe's. So while I'm there I also pick up a loaf of honey whole-wheat sandwich bread (made with only five, whole ingredients).
- **Approximately once a quarter: a different growers-only farmers' market** (farther from home)—I am willing to go the distance to take advantage of the Atherton Market's seafood, pastured lamb products, and organic peaches.
- **As needed: mainstream supermarket** (where I used to do all my shopping)—We do occasionally go back to our original supermarket, but that's only if we forget—or suddenly need—one item. Our chosen "healthier" supermarkets are too far away for quick purchases.

So there you have it . . . I went from drive-through grocery shopping to a much more complex routine. It took some getting used to, but I survived! Just as some might work hard to plan the perfect family trip, or obtain the best seats at a game, or care for a sick family member, we worked hard to change our shopping routine, and this routine is just part of our life now. In my opinion, it's worth the extra effort for higher-quality food.

NAVIGATING SUPERMARKETS

Whether you're shopping at a mainstream supermarket or a healthy supermarket, you still need to pay close attention to what you buy. It can be tricky to find the real-food choices even at your best-option health food store.

8 Tips for Buying Real Food at the Supermarket

1. It's classic good advice for a reason: **shop around the perimeter of the store.** There are a few exceptions like whole-wheat flour, brown rice, and three-ingredient crackers, but other than that most fresh, whole foods, such as produce and dairy, are located around the perimeter of the store.

2. When shopping for produce, **buy organic whenever possible**, especially if the item is on the Dirty Dozen list or is made from a high-risk GMO crop (see box). If your store does not offer any organic fruits or veggies, then check to see if a local farmers' market or CSA (Community Supported Agriculture) program might offer produce that hasn't been sprayed with chemical pesticides or treated with synthetic fertilizers. Remember that not all local farms can afford to be officially certified organic, so just ask how they grow and treat their crops.

3. If you can't find much in the way of fresh organic produce, **frozen produce** is a legitimate alternative. According to Michael Pollan, in his book *Food Rules*, "Freezing does not significantly diminish the nutritional value of produce" (like canning does) because the crops are picked and frozen at the peak of freshness.[1]

WHAT IS THE DIRTY DOZEN LIST?

The Environmental Working Group, an environmental health research and advocacy organization, publishes a Dirty Dozen List that according to the Executive Summary on their website, "will help you determine which fruits and vegetables have the most pesticide residues and are the most important to buy organic." The Dirty Dozen are the most contaminated conventional produce and should therefore be purchased organic, whereas the Clean Fifteen are the least contaminated. But, it's also so important to remember, "eating conventionally-grown produce is far better than not eating fruits and vegetables at all."[2]

WHAT TO BUY ORGANIC

EWG's 2014 Shopper's Guide to Pesticides in Produce™ "Dirty Dozen List"	**Non-GMO Project's list of High Risk GMO Crops**
Apples	Alfalfa
Strawberries	Canola
Grapes	Corn
Celery	Cotton
Peaches	Papaya
Spinach	Soy
Sweet Bell Peppers	Sugar Beets
Nectarines—Imported	Zucchini and Yellow Summer Squash
Cucumbers	+ list of common food additives derived from GMO Risk Crops (see page 28)
Cherry Tomatoes	
Snap Peas—Imported	
Tomatoes	

21 ESSENTIALS FOR FREEZER, FRIDGE, AND PANTRY

Freezer Essentials

1. **Frozen organic berries** for making smoothies or berry sauce
2. **Whole-grain flours**, including whole-wheat flour, masa harina, and whole-wheat **bread-crumbs**
3. **Homemade dishes**, such as soups, sauces, stocks, smoothie pops, and other leftovers
4. **Homemade baked goods** such as pancakes, waffles, and muffins
5. **Extra whole-grain breads and tortillas**, for when you can't make it to the bakery or don't feel like making a fresh batch
6. **Locally and humanely raised meats and wild-caught seafood** that you stock up on when you find a good source
7. **Frozen organic vegetables**, such as peas and corn (frozen are more nutritious than canned)

Fridge Essentials

8. **Dairy products** like milk, cheese, cream cheese, and plain yogurt
9. **Eggs**
10. Perishable **fruits and vegetables**
11. One-ingredient **peanut butter** and all-fruit **preserves, jam, or jelly**
12. **Cooking fats,** such as unsalted organic butter, ghee (clarified butter), and lard
13. **Snacks**, including olives and pickles
14. **Spreads, sauces, and condiments**, such as hummus, onion dip, soy sauce, maple syrup, mustard, and homemade salad dressings

Pantry Essentials

15. **Nuts** (including raw cashews, almonds, and pecans) and **seeds** (such as raw pumpkin and sunflower). The pantry works for short-term storage, but if you don't go through these items fairly quickly, store them in the freezer.
16. **Dried fruit** such as raisins, dried apricots, and dried apple rings. One-ingredient organic applesauce is also great to have on hand when you are out of fresh fruit.
17. **Baking ingredients and other seasonings,** including honey, vanilla extract, spices, oils, salt, and baking powder/soda
18. **Whole-grain products**, including whole-grain sandwich bread, whole-wheat pasta, brown rice, quinoa, whole-wheat couscous, whole-wheat pretzels/crackers, etc.
19. **Whole-grain cereals**, such as raw oats (for oatmeal), homemade granola, and shredded wheat cereal
20. **Fresh fruit** that doesn't need to be refrigerated, such as bananas, peaches, apples, pears, and tomatoes. We keep these items in a big fruit bowl on the kitchen table.
21. **Staples**, including potatoes, onions, garlic, dried/canned beans, and canned tomato products

4. Pollan advises that we **"avoid food products that make health claims"** because there's probably a catch.[3] Look to the ingredients list to tell you what's really in your food. And don't overlook apples or other produce items, which don't showcase fancy health claims at all (or ingredient labels, for that matter).

5. **Buy products that either don't have an ingredient list** (because they're a one-ingredient whole food) **or that display a short list of ingredients** that you can easily pronounce and understand. We like to draw the line at five ingredients, as long as all of those ingredients are whole foods.

6. For bulk products, such as organic brown rice, raw nuts, whole-grain flours, coconut oil, or organic dried fruit, **consider shopping online**. It may actually be cheaper than buying them from a supermarket. Whether you utilize Amazon Prime or Amazon Subscribe and Save or shop at an independent retailer like Azure Standard (azurestandard.com), you can easily find nonperishable (or at least slow-to-perish) real-food staples online.

7. Whether from your supermarket or a local farmers' market, when you find great products at a low price, don't be afraid to **stock up so you can preserve some for later**. We actually bought an extra freezer just for this purpose; there's nothing like having quality grass-fed beef available whenever you need it!

8. Consider **growing your own produce**, even if only to supplement other purchases. You don't need an elaborate garden to get started; a pot, some soil, a bag of organic fertilizer, and a few seeds will do (see page 64 for ideas).

Note: Beware of the supermarket bakery! Whatever delicious smells may be wafting from that direction, it's likely that they're actually baking highly processed dough (full of dough conditioners and other additives) that's made in a central location and shipped to each store. The only way to know for sure is to—you guessed it—check the ingredients!

My Weekly Real-Food Grocery List

Here's a peek inside my shopping cart (or farmers' market basket!). These are the staples* we pretty much always have on hand, including brand names where appropriate.

Produce

- Weekly fruit: apples, bananas, pears, oranges, and usually kiwi
- Seasonal fruit: berries, cherries, peaches, and tomatoes

**I buy the organic version of everything whenever possible. We also make some items from scratch that are not listed as purchases (such as chicken stock, as on page 322) and harvest food from our family garden (see page 64).*

- "Lunch-box fruit" (will hold up well in the lunch box): melons, grapes, oranges, mango, and sometimes pomegranate
- Lettuce and/or fresh spinach
- Carrots and cucumbers
- Onions and garlic
- Lemons, limes, and sometimes grapefruit
- Other items as needed for dinners and recipes: bell peppers, broccoli, kale, asparagus, potatoes, cucumbers, squash, mushrooms, eggplant, celery, cauliflower, green beans, gingerroot, shallots, fresh herbs, avocados, hot peppers, and so on

Grains / Bulk Section*

- Rolled oats—we go through a lot of oats!
- Wheat berries (I grind them myself to make flour; it's easier than it sounds and simply requires a grain mill, which operates much like a coffee grinder!)
- Raw nuts: cashews, almonds, pecans, walnuts, and pine nuts (for pesto; see recipe page 274)
- Dry-roasted salted nuts (for snacking)
- Raw sunflower and pumpkin seeds
- Dried pinto beans (for refried beans; see recipe on page 155)

**Most items in bulk bins cost about 20 percent less than their packaged counterparts. Check the interior aisles for the listed items if your store doesn't offer them in bulk.*

- Organic popcorn kernels
- Quinoa
- Whole-grain spelt flour

Interior Aisles

- Store-brand whole-wheat pasta
- Ak-Mak whole-wheat crackers
- Masa harina (whole-grain corn flour)
- Brown rice (I like the quick-cooking variety by Nishiki, found in the ethnic aisle, or choose any other organic brand)
- King Arthur organic whole-wheat flour
- Store-brand unsweetened shredded coconut
- Local raw honey
- Store-brand organic pure maple syrup (grade B)
- Store-brand (grind it there) organic one-ingredient peanut butter
- Barbara's shredded wheat biscuits (one-ingredient cereal)
- Freshly baked whole-wheat bread (usually from a local franchised bakery and made with only five ingredients)
- Store-brand organic pasta sauce
- Wine (mostly red, some white) and quality beer

Dairy and Other Cold Items

- Homestead Creamery brand whole milk, which is non-homogenized and is pasteurized at 161°F through a process called high-temperature, short-time (HTST) pasteurization. Standard organic grocery store milk is ultrapasteurized at temps up to 280°F.
- Cheeses such as Monterey Jack, Parmigiano-Reggiano, sharp cheddar, mozzarella, blue, and feta
- Local goat cheese
- Kerrygold or Organic Valley pastured butter (both salted and unsalted)
- Purity Farms organic ghee (clarified butter)
- Organic Valley or Nancy's organic cream cheese
- Stonyfield or Seven Stars Farm plain organic whole-milk yogurt
- Organic Valley sour cream
- Organic heavy cream
- Trader Joe's plain organic hummus
- Organic olives
- Frozen store-brand organic peas
- Frozen store-brand or Cascadian Farm organic mixed berries (for smoothies)

ARE BROWN EGGS BETTER?

Brown eggs aren't better, they're just different: The color depends on the kind of chicken that lays them. As long as the eggs come from a pastured, humanely raised animal, it doesn't matter what color they are on the outside. All pastured eggs, though, will usually have a bright orange yolk on the inside! Quite a contrast from the pale yellow yolks you'll find at the grocery store.

Meat, Seafood, and Eggs (almost always farmers' market purchases)

- Grass-fed ground beef
- Whole pastured chicken
- Bacon, prosciutto, ground pork
- Wild-caught seafood
- Lots of pastured eggs
- *Occasionally* leaf fat (to render into the occasional batch of pastured lard, which we use primarily for tortillas; see recipe on page 326) and lamb

Other Staples

Oils, Vinegars, and Condiments (see pages 60–61 for details on ketchup, mustard, and mayo)

- Trader Joe's organic coconut oil
- Store-brand extra-virgin organic olive oil

- Organic vinegars, such as white wine, red wine, rice wine, apple cider, and good-quality balsamic
- San-J organic tamari soy sauce (reduced sodium)
- Store-brand organic mustard
- Store-brand organic sesame tahini (sometimes found in the ethnic section; for hummus and for the salad dressing on page 313)

Grains and Other Dry and Canned Goods

- Store-brand organic whole-wheat couscous
- Store-brand organic canned black beans
- Dried garbanzo beans (for making homemade hummus)
- Farmer's Market brand organic pumpkin puree (for making the Whole-Grain Pumpkin Muffins on page 165)
- Muir Glen organic (plain) tomato sauce
- Organic unsweetened raisins
- Trader Joe's organic espresso blend
- Whole-wheat pretzels (either the Unique Sprouted "Splits" from the Fresh Market or Trader Joe's 100% whole-wheat)

Baking Needs

- Hershey's special dark cocoa
- Ian's whole-wheat panko breadcrumbs (in case I'm out of the homemade Whole-Wheat Breadcrumbs, page 331)
- Whole-grain cornmeal (both fine and coarse)
- Arm & Hammer baking soda
- Rumford baking powder

Exceptions to the 100 Days of Real Food Rules (used sparingly, with the exception of dark chocolate)

We are no longer on a strict pledge, and certainly no one is perfect!

- Store-brand organic ketchup (I've tried making my own, but we use ketchup so rarely this is just easier—and tastes better, in my opinion)
- Spectrum organic mayonnaise with olive oil (for occasionally making egg salad or chicken salad)
- Organic refined white and brown sugar (for homemade treats, such as cookies or cake, although we usually use maple syrup or honey)
- Organic very dark chocolate bars . . . 85% dark!

My Most Frequently Used Dried Spices

- Cinnamon
- Ginger
- Nutmeg
- Cumin
- Chili powder
- Onion powder

- Garlic powder
- Paprika
- Thyme
- Italian seasoning
- Black pepper (both peppercorns and ground)
- Red pepper (both crushed and ground)
- Celtic or Real salt (these are the unrefined options; don't overlook the ingredients even on something as simple as this, because not all salts are created equal!)

THREE TRICKY PACKAGED FOODS TO AVOID

1. Pre-flavored packaged products

There's a wide range of "flavored" products available these days, including everything from beverages to yogurts to oatmeal to cream cheese. Trust me, food factories are going to use a lot more sugar, salt, refined oil, and unrecognizable ingredients than you would if you made them at home. Many of these are disguised simply as "natural flavors" or "artificial flavors" on the ingredient label.

Instead: Buy plain and flavor and/or sweeten it yourself (naturally). When it comes to drinks, squirt some lemon (or other citrus) in your water or sparkling water to kick things up a notch.

TOP 10 KITCHEN TOOLS AND APPLIANCES

I reach for these most frequently to help meet our family's real-food goals.

1. High-quality food processor
2. Set of mixing bowls (10 nesting bowls)
3. Stainless-steel measuring cups and spoons
4. Glass measuring cups of varying sizes
5. Good-quality knives and cutting boards
6. Slow cooker
7. Countertop blender
8. Handheld immersion blender
9. Salad spinner
10. High-quality stainless-steel pots and pans

2. Seasoning packets

Little packets of seasoning mix for tacos, ranch dressing, sloppy joes, and even brown gravy are tempting—but trust me, turn the other way! I couldn't believe it when I noticed that the first ingredient of a popular brand of taco seasoning (and what it contains the most of) was maltodextrin, a highly processed additive made from corn. And, I promise, the others are not much better.

Instead: Make your own, of course. Check out the seasoning blend in Taco Night! on page 264 and the ranch dip and sloppy joes recipes on the blog (100daysofrealfood.com).

3. Imitation foods

This includes anything that pretends to be something it's not—things like margarine (or vegan "butter"), processed cheese products, imitation crab meat, pancake "syrup," and "lemonade" powder (which likely contains no lemons at all). Believe it or not, there used to be a regulation requiring manufacturers to clearly label foods like these as an imitation, but it's no surprise that the ever-so-powerful food industry got that regulation thrown out the window. The bottom line? Imitation foods are highly processed "fake" versions of the real thing.

Instead: Buy real! Real butter, real cheese, real crab, real pure maple syrup. And make lemonade with real lemons, not with artificial powder.

CONVERTING YOUR FAVORITE RECIPES

Being on a real-food diet doesn't mean you have to toss all your favorite old recipes! Here are some suggestions to convert them to real-food recipes:

Processed Ingredient	Real-Food Substitute*
All-purpose white flour	Whole-wheat flour
Vegetable or canola oil (for baking)**	Melted butter or melted coconut oil
Vegetable or canola oil (for sautéing at low temperature)**	Olive oil, butter, or ghee (clarified butter)
Vegetable or canola oil (for sautéing at high temperature)**	Ghee (clarified butter), coconut oil, or pastured lard
Vegetable or canola oil (for deep frying at high temperature)**	Pastured lard or coconut oil
Margarine or other butter substitute	Butter
Solid vegetable shortening	Solid (cold) coconut oil
Refined sugar	Honey or maple syrup***

Processed Ingredient	Real-Food Substitute
Artificial sweeteners	Honey or maple syrup***
Cornstarch	Arrowroot powder
Corn syrup	Pure maple syrup
Chocolate syrup	Simple Chocolate Sauce (page 338)
Chicken stock	Overnight Chicken Stock in the Slow Cooker (page 322)
Canned cream of mushroom soup	Homemade Cream of Mushroom Soup (page 314)
Packet of dried onion soup mix	Homemade Dried Onion Soup Mix (page 317)
Pancake or "table" syrup	Pure maple syrup
Imitation vanilla extract	Pure Vanilla Extract (page 337)
Cool Whip topping	Homemade Whipped Cream (page 339)
Refined breadcrumbs	Whole-Wheat Breadcrumbs (page 331)
Velveeta	Basic Cheese Sauce (page 324)
Low-fat or fat-free products	Full-fat version
Artificial food coloring (you know, the colorful ones in the little squeeze bottles)	Store-bought natural food colors (such as India Tree brand from Whole Foods or Amazon.com) or homemade (like beet juice, kale or spinach juice, blackberry juice, turmeric powder, and carrot juice)

**All suggested substitutes are 1:1 (except when using honey instead of sugar; see below).*

***Refined vegetable oils could come in the form of canola, soybean, corn, safflower, or grapeseed oil, but "vegetable oil" and "canola oil" are the most common labels you will encounter.*

****Honey is more concentrated than refined sugar, so start with half the amount or even a little less. If a recipe calls for just a small amount of sugar (1 teaspoon or tablespoon), I usually leave it out altogether. If a recipe calls for a great deal of sugar (1 cup), I add half the amount of honey and hope for the best, since I'm replacing dry sugar with a liquid. The results are usually satisfactory.*

REAL-FOOD CONDIMENTS: DO THEY EXIST?

I get a lot of questions about condiments. And surprisingly (since I have such a sweet tooth), condiments were one of the things I missed the most during our 100 Days of Real Food pledge. They're like the little things you don't pay much attention to until they're suddenly gone. So here's the deal on what's real and what's not, and what we use now that our pledge is over.

Mayonnaise

Just about all store-bought mayos are made with refined oils (such as canola oil), even if it says something catchy on the front like "made with olive oil." Just read the ingredients and you'll see what I mean. And no matter what oils are used, there are no easy-to-find brands (to my knowledge) that contain five or fewer ingredients, which was one of our real-food pledge rules.

You can certainly make homemade mayonnaise yourself, but I'll tell you right now that based on my experiences it won't be the same fluffy white stuff that you buy from the store. I've decided that **homemade mayo and store-bought mayo are just two completely different products** and—right or wrong—I like and prefer the fluffy white stuff.

What's the solution?

You can try to make homemade mayo using unrefined oils and pastured eggs, but most recipes call for raw eggs. I'm still on the fence about giving uncooked eggs to my kids, so after a few different "cooked-egg" mayonnaise failures I honestly just gave up on it. So during our 100 Days pledge we basically abstained from mayonnaise altogether (gasp)!

Some people successfully **substitute plain Greek yogurt** for mayo in recipes like egg salad and chicken salad, but I'm just being honest here: I've tried it and am not sold on the idea.

Now that our strict 100 Days pledge is over, we just buy a minimally processed (meaning: small number of ingredients) organic mayonnaise from the store. Yes, it's the organic Spectrum brand that says "made with olive oil," even though I know it also contains highly refined canola oil, but occasionally convenience wins around here. That said, we **use the store-bought stuff in great moderation** (probably only once a month at the most, in dishes like egg salad).

Ketchup

There's no such thing as ketchup without added sweeteners. For better or worse, that's just what ketchup is—sweetened tomato sauce. Ketchup is basically two parts tomato and spices and one part sugar. That means **for every tablespoon of ketchup you eat, you're consuming 1 teaspoon of sugar.** Yikes!

There seem to be all sorts of ketchup options these days, both organic and conventional, that are sweetened with everything from high-fructose corn syrup to sugar to agave nectar. Just because some added sweeteners are less refined than white sugar—such as honey and maple syrup—please remember that **added sugar is added sugar and all should be consumed in moderation.**

What's the solution?

Clearly you can simply **reduce your consumption of ketchup**. I know some parents say their kids love to dip anything and everything in ketchup, so if that's the case I'd recommend introducing some new and different real-food dips, such as hummus, homemade onion dip (see page 189), or homemade ranch dip.

During our 100 Days pledge, we tried making homemade ketchup with honey (because honey was one of our "allowed" sweeteners), but frankly the result wasn't all that great. So now we just buy organic ketchup made with sugar, and just as with mayo, **we use it in great moderation** (probably about once a month).

Barbecue Sauce

I hate to break it to you, but just like ketchup, **pretty much all tomato-based barbecue sauces contain added sweeteners.** And even if you make your own homemade barbecue sauce, which I highly recommend over the store-bought stuff, most call for ketchup as an ingredient.

What's the solution?

I may sound like a broken record, but due to the added sweetener issue (see ketchup explanation above), it's best to **simply reduce your overall consumption of barbecue sauce.** We didn't have it at all during our 100 Days pledge, but that's because I hadn't yet played around with creating a satisfactory version made with maple syrup or honey (see page 316). Let's face it: Barbecue sauce is pretty awesome.

Mustard

After all that bad news, here's the good news: **There are actually quite a few real-food store-bought mustards out there!** Several organic yellow and Dijon mustard brands contain simply vinegar, mustard seed, and spices, which is all pretty innocent stuff.

FARMERS' MARKET SHOPPING 101

One of the best things you can do to kick-start your real-food lifestyle is to visit your local farmers' market . . . no knowledge about ingredient labels necessary! Until our family cut out processed food, I'd actually never before shopped at a farmers' market, and I admit to having been a little overwhelmed at first. I wasn't sure what questions to ask, what vendors to peruse, or what products to buy. But, after reading *In Defense of Food*, I did know that the produce in the supermarket (whether organic or conventional) travels on average fifteen hundred miles from the farm to your plate, and not only is all that travel taxing on the environment, but it also gives the produce a chance to lose a lot of nutritional value along the way. Local produce at the farmers' market is in season and picked at the peak of freshness.[4]

You'll be pleasantly surprised to find many varieties of produce at the market—including heirloom vegetables—that you've never seen before, because they just won't hold up on grocery store shelves for weeks at a time. Our choices at grocery stores are really quite limited.

Here's an interesting quote from Barbara Kingsolver's book *Animal, Vegetable, Miracle*, about her family's mission to eat almost 100 percent local (off their own farm and from other surrounding farms) for an entire year:

> According to Indian crop ecologist Vandana Shiva, humans have eaten some 80,000 plant species in our history. After recent precipitous changes, three-quarters of all human food now comes from just eight species, with the field quickly narrowing down to genetically modified corn, soy, and canola.[5]

Now for most of us—our family included!—it's just not realistic to eat local 100 percent of the time, but it's certainly possible for everyone to incorporate some local foods into their diets every week. So I finally got the hang of farmers' market shopping, and here are some lessons I've learned.

10 Farmers' Market Shopping Tips

To find a farmers' market near you, search localharvest.org and eatwild.com.

1. **Find and shop at a growers-only farmers' market.** This ensures that all products are locally grown/raised. In South Charlotte, we love to shop at the Matthews Community Farmers' Market because it's close to home, but it's also the biggest growers-only market in the area. I once went to our regional farmers' market, which allows third-party vendors, and saw blueberries for sale that came all the way from Chile, so it's very important to make sure you're in fact buying local food. Growers-only markets make that part easy, because it's all they allow! If you have to shop elsewhere, including roadside fruit stands, be sure to ask where the food came from.

2. **Ask if the market manager sends out an e-mail or newsletter** showing what you can expect to find on upcoming market days, because it can be a big help with meal planning. Some markets have Web sites that show when different foods will be in season in their area, so you can have an idea of what products you might find in the coming weeks.

3. **Arrive as close to the opening time as possible,** because the "good stuff" can run out really quickly. I also prioritize my shopping list. For example, if it's the first weekend that greenhouse tomatoes or field-grown corn are available, I go to those vendors first because I know their produce will be gone in no time.

4. On the flip side, if you show up **at the end of the market you might find some smashing deals,** because no farmer wants to transport his or her produce back home. I once scored a great deal on zucchini blossoms that I would have never purchased otherwise, and they made for a great appetizer after we stuffed them with goat cheese, then battered and pan-fried them.

5. **Map out which farmers are certified organic or follow organic practices (but are not certified)** and be sure to give them most of your business. Just ask if they use chemical pesticides and synthetic fertilizers (or more natural methods), and if you're at a growers-only market they'll surely know the answer. If the vendor seems to have no idea what you're talking about, there's only a slim chance he or she is selling organic produce. When farmers grow their crops naturally, they're proud of it, it costs them time and money, and they know it gives added value for consumers. (By the way, if you find yourself struggling between the choice of local/conventional produce versus organic/well-traveled produce, I hate to tell you, but there is no perfect answer.)

6. **If you have kids, let them tag along** and give them a buck or two to buy something. My older daughter never used to eat cucumbers at home, but for some reason she likes to buy them herself at the market and take a couple big bites while we're shopping. This took me happily by surprise and led to her newfound love for cucumbers!

7. **If you're looking for something specific, ask questions:** "Does anyone sell ground beef around here?" or "Do you know where I can find goat cheese?" You may not see a sign for something, but it might be there—or someone there may know about it.

HOW TO EAT LOCAL YEAR ROUND?

If your farmers' market is closed in the winter, the key to eating local foods all year is to preserve the summer's bounty when it's fresh. Produce like strawberries, blueberries, corn kernels, roasted bell pepper chunks, and sliced peaches can be frozen on baking sheets, then transferred to bags or other freezer-proof containers. Tomatoes can be cooked in soups and sauces, then frozen (or canned). Green beans, leafy greens, and other vegetables can be steamed and frozen for a rainy day. And there's always the fun kitchen project of making jam.

8. **Don't be fooled by the baked goods.** Sure, the muffins for sale are a far better option than the highly processed ones you'll find at the coffee shop, but chances are a lot of them are still full of refined grains and sweeteners, so just know what you're buying. It all goes back to asking questions!

9. Don't forget to **bring cash and reusable shopping bags** or a cooler with ice packs if it's a hot day.

10. **Enjoy the sense of community** and get to know the hand that grows the food you feed your precious family.

Now that I'm more comfortable with farmers' market shopping, I'll occasionally ask friends and family members if they shop at the market as well, and I'll get responses like, "It's not really at a convenient time for me," or "I'm never in that part of town on Saturday mornings." Once again, eating real food is not about convenience . . . it's about prioritizing so you can do what's best for the health of your family. So put the next market date on your calendar, set your alarm, and make a point to be there! Don't forget that we are voting with our dollars each and every day and it's so important to "vote" local whenever possible.

GARDENING: DON'T BE INTIMIDATED!

Aside from the items that we purchase from the grocery store and the farmers' market, we also routinely utilize food from our family garden. For years I'd considered starting a garden, but I always felt intimated by the idea. But gardening doesn't have to be complicated! You can start really small with one pot, a simple tomato plant, a bag of organic fertilizer, and some TLC. Fresh herbs are another great way to kick-start your first garden. It's hard to beat walking out your back door to gather some fresh basil off your very own plant.

Our rather small beginner garden plot has expanded over time. First we had some pots of fresh herbs on our back deck, then my handy husband added five raised boxes in the backyard. Over time we've added two more boxes and five large half barrels. Our garden doesn't exactly feed the neighborhood but at about 150 square feet, it's a great size that we can handle without being overwhelmed.

Herb Gardens

Fresh herbs are probably the easiest way to start growing your own food, and doing so can save you lots of money as well! Forget paying two or three dollars per pack of fresh basil when you can pay once and have access to your very own prosperous plant all summer long. Some great herbs to start with—and that should be planted in the late spring/early summer—are basil, rosemary, thyme, oregano, and sage. Mint is another good one, but you must plant this herb in a pot (rather than the ground) because it will spread like wildfire through your garden (one of the many things I've learned the hard way). We also love to grow our own fresh cilantro, but it's a cool-weather plant that does best in the fall and spring in our gardening zone.

Summer and Winter Gardens

When most people think of gardening, they picture themselves picking a bright red tomato right off the plant on a hot summer day. But in climates that allow them, winter gardens are just as much fun, and in some cases even better! In North Carolina you can plant winter crops twice (in the fall and then again around Valentine's Day), and cold-weather crops require very little maintenance. Greens, broccoli, cauliflower, carrots, and onions don't attract as many bugs or need as much water as their warm-weather counterparts. Also, in the summer, you want to be sure you don't abandon your garden for too many days in a row because a rotting tomato can ruin the whole plant (best to remove them). But winter gardens will likely still be standing even if you ignore them for weeks at a time (I've put this to the test). Plus, it's hard to beat having your very own fresh spinach, kale, and/or Swiss chard leaves to throw into your afternoon smoothie.

Growing summer gardens can take a little more effort, but since homegrown tomatoes are so darn good, it's totally worth it. I've found that the flavor of the tomatoes from our backyard (and the farmers' market) is light-years ahead of the store-bought variety. In our summer garden you'll find multiple varieties of tomatoes (sungold cherry tomatoes are my favorite), zucchini, squash, cucumbers, bell peppers, melons, green beans, berries, and wildflowers.

8 Gardening Tips

1. **Pick a sunny spot.** Summer garden crops need a lot of sunshine to flourish, so be sure to pick a spot that gets plenty of morning and/or afternoon sunshine!

2. **Use organic fertilizer.** Aside from using a good-quality soil/compost base, we also personally use and like Plant-Tone for the majority of our plants. All it takes is a handful of fertilizer around the base of each plant once every three to four weeks and you should be good to go. I did not use any fertilizer the first summer we had a garden and the outcome was rather sad . . . I've found this to be a necessary step! (Plant-Tone works for the majority of what we grow in our garden with the exception of acid-loving blueberry plants.)

3. **Follow the plant spacing guidelines.** It may be hard to believe it when you're looking at tiny little starter plants, but they'll grow right before your eyes and need the space to spread out! Also, it's sometimes a difficult but important part of the job to "kill" some of the plants you started from seed. You typically plant seeds fairly close together to ensure enough healthy plants, but once they start growing, it's important to thin out those starter plants (to the proper spacing) so they can prosper. This advice even pertains to root vegetables like carrots!

4. **Segregate your cucumbers.** I had to learn this one the hard way, but cucumber vines have thin, spiraling tendrils that like to latch on to *everything* . . . including other plants! So the second time I planted cucumbers in our garden I got smart and put them in a round whiskey barrel off all by themselves (with a trellis to climb up), and the outcome was much better. It's also a good idea to give other vine plants (such as pumpkins, fall squash, and watermelons) a little bit of room

to stretch out, although they don't necessarily need to be all on their own.

5. **Use cages for tomatoes and peppers.** With a little support, these plants can do really well; some say the bigger the cages, the bigger your tomato plants!

6. **Don't forget to water.** If you can set up an irrigation system I say go for it. If not, though, be sure your plants get watered two or three times a week—especially in the heat of the summer. This is another great way to involve children.

7. **Keep a journal.** While your summer garden is flourishing, you may have grand ideas about how to plant things differently the following year, but it's amazing how quickly you can forget those plans after a long winter break.

8. **Expect change.** Every season is truly different from another. The way your zucchini grows one season could very well be totally different the next, or one season's drought could be a complete contrast from heavy rains the year before. Gardening is a learning process that takes time, patience, and prac-

tice, but luckily the reward of tasty home-grown food makes it all worthwhile!

So if you're brand new to gardening, do not delay . . . start now by making plans for a sunny spot on your deck or balcony, or in your yard. Even if it's the dead of winter, a couple of pots of herbs or greens will get you inspired to plan for warmer days ahead.

Involving Children

Many tout gardening as a way to get children interested in eating their veggies . . . and it really does help! It's amazing how many kids don't realize that most of their food starts out sitting in a plot of dirt. Gardening together as a family is a great way for children to learn and, hopefully, expand their palates as well. My daughters were very interested in helping me with our garden, but what really took things to the next level was "giving" each girl her very own small raised garden box. When you're a young child, it's hard to beat having something of your very own that you're completely responsible for! So each new gardening season we till up the dirt together, then my daughters get to pick first from my stash of starter plants and seeds. My type-A personality has to get over "like items not being together," but it's all in good fun. And as a result my daughters are more into growing their very own plants—and eating them!—than I could ever have imagined.

GETTING USED TO THE CHANGES

I know it can be tough to go from a theoretical understanding of real food to integrating it fully into your life. Trust me, nobody figures this stuff out overnight; getting settled into a new routine and remembering what to look for at the store is a *loooong* process that can take many months or longer. Throughout my real-food journey I've often been excited to find a "new" 100% whole-grain product, but have completely forgotten to see if there was an organic version. Or I'd select some fresh, wild-caught seafood, but forget to check if it was from North America or a faraway continent. Instinctively knowing what criteria to consider with every single purchase takes time, but eventually it becomes second nature!

3. Making Changes: Don't Overthink, Just Start!

Real-Food Tip: Making some small changes toward a real-food diet is far better than making none at all.

Completely revamping the way you shop for food and cook for your family can be a daunting task. The key is to not get overwhelmed and give up all together! Even some of the smallest changes toward cutting out processed food can really go a long way. Blog readers often ask me where they should start, and the two food groups where I think you can get the most bang for your buck are produce and grains.

TWO SMALL CHANGES WITH BIG RESULTS

Produce. Vegetables and fruit should be the "bread and butter" of everyone's diet. Just take a look at all the different diet trends that come and go and you'll find one common overlap: Vegetables are king! If you haven't been a big fan of vegetables in the past I encourage you to try fresh (local) veggies, new vegetable recipes, and maybe even some new types of vegetables all together. Putting whole foods like fruits and vegetables on your plate will automatically displace some of the processed stuff!

Set a Goal. Eat 1 fruit with breakfast, 1 fruit and 1 vegetable with lunch, and 2 different vegetables with dinner.

Tips. Try raw vegetables with a dip (such as hummus or the onion dip on page 189), try adding minced vegetables to ground meat (in recipes like the tacos on page 264), and try mixing different vegetables together to get more of a variety (in recipes like Veggie Pancakes, page 226).

Grains. Right or wrong, it's a fact that grains make up a very big portion of most people's diets, so switching to 100 percent whole-grain foods could potentially go a long way. This includes bread, buns, crackers, pasta, rice, tortillas/wraps, cereals, snacks, and more. When was the last time you had a meal that didn't include something from this category? So start now by switching to products that are 100 percent whole grain and have a short ingredient list (they're sometimes hard to find). And remember again that "wheat" doesn't equal "whole wheat" (see page 19).

Set a goal. Whether it's a week or a month from now, mark a date on your calendar that you'll aim to have at least two out of your three big meals in a day contain no refined grains. This will give you time to replace products one by one as you run out of them.

Tips. It can be a challenge to find decent 100 percent whole-grain products like bread, for example, that don't also contain forty other ingredients, including unnecessary additives. I've found that the higher quality the product, the better tasting it is. Before our switch to real food I would rather have skipped bread altogether than eat store-bought whole-wheat bread (since I didn't like it). So I understand very well that it's not easy to transition from the taste and texture of white bread (or other refined grains) to whole wheat.

If you don't like whole grains, these tips will help:

1. **Don't settle for mediocre whole-grain products.** One reason I used to despise whole-wheat sandwich bread was that I'd never tried good bread before. Even today I don't like the taste of packaged grocery store whole-grain bread, which was designed to have a long shelf life, not to taste good. So skip the supermarket and look into your local bakery options instead, or try making some homemade bread yourself (see page 332)! It takes only four or five ingredients to make real whole-wheat sandwich bread at home, so look for the shortest ingredient list possible if you aren't going to make it yourself.
2. **Go for a lighter variety of wheat.** Try King Arthur's White Whole-Wheat Flour for baking rather than straight-up whole-wheat flour. Even though it has the word "white" on the label, it's still 100 percent whole grain; it's just made from a lighter variety of wheat than typical whole-wheat flours, and it's a great place to start if you prefer the taste of white flour products.

3. **Mix the old with the new.** If whole-wheat pasta is getting shunned at your house, try mixing white and whole wheat pasta together for a few weeks, gradually increasing the quantity of whole-wheat pasta. The bottom line is that eating some whole grains is better than none! This same tactic could be applied to brown rice and whole-grain flours as well.

4. **Branch out and try some new grains.** If your family is really pushing back on your attempted switch to whole-grain pasta or rice, how about trying a new grain altogether? Take a break from the usual and cook some quinoa, whole-wheat couscous, barley, or whole-grain polenta for a side dish instead.

5. **Add some character to plain brown rice.** Even the most die-hard real foodies get tired of ordinary brown rice, so try to switch things up a bit by mixing in a sauce (such as low-sodium soy sauce; Teriyaki Marinade, page 318; or Basic Cheese Sauce, page 324), adding some great flavors (such as chopped cilantro or garlic), or throwing in some toasted nuts or seeds (such as almonds or sesame seeds). Changing the flavor can make it a whole new side dish.

6. **Use a sweet disguise.** Ease your family into whole-grain eating by making something sweet such as Whole-Grain Pumpkin Muffins (page 165), Cinnamon-Raisin Quick Bread (page 173), or Whole-Wheat Banana Pancakes (or Waffles!), page 129. They probably won't even notice that anything is different. But once they gobble them down, don't keep them in the dark about your secret ingredient!

Another way to make changes is to start with one meal of the day. For example, work on cleaning up breakfast first (check out the recipes on pages 129 through 148) and get comfortable, then move on to lunch and dinner. Breakfast is a great place to start because most people rotate just a few core breakfast staples, so you can clean up your act pretty quickly.

14 WEEKS OF MINI-PLEDGES: DOING 100 DAYS, STEP BY STEP

My family jumped head-first into our 100 Days of Real Food pledge, but I'm well aware that going cold turkey isn't for everyone! So I developed a slower-paced, step-by-step plan in which you focus on one part of your diet each week over a 100-day (or so) period.

Week 1: Two fruits and/or vegetables per meal

Eat a minimum of two different fruits or vegetables (preferably organic) with every breakfast, lunch, and dinner meal.

Week 2: "Real" beverages

Beverages are limited to coffee, tea, water, and milk. For sweetener, if you need it at all, use a little honey or 100 percent pure maple syrup. You are allowed a total of one cup fruit juice for the whole week, and wine—preferably red—is allowed in moderation (no more than one drink per day).

Week 3: Local meat and reduced consumption

Consume only meat that is locally and humanely raised (within 100 miles of your hometown). Limit weekly consumption to three or four servings, and treat meat as a side item or flavoring instead of a main dish (see page 26). All types are allowed, including beef, pork, chicken, lamb, turkey, and even wild game!

Week 4: No fast food or deep-fried foods

No fast food or any foods that have been deep-fried in oil (see page 29).

Week 5: Try two new whole foods

This week, try at least two whole foods that you've never had before.

Week 6: No low-fat, lite, or nonfat food products

Do not eat any food products that are labeled as low-fat, lite, light, reduced-fat, or nonfat (see page 24).

Week 7: 100 percent whole grain

Consume only 100 percent whole grains when eating bread, pasta, and any other products with grains (see page 14 for details).

Week 8: Stop eating when you feel full

Make a special attempt to pay attention to your internal cues and stop eating when you feel full (see page 75).

Week 9: No refined sweeteners

No refined or artificial sweeteners, including (but not limited to) white sugar, brown sugar, raw sugar, Sucanat, Splenda, stevia, agave, corn syrup, high-fructose corn syrup, brown rice syrup, and cane juice. Foods and beverages can be sweetened only with a small amount of honey or pure maple syrup (see page 21).

MINI PLEDGE TRACKING CHART

If you're interested in giving these weekly challenges a shot, you can start right at the beginning or go in whatever order you like. You can also build each week on top of the next or tackle one weekly challenge at a time. Whatever you choose, these mini pledges will help you gain a new perspective, and you're likely to end up with at least some positive changes that feel right for you to continue. No matter what, these mini pledges will give you a crash course in label reading—if you don't do it already. And be sure to tell friends and family what you are up to because accountability is key!

week	Mini Pledge	Start Date	End Date	Complete?	Notes
1	Two fruits and/or vegetables per meal			Y / N	
2	"Real" beverages			Y / N	
3	Local meat and reduced consumption			Y / N	
4	No fast food or deep-fried foods			Y / N	
5	Try two new whole foods			Y / N	
6	No low-fat, lite, or nonfat food products			Y / N	
7	100 percent whole grain			Y / N	
8	Stop eating when feel full			Y / N	
9	No refined sweeteners			Y / N	
10	No refined oils			Y / N	
11	Eat local foods (one per meal)			Y / N	
12	No sweeteners at all			Y / N	
13	Nothing artificial			Y / N	
14	No more than five ingredients in packaged food			Y / N	

Week 10: No refined oils

No refined or hydrogenated oils, including (but not limited to) vegetable oil, organic vegetable oil, soybean oil, corn oil, canola oil, organic canola oil, margarine, or grapeseed oil (see page 29).

Week 11: Eat local foods

Eat at least one locally grown or raised food at each meal, including (but not limited to) fruits, vegetables, eggs, grains, nuts, meats, and sweeteners such as honey (and no, you can't cheat and put honey on everything!) See page 62 for tips on shopping at the farmers' market.

Week 12: No sweeteners at all

Avoid all added sweeteners, including (but not limited to) white sugar, brown sugar, raw sugar, honey, maple syrup, date sugar, maple sugar, Sucanat, Splenda, stevia, agave, fruit juice concentrate, corn syrup, high-fructose corn syrup, brown rice syrup, and cane juice. Sugar is sugar, so it's a good exercise to see if you can live without any sweeteners at all—refined or not—for a week (see page 19)!

Week 13: Nothing artificial

Avoid all artificial ingredients, including (but not limited to) artificial sweeteners such as aspartame, sucralose, or saccharin and artificial flavors and artificial colors such as FD&C Red No. 40 and FD&C Yellow No. 5 (see page 23).

Week 14: No more than five ingredients

Avoid any and all packaged food products that contain more than five ingredients (see page 15).

THE 10 DAYS OF REAL FOOD PLEDGE

If you're feeling ready to make the switch to real food, I have another great way for you to dive right in! Committing to our 10 Days of Real Food pledge basically means following our same 100 Days pledge rules (page 10) for a shorter period of time. Thousands of blog readers from around the world have completed this challenge and agree it's an enlightening—and in some cases life-changing—experience that gave them a whole new perspective about where their food comes from. Let me give you one hint before you get started, though: Spend a few days cleaning out your pantry and loading it up with real food first!

Participants who complete the 10 Days pledge have a chance to gain the following:

- A **first-hand, eye-opening experience** in identifying real food in our processed-food world.
- At least **one improved health benefit,** such as having more energy, losing weight, improving regularity, or just feeling healthier overall.
- A better awareness that **"food-like substances" don't even taste that good** compared to real food.

PORTION SIZE MATTERS

I don't believe that counting calories, fat grams, and the like is part of eating a real-food diet. On a real-food diet, along with eating a variety of foods, it's important to keep portion size in mind (including eating only until you feel satisfied). But in a world of supersizing, it's harder than ever to know what a realistic portion size is.

Check this out: In her book *French Kids Eat Everything*, which I talk about on page 88, Karen Le Billon notes that in one scientific study, "two researchers (one French, one American) weighed servings of identical meals at McDonald's restaurants in Paris and Philadelphia. The serving sizes were wildly different: a medium-size serving of fries at McDonald's in Philadelphia was 72 percent bigger than at McDonald's in Paris."[1] Let's hope they aren't charging the same price! But kidding aside, what's up with that? And there's more: According to the Centers for Disease Control and Prevention (CDC), over the last fifty years in the United States "the size of a hamburger has tripled, a basket of fries more than doubled, and the average soda has grown from a modest 7 ounces to a jumbo 42 ounces." And some wonder why "the average American is 26 pounds heavier than in 1950. [And] about one third of us are overweight or obese and that number is projected to hit nearly 50 percent by 2030."[2]

As Michael Pollan says, one contributing factor is that instead of using our internal cues to know when to stop eating most of us "allow external, and usually visual, cues to determine how much we [should] eat." So many of us are likely not listening to our guts and instead just continuing to eat until our plates are clean, the package is empty, or the TV show is over. When was the last time you left some food on your plate simply because you were starting to feel full? I'm the first to admit that it's easier said than done![3]

Keeping portion sizes in check is a high priority on a real-food eating plan. I actually think real food is much more filling than the processed stuff, so it doesn't take as much to feel (and keep you) full, which helps prevent all those crazy spikes in hunger and energy levels throughout the day. Good-bye, afternoon crashes!

So don't be fooled by what society is telling you is the right amount of food; eat what's right for you. You can always go back for more, and believe it or not it's okay to feel a bit hungry between meals! Here are some things to try:

- The next time you're at a restaurant, split an entrée with someone at your table.
- Prepare your food on an appetizer plate instead of a standard-size dinner plate.
- Eat more slowly to allow yourself time to feel full before going back for more.
- Stop eating when you feel full . . . don't worry about cleaning your plate or finishing the last bite!

- The **opportunity to show their children** the healthiest way to eat and enjoy the food Mother Nature has given us.
- New knowledge about **how and why to avoid processed foods.**

Hopefully your ten-day experience will convince you to consider making at least some permanent real-food changes in your life. If you complete the 10 Days pledge, you can receive a congratulatory letter and complementary gift: a silicone wristband that you can wear to make sure all your friends know what you accomplished! (Go to www.100daysofrealfood.com/take-the-10-day-pledge/real-food-graduates/ for an application.) Before we mail our pledges their free wristbands, we ask them to fill out a form so that we can hear about their experience. Here's some of the feedback we've received, including the good, the bad, and the ugly.

"I learned that making my health a priority is worth it. It takes some planning and preparation, but is worth it. I felt better and wanted others to join me. It was easier to say no to Doritos and candy bars when I know what is in them instead of just 'depriving' myself of them 'cause they'll make me fat. I also noticed that when I ate better I wanted to become more physically active."

—FORT WORTH, TEXAS

"I learned that my idea of 'healthy eating' was very far from it. We all feel better. I feel more rested and don't crave the three p.m. coffee to pick me up. My husband's headaches are better and IBS is not a problem. Our three-year-old doesn't have constipation issues. My husband and I both lost about 8 pounds each."

—LEXINGTON, KENTUCKY

"The biggest thing for me is that I no longer have stomachaches or bloating. This is just something I had gotten used to over the years. I also lost a couple pounds. I feel empowered that I am making the choices to get healthy and feel good! And now I'm teaching my daughters how to make healthy choices too."

—WHEATFIELD, INDIANA

"I am so happy that I decided to do this. I learned that I can cook from scratch and it tastes good. Cooking the real foods gives me such a sense of accomplishment. The recipes were easy to follow. My daughter's behaviors completely changed. She was much calmer and didn't complain of a stomachache at bedtime once. She normally complains every night."

—MACOMB, MICHIGAN

"I am amazed at all the changes that happened in these last ten days! My husband lost over five pounds and I lost nine pounds! But more than that I am sleeping better, I have more energy during the day, I'm not craving sugar or soda like I used to. My husband has told me that he no longer has heartburn and his knees and ankles don't hurt while he's at work (he's on his feet and walking the whole time). My youngest has never been regular in her whole life and is now. We are all

feeling so much better after just ten days, I can't wait to see how we'll feel as we continue!"

—MOORESVILLE, NORTH CAROLINA

"I cannot believe the difference this made in my family! I have ADHD, and I have never felt so good. My symptoms were almost gone! As were my migraines. You could completely tell the difference in the kids. And we all felt a lot more full so we were not constantly searching out something to snack on. We will be making this a lifestyle change :)"

—PHOENIX, ARIZONA

"As a working mother of two small children, I find it difficult to prepare, cook, and store 'real' food for everyone in our family (including one child who appears to be allergic to everything in sight). However, with a little planning (actually, it took a lot of planning), I was able to map out a week's worth of meals and I discovered that we used to waste so much food. I'm now able to spend the same amount on groceries as before but this time I shop at Whole Foods Market and I get better-quality produce. I just don't buy as much and we eat everything that we buy. The biggest thing I learned, however, is that eating healthy keeps you healthy . . . everyone in my office has been sick this winter season with the flu . . . except for me."

—ALEXANDRIA, VIRGINIA

"I would say the hardest thing was just getting started, but after that it was all very progressive and easy. I took two hours on Saturday morning and stripped my cupboards bare of everything that I no longer wanted to put into my body, then took myself to the shops and stocked up on fresh produce."

—PALMERSTON,
NORTHERN TERRITORY, AUSTRALIA

"I noticed what felt like a 'fog' being lifted from my head. I had a lot more energy and just overall felt wonderful. My husband lost six pounds and I lost one and a half pounds, though we never went into this caring about weight loss—we were just curious what would happen, so we weighed ourselves before we started and after."

—ELWOOD, ILLINOIS

"I was amazed at how many 'health' foods we ate that were actually horrible! I lost about five pounds and gained tons more energy by eating real food. I am hoping to turn these ten days into a lifestyle change!"

—MACON, MISSOURI

"I was surprised how easy it was to cut out bad foods once I committed. Before committing to the ten days, it was so difficult. But once I had filled out the pledge form, it was much easier. I definitely do not get bloated anymore, have a flatter stomach, feel better, and am more regular. I'm hoping my skin will improve the longer I do it."

—MOUNT PLEASANT, SOUTH CAROLINA

"I've got a rare autoimmune disease and noticed a huge decline in my inflammation on a real-food diet—and we haven't even been doing it for very long or very hardcore yet!"

—LONDON, ENGLAND

"I thought it would be harder. I have eleven-month-old twins and life can be pretty chaotic. I'm used to grab-and-go with food. But I found that the planning and thoughtful preparation of my food was cathartic and made me healthier and more relaxed because it put me in control, not my emotions. For once I felt like I was taking care of me :)"

—SWAMPSCOTT, MASSACHUSETTS

"The first week and in particular the first couple of days were the hardest. I went through major sugar withdrawal and got pretty bad headaches at first but then it started to get easier. It almost felt like I was detoxing in a way . . . I have a sweet tooth so I have missed chocolate a lot but I think I was a bit of a sugar addict before, so it was time I did something drastic!"

—ARVADA, COLORADO

"I have completely changed the way I eat and what I serve to my husband and sixteen-month-old daughter. Before I even discovered your blog, I lost about eighty pounds after giving birth to my daughter. I believed I was eating really healthfully, but this blog has opened my eyes. I was previously obsessively counting calories to make sure that I at least kept off the weight I'd worked so hard to lose. Now, I do not have to count calories. When you eat real food, it fills you up like food is supposed to, so I eat the right amount and do not have to count calories and I do not gain weight. I am still watching my portions, but this way of life that you blog about is so much more simple and it just makes sense. I have more energy and feel much better. I have noticed that my skin seems to be clearer, too. Crazy how much our diet truly affects our health."

—LAWRENCEVILLE, GEORGIA

"We learned that it's not as hard as we thought it would be to find and eat real food. We also noticed that we didn't have any gastrointestinal problems the whole time, which is very uncommon for our house."

—MISHAWAKA, INDIANA

"More than anything, I am proud of myself for taking charge of what goes into the mouths of my loved ones. I'm disgusted with what we have all come to think of as food, and getting back to the basics of eating is a new passion of mine. The kids rebelled, but I stayed strong and kept telling myself that I love them too much to argue about it. We survived our ten days. It was hard and took a lot of planning and mindful eating. But it showed us that we can do it, and that we should continue it. I agree some cheating is okay . . . you do have to live a little and fit into this fast-paced world. But overall, it's most important to take control and not fall victim to the processed-food giants!"

—LENEXA, KANSAS

"The biggest challenge personally was sugar. I have a big sweet tooth that was initially hard to ignore. But with some tweaks here and there I was able to create some goodies that filled the void. My favorite discovery was using frozen bananas to create an ice cream substitute."

—HOLLAND, PENNSYLVANIA

A REAL FOOD TRANSFORMATION

Darcy Struckmeier, one of our real-food pledges, experienced such a dramatic and inspiring change after cutting out processed food that her story was featured in the book *Pandora's Lunchbox* by Melanie Warner. Melanie visited Darcy and her family at their home in California, and what she learned is nothing short of amazing. And, not to bring on the cheese, but reading about their experience honestly brought tears to my eyes. Stories like this are absolutely what keep me going on this real-food mission!

For years the Struckmeiers had to find a way to manage their son Cameron's behavioral problems. The oldest of four children, Cameron was exceptionally stubborn and willful, especially when it came to food. He subsisted on a diet of crackers, milk, refined pasta, and fruit; would often complain of stomachaches; and at times would even throw up on his plate if there was a food he didn't like. Darcy also shared that "he never really seemed happy or joyful like most kids do. It was hard to get him to smile."

As Cameron got older he learned to articulate how he felt, stating that his "insides were being stretched like a rubber band, as tight as possible and about to break" and that he often felt angry without any explanation. After rounds of doctors' visits, medications that didn't help, and chasing after suspected conditions that included everything from ADHD to food allergies to even Asperger's, they were at a loss. With no official diagnosis—or solution—the Struckmeiers finally settled on dealing with Cameron's "sensory processing issues" through love and support like they always had.

Then one day, with personal weight-loss goals in mind, Darcy came across my 100 Days of Real Food blog and the invitation to take the 10 Days pledge. Thinking she'd do it on her own, she was surprised but pleased when the whole family (including Cameron, who was now in middle school) wanted to join her. The Struckmeiers went from a diet that regularly consisted of fast food, frozen dinners, and pizza delivery to homemade stir-fry with brown rice, whole-wheat spaghetti with meatballs, and tacos with tortillas made from scratch. The new dishes that were starting to appear on the family dinner table were well received, and then suddenly, on day seven of their pledge, Cameron told his mom, "I feel like I've been lifted from a fog. I feel like I can think better." Darcy was absolutely stunned.

Shortly thereafter Darcy began to notice the changes in Cameron herself. She caught him smiling out of the corner of her eye and thought, *There you are.* Looking back, Darcy marvels, "It's like he's a different child. There was something there before preventing him from being happy." (Now do you understand why this story brings me to tears?)

Although Darcy isn't sure what aspect of their processed-food diet was causing her son so much turmoil—was it the refined sugar, the food dyes, the artificial ingredients, or even all three?—she's now sure that processed foods were the trigger. After completing their 10 Days pledge, the Struckmeiers went on a family trip. They finished up all the real food they'd taken from home and started frequenting some fast-food joints and ice cream shops. Writes Melanie Warner, "Four days into the vacation, Cameron started having angry outbursts and refused to leave the hotel room. When his parents sat down to talk to him he said he just felt awful, and his stomach hurt and he wanted to 'punch everybody.'" As soon as they got home they went back to their real-food diet, and four days later his anger, stomach pain, and antisocial behavior disappeared again.[4]

Hearing this remarkable story reminds me of a powerful quote from Dr. Kenneth A. Bock in the foreword of Robyn O'Brien's book *The Unhealthy Truth*. Dr. Bock believes that our children are the "canaries in a coal mine" in our world of processed food. Dr. Bock believes that the dramatic rise of autism, allergies, ADHD, and asthma in our children today is our warning. With the increasing amount of food additives, artificial ingredients, and GMOs constantly being added to our food supply, something is very wrong—and it's not something that we should just sit back and accept.[5] I can't imagine any better example than the Struckmeier family's experience to prove this very point.

Of course, not everyone can expect to experience such an immediate and dramatic change from cutting out processed food, but if it could make such a difference in young Cameron's life, it's hard not to wonder what it might do for the rest of us.

If you'd like to officially sign up for the 10 Days pledge yourself, please do so at http://www.100daysofrealfood.com/take-the-10-day-pledge/. There's nothing like putting such a promise in writing; accountability is key when it comes to successfully completing challenges like this!

BEING PERFECT IS OVERRATED

The purpose of following our rules for 10 days or 100 days (or however long you choose) is to gain a new perspective that will allow you to make some realistic and positive long-term changes for life. You can't gain that perspective if you're constantly making exceptions. But beyond the period of your real-food pledge, it's important to remember that some flexiblity and some occasional rule breaking might actually be good for your health, too! Unnecessary stress certainly never did anybody any good.

Now that our family's official pledge is over, we typically indulge in about one special treat a week. If our girls happen to be invited to two birthday parties in one week, we honestly don't fret too much (I don't want to give them a complex), but there are many weeks where homemade organic ice cream (see page 290) or whole-wheat Peanut Butter Cookies (page 302) count as our special treat.

So when we do indulge, we do it in true moderation. If I had a penny every time someone said to me, "It's just this one time," or "Halloween is only once a year," I think I would be rich. All those holidays, school celebrations, sports snacks, church activities, birthday parties, special occasions, and other "just one times" can add up to *a lot*. So as much as it's good to be flexible, it's also important to find a middle ground that will keep you in control. Whether you decide to practice an "eighty-twenty" rule (real food 80 percent of the time) or stick to real food at home but not necessarily outside the house, it's up to you to decide what's realistic for you and your family.

It's also important to decide how far you want to go on your mission. When readers tell me using my microwave is toxic (I don't believe it is) and my slow cooker is leaching lead into my food (I don't believe it is) and wheat is making me ill (even though I feel fine), it's clear that different people have different priorities. When our initial 100 Days pledge ended, it took some time for us to find our happy medium, but at this point I'm very pleased with where we've ended up. I like to think of our family as people who stand up for—but don't obsess over—what we believe is right.

And since I know not everyone is aiming for perfection 100 percent of the time, I think it's helpful to break down food choices into three distinct categories: bad, better, and best.

SINCE NO ONE IS PERFECT

Bad	Better	Best	Why
Bag of artificially flavored, crunchy chips deep fried in refined oil	Bag of crunchy nuts baked in refined oil and salted by a food factory	Raw nuts (or homemade organic popcorn, page 192)	Nuts and organic popcorn are a whole food, especially when there are no unhealthy additives like refined oil and/or excessive amounts of salt.
Boxed orange (artificially colored) macaroni and cheese	Organic (but still refined) boxed macaroni and cheese	Homemade whole-grain Macaroni Casserole (page 252)	The organic boxed macaroni and cheese is of course organic, which means it doesn't have any artificial ingredients or food dyes, among other things. However, it is still highly processed, since the noodles are made with refined grains. The homemade version is actually fairly simple to make, can be organic, and incorporates 100 percent whole-grain noodles. Even if the boxed version says "whole-grain" on the front it may not be 100 percent whole-grain.

Bad	Better	Best	Why
Artificially colored boxed cereal	"All-natural" store-bought boxed cereal that is 100 percent whole-grain (or close to it)	Homemade Granola Cereal (page 134)	If you choose to buy store-bought boxed cereal, at least buy a version that is 100 percent whole-grain, is low in added sugar, and does not contain any artificial additives, such as food coloring.
Artificially flavored and/or colored ice cream	"All-natural" vanilla boxed ice cream made with a few ingredients, including refined sugar	Organic ice cream made at home with a fraction of the sweetener used in the store-bought stuff (see page 290)	Boxed "all-natural" ice cream with a few simple ingredients is far superior to store-bought ice cream made with artificial additives and colors. But even if you buy ice cream made with only a few simple ingredients it could still contain far more sugar than is necessary. Making it yourself is easy (with a modern ice cream maker) and the only way to regulate how much—and what—sweetener is added.
Orange fish crackers	Organic (but still refined) cheddar-flavored bunny crackers	Homemade organic, whole-wheat cheese crackers (www.100daysofrealfood.com/easy-crackers/)	The biggest problem with the store-bought crackers is that, organic or not, they are both made with highly refined white flour. Even if the package says "whole-grain" on the front, chances are they're not 100 percent whole-grain. Making your own homemade cheese crackers (page 190) is surprisingly simple and can be made 100 percent whole-grain. (They can also be frozen for later use.)
Store-bought white sandwich bread	Store-bought whole-wheat sandwich bread that was made in a factory or in the supermarket "bakery" and contains 30 or 40 ingredients	100% whole-wheat bread made from 4 or 5 fresh ingredients from a local bakery or made at home (see page 332)	Whole-wheat bread that was made in a factory might contain some whole-grain flour, but it usually also contains a bunch of other refined additives on the list of 30 to 40 ingredients. Whole-wheat bread from supermarket "bakeries" is usually made with dough sent in from central locations that also contains equal amounts of unnecessary additives, including dough conditioners. It is certainly a step up from "white" bread or "white wheat" bread, which are both made with only refined grains. In most cases, buying your bread from a bakery or making it yourself is the only way to get fresh bread made with only a handful of the intended ingredients.

Bad	Better	Best	Why
Coffee flavored with an artificial sweetener	Coffee flavored with a refined (but natural) sweetener, such as white sugar	Coffee flavored with a small amount of a natural (and unrefined) sweetener, such as honey or maple syrup—or no sweetener at all, of course	Sugar is sugar, but at least honey and maple syrup have some trace nutrients and are mostly processed in nature. No matter what kind of sweetener you use, it's always best to go with a natural product over artificial, and always consume it in moderation.
Jelly sweetened with high-fructose corn syrup	"All-fruit" jelly spread sweetened with fruit juice concentrate	Freshly mashed fruit (like bananas or strawberries)	"All-fruit" jellies, jams, and preserves that are sweetened naturally with fruit juice concentrate are far superior to varieties that list sugar or high-fructose corn syrup as the first ingredient. But it is also fairly easy to mash up some fresh fruit with a fork, which of course would be the best choice since there's no added sweetener at all.
Store-bought conventional meat	Store-bought organic meat	Local grass-fed, organic meat	The only way to truly know if the animals were humanely raised and fed a proper diet is to ask the farmer yourself, although I would certainly choose organic meat from the store if I didn't have access to any locally raised options.
Conventional grocery store eggs	Organic grocery store eggs	Pastured, organic farmers' market eggs	Eggs from chickens that are able to roam a grassy pasture provide the most nutrients, but if I didn't have access to that option, store-bought organic would be the next best bet.

4. Getting Your Family on Board

Real-Food Tip: It's much easier to avoid eating processed food if it's not in the house.

At first, the transition from highly processed to real food can feel intimidating, overwhelming, and even impossible. I lost a couple nights of sleep myself when our family first started cutting out processed food, mainly because I didn't really know where to start and had an irrational fear that we might starve before I figured it out! But after lots of practice our new way of life has come to be second nature to us, and honestly our meals look a lot like they used to, except they're made from much higher-quality ingredients. So instead of frozen pizza, it's a homemade one with whole-wheat crust, organic tomato sauce, and freshly grated cheese—better for us, and in my opinion, so much better tasting! This isn't about giving up cheeseburgers for sprouts and tofu (although those are both suitable real-food options). It's about using better-quality organic, fresh, whole, and humanely raised products. So just start by taking a deep breath and remembering it doesn't have to be all or nothing out of the gate . . . you can do this!

KIDS AND REAL FOOD

Do you have a couple of picky kids at your house, or maybe a reluctant spouse? In some ways it's helpful for people to come around on their own

> **LISA'S TIP:** Offer your kids more real food. If junk food is no longer a choice they might just surprise you!

> "Tacos, macaroni casserole, and spaghetti and meatballs are three of my favorite dinners!"—SIENNA, AGE 7

when it comes to making the transition to real food, but there are *plenty* of things you can do to help nudge them along the way.

12 Tips for Converting Picky Eaters

These tips won't completely convert every kid, but for most otherwise healthy children, they can help you make some headway. The important thing to remember is that it can take many months or a year to win over your picky eater so, just like potty training, don't give up if a certain tactic doesn't work right away.

1. Start by switching out some of the refined and processed meals they love for the real-food versions. Some recipes to consider: Macaroni Casserole (page 252), Homemade Chicken Nuggets (page 244), Whole-Wheat Pizza (page 250), and Whole-Wheat Banana Pancakes (or Waffles!), page 129.

2. Give your child a good first impression of the real food you want her to try, even if it means deep-frying sweet potatoes to make French fries, making sweet zucchini bread, or topping broccoli with Basic Cheese Sauce (page 324). Once your child thinks she likes zucchini, you'll have a better chance of getting her to eat it next time (even if you cook it differently).

3. If you like to hide veggies in your kids' food, *please* do me a favor and tell them about it while they're eating it, or at least afterward. They need to know the hidden ingredient isn't so horrifying after all. Plus, what happens when they turn eighteen and think they hate foods they've secretly been eating all this time? They'll still avoid them, and their diets will suffer.

4. Bribe them to eat real food with other real food. Parenting experts probably won't like this advice, but let's face it, most parents already bribe on occasion. Just remember that it does not always have to be about sweets and junk food. For example, my younger daughter absolutely loves organic cheese sticks and will do just about anything for one . . . including eating a bite of her veggies!

5. Let them pick out their own fruits and vegetables at the store or farmers' market. Better yet, let them help you grow some produce in a few pots or in a small garden in your very own backyard (see page 64).

6. Get them involved in picking out dinner or breakfast recipes and helping you cook the

meal. Even kids as young as one or two are great at stirring (see page 89 for more ideas). I started letting my older daughter flip pancakes under close supervision at six years old, and today she gets great satisfaction at the idea of cooking for the family. Most kids will at least have a taste if they helped make the meal.

7. Make a strict "one-bite rule," that is, kids have to at least try a food. Remind them that it won't hurt them if it tastes bad. Do this at every meal and they'll learn to expect it. Allow them to wash it down with their drink as opposed to spitting it out. You may only win them over once in a blue moon, but that one time makes it so worth it! Neither of my daughters liked my recipe for refried beans (see page 155) when I first introduced it, but when I'd be eating some for lunch I'd say, "But it's *sooo* good! C'mon, try a bite." I did this over and over and now—no joke—it's one of their favorite meals.

8. Don't pressure or upset your kids too much over trying a new food. There's a sweet spot between giving up too easily and pushing too hard. This is why I like our "one-bite rule," because we're consistent and our kids know what to expect if there's a new food on their plate. You definitely don't want them to have any negative feelings toward food or mealtime. You should know pretty quickly when you're taking things too far.

"I can't pick my favorites because my mommy cooks too many yummy things."—SYDNEY, AGE 9

9. If your child is especially resistant, put only one new food on his plate at a time, along with other real food that you already know he likes, so he doesn't get overwhelmed.

10. Talk to older children about why it is important to make these changes and consider inviting them to watch the documentary *Food, Inc.* with you. Sit down with them and discuss the list of top ten reasons to cut out processed food (see page 12). Most kids want to be healthy and do the right thing, and I promise the transition will be much easier if they're on board with making changes.

11. Make sure you have the right expectations. Converting your child or your entire family over to real food won't happen overnight; in fact, it could take many months or longer. Shopping for, prepping, and cooking wholesome meals is going to be more work than ordering takeout. Just remember that the changes you'll see in the health and well-being of your family will be more than worth it in the long run!

12. It really does take a dozen or more times for a child to realize she might like a new food. It took a lot of patience on my part, but I think I offered my youngest daughter green bell peppers as many as two or three dozen times before she one day decided she liked them (much to my surprise!). So remember . . . *gentle* persistence is key. Don't give up!

Advice from the French

When it comes to handling those picky eaters in the family, there is a *very* inspiring book that I always recommend to blog readers called *French Kids Eat Everything* by Karen Le Billon (I mention it in chapter 3). Karen is Canadian but transplanted her family, including her two young daughters, to France for a year to live in her French husband's childhood village. She went into the experience with two kids who were used to being accommodated with "kid food," eating snacks whenever they pleased, and not necessarily being required to eat their vegetables. And after a bumpy start with her immersion into French culture, Karen managed to completely turn things around in their year abroad and come out of it with some valuable lessons learned—not to mention two very good eaters.

Karen summarizes her experience with ten important French food rules, which she expands upon in her book.

OPEN YOUR MOUTH, CLOSE YOUR EYES . . .

And you will find a big surprise! I play this game with my daughters, and by now they know the rules: *If you cooperate, most of the time I'll put something yummy that I know you love in your mouth, but every now and then it will be something unexpected and new!*

And maybe one out of five times my daughters decide they actually like the new item (which makes this game worth it!), but sometimes I take it too far with trying to feed them things like olives or raw broccoli. It's all in good fun, though, and yes, they still trust me. Again, they know the rules! Go to 100daysofrealfood.com and type "Taste Testing Games" into the search bar for more fun ideas including a free, downloadable worksheet for your little ones.

French Food Rules

1. Parents: *You* are in charge of your children's food education.

2. Avoid emotional eating. Food is not a pacifier, a distraction, a toy, a bribe, a reward, or a substitute for discipline.

3. Parents schedule meals and menus. Kids eat what adults eat: no substitutes and no short-order cooking.

4. Food is social. Eat family meals together at the table, with no distractions.

5. Eat vegetables of all colors of the rainbow. Don't eat the same main dish more than once per week.
6. For picky eaters: You don't have to *like* it, but you do have to *taste* it. For fussy eaters: You don't have to *like* it, but you do have to *eat* it.
7. Limit snacks to one per day (ideally, but two maximum), and not within one hour of meals.
8. Take your time, for both cooking and eating. Slow food is happy food.
9. Eat mostly real, homemade food, and save treats for special occasions. (Hint: Anything processed is not "real" food.)
10. *(The Golden Rule)* Eating is joyful, not stressful. Treat the food rules as habits or routines rather than strict regulations; it's fine to relax them once in a while.[1]

Even if you don't apply every single one of these rules to your life, you'll quickly see that kids really don't have to be so limited when it comes to their food. I never understood why so many Americans (especially in the form of kids' menus) think children will eat only hot dogs, pizza, or plain white pasta with butter!

Age-Appropriate Kitchen Chores for Kids

Just getting your kids into the kitchen may help turn them on to the idea of eating new foods, and, whether you've got a toddler on your hands or a child in middle school, there are plenty of kitchen jobs for kids of all ages. We've personally turned the corner in the last couple years, and at seven and nine our kids are now old enough that their "help" in the kitchen is actually pretty useful. My husband and I have decided that we don't want to "reward" them for pitching in (by giving them a marble or a check mark or an allowance); instead we want them in the habit of emptying the dishwasher (for example) in exchange for having a roof over their heads. Lots of work goes into providing real-food meals every day, so it only makes sense for everyone to pitch in and do their part! Here are some good tasks for children of every age, under supervision as needed:

Toddler

- Stirring pancake or other batter, mixing eggs with a fork or whisk
- Mashing bananas for pancakes, bread, or muffins
- Wiping easy-to-reach surfaces after meals

Preschool

- Setting and/or clearing the dinner table
- Washing and drying vegetables, lettuce, and other produce (kids love using the salad spinner!)
- Assisting with simple food prep, like snapping off the ends of green beans, peeling

hard-boiled eggs, and cutting soft foods (like bananas) with a dull knife

- Sprinkling salt, pepper, and dried herbs
- Unloading (dull) silverware from the dishwasher

Elementary School (Kindergarten to Second Grade)

- Picking out one or two dinner recipes for the week
- Adding items to a food shopping list (and helping mark off those purchases in the store)
- Putting groceries away after a shopping trip
- Cooking simple things at the stove (with assistance), like scrambled eggs, grilled cheese, oatmeal, and pancakes
- Helping to operate some appliances such as the stand mixer
- Independently preparing other basic dishes, such as sandwiches, salads, and toast, and heating up leftovers
- Assisting with the preparation of a more complex meal: getting out ingredients, chopping foods with a dull knife (or with a sharp knife under close supervision), assembling meatballs, peeling shrimp, measuring out spices, and grating cheese
- Filling water glasses for dinner
- Putting away perishables after dinner
- Sweeping or vacuuming the kitchen floor after meals
- Completely emptying the dishwasher and placing hard-to-reach items on a dish towel (or using a stool to put them away)
- Packing school lunches
- Harvesting produce from the garden
- Folding and putting away clean dish towels
- Ironing cloth napkins with supervision

Elementary School (Third to Fifth Grades)

- Taking over more complex prep jobs, like peeling carrots/potatoes, grating cheese, and chopping ingredients
- Independently following and preparing simple recipes, such as baked potatoes, steamed broccoli, popcorn, salad dressings, cookies, and smoothies
- Helping with more complex foods at the stove, such as stir-fry, chicken nuggets, and sautéed vegetables
- Loading dirty dishes into the dishwasher
- Hand-washing larger dishes
- Taking out the kitchen trash (and/or compost)

Middle School

- Planning and preparing dinner for the family one day a week
- Independently making straightforward recipes, including muffins, granola cereal, chili, chicken noodle soup, and tacos
- Grilling foods under close supervision
- Preparing foods that require the use of appliances, such as a food processor or an electric mixer
- Doing a complete cleanup job after dinner

High School

Planning the meals, driving to the store, purchasing all the groceries, cooking for the family, and cleaning up afterward! Ha—this is my dream, at least. But in reality, if they're given direction, teens can do any kitchen chore an adult can do; it's just a matter of getting them to contribute.

PACKING WHOLESOME SCHOOL LUNCHES

As I touch on in chapter 5, planning ahead is key, and school lunches are no exception. You don't need to have every detail figured out for an upcoming week's worth of lunches, but simply having a few homemade items on hand in your freezer (such as muffins and soups) will make the lunch packing process much easier. And packing lunches and setting up for breakfast the night before makes the morning so much less hectic (see my routine below).

Having the right tools makes all the difference. Some of my favorite lunch packing resources include divided lunch containers (I like the ones by Ziploc because they're lightweight and leak-proof), insulated water bottles and containers (I like Thermos brand), ice packs, Norpro ice pop molds, reusable napkins and silverware, silicone muffin liners, and insulated soft lunch "boxes" (by Land's End). I send hot oatmeal (my daughters' typical morning school snack) in Thermos food jars each day, which go in a separate reusable bag with a cloth napkin and spoon. I also use the insulated food jars once a week to send hot soup for lunch, in which case they go in the lunch boxes. I use jumbo silicone muffin liners inside the divided lunch container's large compartment when I need to separate additional loose items, such as popcorn or trail mix. Check out 100daysofrealfood.com/schoollunchsupplies for pictures of all these items!

PLANNING AHEAD FOR SCHOOL LUNCHES

Weeks in Advance: Make-Ahead Items for School Lunches

- **Freeze in individual-size freezer-safe jelly jars (or other small containers)** *(leave room at the top of glass jars for liquid to expand without cracking the glass)*

WHERE'S THE PROTEIN?

I post pictures of my daughters' school lunches almost every day on my Facebook page, and when I don't serve meat, readers commonly ask me, "Where's the protein?" We don't actually track individual nutrients (including protein) because we believe that if you eat a variety of colorful whole foods, the rest will fall into place. There are many sources of protein apart from meat, including dairy products, eggs, beans, nuts, and seeds, and according to the Centers for Disease Control and Prevention, protein deficiency in people who eat a varied diet is actually quite rare.[2]

Homemade Chicken Noodle Soup (page 260)

Slow-Cooker Potato Soup (page 276)

Vegetable Chili (page 248)

Veggie Corn Chowder (page 271)

Tomato Bisque (page 177)

Meatballs (see page 256) with Homemade Tomato Sauce (page 320)

Easy Slow-Cooker Refried Beans (page 155)

Macaroni Casserole (page 252)

- **Freeze in ice cube trays**

Applesauce

Homemade Tomato Sauce (page 320; can be used for homemade pizza "lunchables")

Hummus

Sweet and Tangy BBQ Sauce (page 316)

Pesto sauce (see page 274; for paninis, pasta, and more)

- **Freeze in one layer on trays then transfer them into bags or other freezer-safe containers**

Whole-wheat waffles or pancakes (see page 129; for sandwiches filled with cream cheese and jam)

Mini Lunch-Box Quiches (page 171)

Grilled Caprese Paninis (page 181)

Whole-Grain Pumpkin Muffins (page 165)

Cinnamon-Raisin Quick Bread, sliced (page 173)

Pizza Bites (page 163) and/or pizza crusts baked plain (see page 250; for homemade pizza "lunchables")

Grandma Esther's (Whole-Wheat) Crepes (page 132)

Homemade Chicken Nuggets (page 244)

Corn muffins (to go with the chili!)

Homemade "Pop Tarts" (on the blog)

Grilled cheese sandwiches

- **Freeze in ice pop molds**

Smoothies! (see pages 179 and 201)

Days in Advance: Prep Items to Have on Hand

- Peel and chop carrots or other veggies
- Boil eggs and/or noodles
- Make a dip for veggies and pretzels (see pages 189 and 195)

Night Before: Start Packing Divided Lunch Container and Set Up for the Morning

- Add any frozen items that need to defrost into the divided container (such as a muffin) and let them defrost overnight in the fridge
- If serving soup, let it defrost overnight in the fridge
- Add fruit and/or veggies, whole-grain crackers or other grains, and/or dipping sauce to the divided container
- Make a sandwich or wrap if you don't think it will get soggy overnight
- Fill the insulated bottle with water or milk and store in the fridge
- Set out the lunch box, reusable napkin, silverware, and so on, as well as any items needed for breakfast such as cereal bowls (for a video of me setting up for school lunches go to 100daysofrealfood.com/lunchsetup)

Morning Of: Finish Assembling

- Reheat any soups, oatmeal, or other items as needed and add them to the insulated food jar(s)
- Get out the frozen smoothie pops and place them in the large compartment of the divided container (you'll need to "break" them up somewhat and bend them to fit). They'll partially defrost by lunchtime.
- Assemble and pack any other items you didn't make the night before (such as sandwiches)
- Add several ice packs to an insulated lunch box/bag to keep the perishables cold

I don't always plan ahead as much as I'd like to, but when I do it really makes figuring out lunches a breeze. On the days when I'm not so organized I rely more heavily on items that can be thrown together without any advance preparation, many of which are featured in my lunch packing chart on page 183.

RELUCTANT SPOUSES

Believe it or not, for years I was the reluctant spouse in our marriage. My husband had been hinting around with his whole-wheat bread and *real* maple syrup for years, but I just wasn't buying it. We never really had a serious discussion about it, and I was the key decision maker when it came to food shopping and meal planning for our family. Since I almost always "cooked" homemade meals and wasn't one to rely on pizza delivery or takeout, I honestly didn't think I was doing so badly.

But as I mentioned in the Introduction, I finally got my wake-up call thanks to Michael Pollan's book *In Defense of Food*. I think allowing the adults in your house to have their own "aha" moment (even if you're the one providing them the resources!) can go a long way. Many blog readers tell me it was the birth of their first child or a health scare that got them on board with cutting out processed food, but it doesn't have to be triggered by something so dramatic. Some basic education, and even trying to eat this way for a short period of time, can convert even the most skeptical of people.

Tactics for convincing a reluctant spouse (or other family member) to make the switch

1. Watch the documentary *Food, Inc.* together; it's only ninety minutes! Another good, newer documentary is *Fed Up*.
2. Convince him or her to read Michael Pollan's *In Defense of Food* (or at least listen to the audio version).
3. Make some yummy real-food meals to show how good and filling they really are, and switch up familiar recipes with better ingredients. Try Slow-Cooker BBQ Ribs (page 281) made with local pork; organic baked potatoes; and local green beans.
4. Don't tell your family member up front that you're making changes . . . just stop buying and serving the processed and refined junk and see what happens.
5. Buy different and better versions of familiar products, such as peanut butter, pasta, and dairy products.
6. Slowly incorporate more vegetables into your weekly menu, and be sure to serve fresh, in-season, and well-prepared produce to those who don't think they like veggies (the taste is quite different from what comes out of a can). Alternatively, you could sneak veggies into meals, but only if you tell them about it afterward!
7. Occasionally share facts and tidbits on why one should cut out processed food (check out the list on page 12) as well as the success stories of people who have taken the 10 Days pledge (pages 76–78).
8. If you have children, agree to work together to set a good example for them.

9. Track and share spending at fast food joints and other restaurants versus eating at home and packing lunches.
10. Tell them to eat what you're serving—or to make their own dinner!
11. If your family members don't like a certain real-food meal, don't keep making it; move on to other real-food options.
12. Make changes for yourself (and your children, if you have them) and hope your reluctant spouse will eventually come around.
13. Moderation is key; don't harp on the occasional junk food!
14. As with any unwilling or picky family member (young or old), remember to practice patience and *gentle* persistence.

GATHER AROUND THE FAMILY DINNER TABLE

Now that you (hopefully) have your kids and spouse at least considering the idea of real food, how about creating an environment where you can sit down and enjoy a great meal together?

Tips for a Peaceful Family Dinner

- **Pitch In:** Get everyone to pitch in by setting the table, filling water glasses, and carrying dishes to the sink when it's time to clean up (see page 89 for ideas). We personally like for our daughters to empty the clean dishes out of the dishwasher while we work on making dinner—that is, if they aren't helping us cook!
- **Set the Tone:** Dim the lights, turn on some soothing music, switch to cloth napkins (which is also good for the environment), and even light some candles. Set aside enough time to enjoy a special dinner, even if it's just once a week.
- **Stay Calm and Stay Put:** Consider creating a "race-car seat belt" out of a belt for younger, antsy ones or using a child-size apron to loosely "tie" them into their chair to help them learn to stay put. No getting up for any reason without asking to be excused.
- **No Pressure:** If there are some exceptionally picky eaters at the table, do your best to take the focus off of them and what foods they *should* be eating. Sometimes changing the subject is all it takes with younger kids.
- **Set Some Expectations:** It's never too late to start enforcing good table manners like using silverware instead of hands, not interrupting, asking to be excused, and so on. Give children three "strikes" before they're "out" (asked to leave the table).

Family Dinner Questions

At family dinners when I was growing up, my parents asked each person at the table these three questions:

- What was the best thing that happened to you today?
- What was the worst thing?
- What's one thing that you learned?

We usually follow this same structure, but I personally like to use this as our third question instead:

- Did anything funny happen today that made you laugh? What was it?

Here are some other questions to (hopefully) spark pleasant conversation at your dinner table.

Questions that can be asked every week

- Name one thing you're thankful for today.
- What is one thing you are most proud of from this past week?
- What are you most looking forward to tomorrow (or this week)?
- If you were given an extra hour today, what would you do with it?
- When was the last time you were embarrassed, and why?
- If you could take back one thing you did in the last week, what would it be?
- When was the last time you felt scared, and why?

Questions that can be asked once in a blue moon

- Share one thing that you love (or appreciate) about each person at the table.
- If you were to become an author one day, what would your book be about?
- Name one place you'd like to travel to (or live) if you could leave tomorrow and go anywhere.
- If you could have one special power, what would it be?
- What's your favorite holiday, and why?
- What do you want to be when you grow up? (Even the adults can answer this one!)
- What's your favorite dinner dish of all time?
- Name one person you find inspiring, and explain why.
- What's one adventurous activity you'd like to try in your lifetime?
- What's a topic you know more about than anyone at the table?
- If you could create a new law (or new rule at school), what would it be?
- If you had to give up one of your five senses, what would it be, and why?
- What's your favorite season of the year, and why?

- If you were going to wake up as an animal tomorrow, what would you be, and why?
- What's one thing you wish you'd known one year ago?
- If someone handed you a free twenty-dollar bill, what would you do with it?
- If you could snap your fingers and be invisible for a day, what would you do?
- What do you like best about yourself?
- If you could invent something that doesn't currently exist, what would it be?
- What's your favorite vegetable?
- What's your favorite fruit?
- What's one rule you have to follow that you disagree with?
- What's the most important quality for a friend to have?
- What's the hardest decision you've had to make in the last week?
- What's your favorite family tradition?
- What's your favorite game to play?
- If you could hear what everyone was thinking for a day, would you do it?
- If you could be a character in one TV show for a day, who would it be?
- Describe yourself using three words.
- Name one thing no one in this room knows about you.
- If you had a time machine, what year would you go to, and why?
- What is the best gift you've ever received?
- What would you like to be known for when you die?

Thought-Provoking Discussions

On a more educational note, consider picking out different admirable character traits to discuss around the dinner table. Let everyone (even young kids!) take turns sharing examples of when they've seen someone demonstrate traits such as courage, kindness, self-confidence, generosity, trustworthiness, thoughtfulness, appreciation, compassion, and/or perseverance.

EXPLAINING YOUR REAL-FOOD MISSION TO FAMILY AND FRIENDS

As with any special dietary needs, whether it's a food allergy or the choice to be vegetarian, feeling passionate about your real-food mission can add some complexity when others are involved.

Dining with Others

I think it's important to not offend loved ones, especially when they're the ones feeding you. But would you expect a committed vegetarian to eat meat just to be nice? Of course not. So there's a fine line between honoring your values and being polite, but it's not always easy to know where to draw that line.

If you'll be dining with a close family member or friend, let's hope you can share what changes you're making and why (and that they'll respect your desires). Who knows, maybe he or she will be interested in learning more, or even in trying the 10 Days pledge! That would be great, but if you'll be dining with extended family members or acquaintances I wouldn't expect them to go out of their way to accommodate you, or even to really understand your real-food needs.

We've found the following tactics helpful for when we're dining at a friend's house:

- **Offer to bring a dish:** A yummy real-food dish to share, of course! I sometimes feel it's my mission in life to share real food with others, and it's also a great conversation starter: "Oh, yeah, I got this dip recipe from a new real-food cookbook. We're trying to eat better, blah blah blah."

- **Eat a little beforehand:** I hope none of my acquaintances reading this are feeling offended by my little secret, but we sometimes—although not always—eat a little before we go to parties. There's nothing like a big salad or some fresh whole-wheat bread to fill up on "just a little bit" in case the dinner spread you encounter doesn't exactly meet your needs.

- **Fill up on the good stuff:** If the meal you're eating is buffet or family-style, fill your plate with likely whole food items and maybe just a little bit of the stuff you aren't sure about.

- **Avoid the meat:** Not eating factory-farmed meat is something I personally feel very strongly about, so, whether we're at a friend's house or a restaurant, if I don't know where the meat came from I usually try to eat like a vegetarian.

Now, during our 100 Days pledge, we certainly could not be this flexible when at a friend's house. For that brief period of time we took all our food with us, and thankfully no one disowned us!

People sometimes imply that we don't eat processed food because my husband and I "can't," but the truth is at this point we don't want to! If I see a casserole at someone's house that I know is topped with a tube of crescent rolls, I'll avoid it like the plague. Since experiencing a change in our palates, highly processed foods just taste, well, highly processed to us now, and we simply don't enjoy them. (That alone would be enough to keep us away, even without thinking about how many unwanted chemicals and additives go into those types of foods!)

When Your Kids Are with Friends

As I've mentioned, now that we're no longer on a strict real-food pledge, I honestly don't make too big a deal about what my kids may or may not eat at a friend's house—although at this point most of our acquaintances know where I stand. My goal is a big-picture one: to empower my children to make the best choices (and not feel too much guilt about the not-so-great choices) when they're away from home. If my children grew up not eating processed food simply "because Mommy said so," I would expect a rebellion at some point. As much as possible, I like to explain things to them on their level, including showing them ingredient labels and sharing the reasons behind a lot of my decisions.

I've also coached my kids a little on how to handle situations, such as when someone offers them a Chips Ahoy! cookie and some chocolate milk. Politeness is first and foremost, of course! But I tell them just to take one cookie (not two) and ask if they can have some water for a drink instead. I never want my children to ask other adults to go out of their way for them, but my kids know that it's never too much trouble to ask for water. And if they're already eating a birthday cupcake or whatever it is, they know to try not to add juice or other sweetened beverages on top of that. We've also discussed not inflicting our viewpoints on others unless asked (after a conversation we had when one of my daughters at the grocery store said, "Mommy, look at all the processed food that lady has in her grocery cart!").

I know I can make my children feel like the most special and loved girls in the world without giving them highly processed junk food, but I also know there's a social aspect to it. When the ice cream truck comes down the street or vendors are selling cotton candy at the ball game, I tell my husband all the time, "We've been there, done that," so it's very easy for us to give those things up. But our children haven't had those experiences yet, so I don't close them off entirely. Again, the last thing I want to do is give them a complex about the food they eat. But I do want to show my girls that their mommy stands up for what she believes in, and so I try hard to instill balance. It's easier said than done, though, because many times I honestly don't know the "best" or "right" answer when faced with a food decision; but all I can do is try my best and not spend too much time sweating it!

Entertaining with Real Food

People sometimes ask what our friends think of eating only real food when they come to our house for dinner (I confess that I like to entertain). They love it, of course! Just as any other hostess would do, I try to serve real-food versions of dishes I know my guests will enjoy (for example, I have a hunch my dad would turn up his nose at veggie burgers, so I'd serve him grass-fed burgers instead). I won't succumb to Goldfish to try to accommodate my daughters' friends, but my alternative choices are very kid-friendly—things like popcorn (see page 192) and Frozen Yogurt Pops (page 298). Most of the time no one even notices that something might be slightly different about the food, not even the kids. Most real-food dishes truly are "normal," tasty meals, just made with higher-quality ingredients!

"MAKE-YOUR-OWN" FOOD BAR PARTY!

Whether you're throwing a dinner party, a slumber party, or a birthday party, inviting guests to make their own customized meal from a variety of ingredients can be a really fun activity for kids and adults alike. We even do this at home with just our family on occasion and it never disappoints!

PIZZA BAR

This would be great for a slumber party with older kids or a fun potluck-style dinner with friends (the host makes the crust!).

INGREDIENTS

Whole-Wheat Pizza dough (page 250; 1 recipe per 4 to 5 people)
Homemade Tomato Sauce (page 320) or store-bought organic red pizza sauce
Freshly grated mozzarella cheese
Little bowls filled with some or all of the following toppings:
- Cooked, crumbled sausage
- Sautéed mushrooms
- Freshly grated Parmesan cheese
- Pesto sauce (see page 274)
- Torn fresh basil leaves*
- Crumbled goat cheese
- Fresh arugula*
- Diced roasted bell peppers
- Olives
- Caramelized onions
- Pulled pork (see page 286) or shredded barbecued ribs (see page 281)
- Fresh cilantro (great with barbecue flavor)*
- Diced raw red onions

Add after pizza is baked.

EQUIPMENT

Rolling pin(s)
Baking sheets
Large cutting board and sharp knife (or pizza wheel)

TECHNIQUE

Set up a large counter or table with all the necessary supplies and preheat the oven to 500°F. Give each person a large fist-size chunk of raw pizza dough (I usually make 4 to 5 personal-size pizzas out of one recipe). Take turns with the rolling pin so each person ends up with his or her own round of pizza crust. We like to fold the half-inch or so of the crust around the edges and mash it down with a fork; we call this "fancy crust." Next, everyone can start adding sauce and toppings in whatever manner their heart desires. Don't judge the unusual combinations! Bake the pizzas (see page 250) in batches if necessary and enjoy.

"A 'make-your-own' bar is the new buffet!"

TACO BAR

Whether it's Cinco de Mayo or the Super Bowl, tacos are always a crowd-pleaser (especially when you can assemble your own!).

INGREDIENTS

Whole-grain Corn Tortillas (page 329) or store-bought
Whole-Wheat Tortillas (page 326) or store-bought
Lettuce (chopped if you want to offer a taco salad option, or as whole-leaf lettuce cups if you want to offer them as an alternative to tortilla shells)
Ground pork taco meat (see page 264)
Flank steak fajita meat (see page 282)
Easy Slow-Cooker Refried Beans (page 155)
Freshly grated Monterey Jack cheese
Diced tomatoes, salsa, or pico de gallo
Avocado slices or homemade guacamole (see page 175)
Sour cream
Diced hot peppers
Fresh cilantro
Lime wedges

TECHNIQUE

Prepare and cook all the tortillas and meat and bean fillings in advance. Keep the warm items wrapped in foil in an oven on low heat (200°F) until your guests arrive. A plastic or ceramic tortilla warmer with lid can also come in handy. On a large countertop or table, put out bowls with a selection of the other toppings. Set out the warm items once guests arrive and allow everyone to assemble their own!

PANINI BAR

Whether you're hosting a luncheon or just trying to figure out what to feed a houseful of overnight guests, a panini bar is the way to go.

INGREDIENTS

Everyday Whole-Wheat Bread (page 332) or store-bought, or whole-wheat pitas
Some or all of these fillings:
- Mozzarella and/or Havarti cheese slices
- Goat cheese, blue cheese, or pimento cheese (see page 190)
- Pesto (see page 274)
- Prosciutto
- Tapenade
- Fresh basil leaves
- Sliced tomatoes
- Roasted bell pepper and/or zucchini slices
- Grilled portabello mushroom slices
- Cooked and sliced or shredded chicken or steak

Olive oil for greasing the panini grill
Good-quality balsamic vinegar for dipping

EQUIPMENT

Panini grill or George Foreman grill, or use a sauté pan or griddle and prepare them as you would a grilled cheese sandwich (see page 153)
Large cutting board and sharp knife

TECHNIQUE

Display all the ingredients on a large countertop or table. Have the guests assemble their own sandwiches (each on their own plate) and line them up to take turns cooking in batches in the panini grill. Serve with side dishes such as pasta salad, Fruit Salad with Orange Zest (page 137), raw vegetables, and/or something crunchy like whole-grain pretzels.

CREPE BAR

You can easily pull off a crepe bar, which is especially fun for kids, for breakfast or dessert! If whole-wheat crepes (see page 132) seem too time-consuming, just substitute whole-wheat waffles (see page 129) instead. I promise you won't hear any complaints.

INGREDIENTS

Grandma Esther's (Whole-Wheat) Crepes (page 132, made in advance)
Some or all of these fillings:
- Sliced bananas
- Diced strawberries (or other berries)
- Homemade ice cream (see page 290)
- Whipped cream-cheese frosting (see page 308) with orange zest added

Some or all of these toppings:
- Homemade Whipped Cream (page 339)
- Simple Chocolate Sauce (page 338)
- Berry Sauce (page 334)
- Pure maple syrup

EQUIPMENT

Reusable plastic squeeze bottles for the chocolate and berry sauces (I often cut off the tip to make the dispenser hole bigger for the thick berry sauce.)
Whipped cream dispenser (Whip-It! brand makes a great one)

TECHNIQUE

Set out all ingredients including the prepared crepes. Instruct your guest to take a folded crepe, open it up, put the fillings inside, fold it back up, and then top it off with desired toppings.

SUSHI BAR

It may seem tricky, but adults and kids alike will have a surprising amount of fun making their own sushi. Just be sure you have ample time for this one, since the technique can take some practice.

INGREDIENTS

Short-grain brown rice (6 cups cooked rice mixed with 4 tablespoons rice wine vinegar)
Nori (dried seaweed sheets)
Some or all of these fillings, cut into sticks:
- Cucumber
- Avocado
- Carrots
- Cooked shrimp (stick a skewer through from end to end before boiling)
- Cooked crab meat (not imitation)
- Smoked salmon
- Cream cheese
- Raw sushi-grade tuna, salmon, and other seafood as desired
- Soy sauce
- Toasted sesame seeds
- Wasabi

EQUIPMENT

Bamboo rolling mats
Plastic wrap
Large cutting board(s)
Very sharp knife
Small bowl of water (wet fingers make it easier to handle the sticky rice)
Chopsticks
Wooden or bamboo spoon

TECHNIQUE

Search for sushi-making diagrams and instructions on the Internet and familiarize yourself with them (do a test run a few days ahead if you think it's necessary). On a large countertop or table, put rice out in a large bowl and put the other ingredients on a large platter or two. Give each person a cutting board to use as their work surface, get to work, and have fun with it!

"For my daughter's slumber party for her ninth birthday I served a taco bar for dinner and a crepe bar for breakfast—it was a *huge* hit with all of her friends!"

Starting a Real-Food Dinner Club

My husband and I especially enjoy being part of a dinner club. This is an adults-only, often upscale affair and always loads of fun. I just love the excuse to throw a dinner party, and knowing it will soon be reciprocated by others in the group makes it all the more worthwhile.

- Think of friends, even those that you don't know very well, who enjoy and appreciate good food and consider inviting them to join. We feel eight adults (or four couples) is a good number, especially if it's not going to be a potluck affair.
- Offer to host the first dinner gathering, but first set some ground rules:

  How often will you meet? *A common frequency is once a month or once every two months. If you don't pick a day, such as the second Saturday of the month, whoever's turn it is to host next should be in charge of setting the date.*

  Will the dinners be fully prepared by the host or will it be a potluck gathering? *I'm personally a big fan of having complete control over the dinner when it's my turn (yes, if you haven't already caught on, I'm Type A!), because it allows me to create a theme, have some fun with a little coordinating décor, keep an element of surprise, and even incorporate wine pairings if I'm really into it. (It also means that when the calendar turns and we're guests instead of hosts, we're in the clear and don't have to prep anything.) Although dinner gatherings with friends do not have to be elaborate to be a good time; a themed potluck event is just as much fun to have on the calendar. I personally just get this entertaining bug every so often and our dinner club helps me fulfill those desires.*

  How about a break between hosting rounds to go out to dinner? *Our dinner club members take turns hosting, and then before it's the next couple's turn we go out to dinner together. It's a nice break where no one is left with a kitchen full of dirty dishes, and with these outings added into the rounds we each end up only hosting less than once a year (which I think is a pretty manageable frequency for most).*

Entertaining Tips

Along with all of the fun, of course, comes a lot of work. When hosting such an event we aim to do the following:

- **Plan** the menu weeks in advance.
- **Practice** new recipes that we've never made before so we can make any necessary adjustments.
- **Purchase** all groceries at least two days in advance.
- **Set up the table** and décor a day or two beforehand.
- **Prep cook** the day before as much as possible, including chopping, making sauces, preparing garnishes, and so on.
- Welcome guests into a **clean kitchen**, which may mean running partially full loads of dishes early in the day.
- And if I could leave you with one more important, albeit random, entertaining tip, it's to set the tone by turning on some nice music and **buying a dimmer** for your dining room light! Seriously, while entertaining you should only have the ceiling light on the brightest setting if you're looking for someone's lost earring. Okay, glad to get that little tidbit off my chest.

No matter how prepared we try to be when we entertain, there always seems to be room for improvement, whether it's having all of the prep cooking completed before guests arrive, being showered and ready on time, having the kids settled upstairs, or ensuring each dish is served promptly and at the right temperature. We don't always pull everything off flawlessly when it's our turn to host, but we certainly have fun trying!

RESTAURANTS AND TRAVEL

How to order real food in restaurants

During our 100 Days pledge my husband had to travel on business quite frequently so we learned a lot about how he could find real food in restaurants. Here are some general tips:

- **Bread items** such as rolls, breadcrumbs, tortillas, pasta, breading, crusts, and the like are typically not 100 percent whole wheat (and likely contain no whole wheat at all). Some restaurants may be able to confirm the ingredients for you.
- If the waiter or chef doesn't know (and can't find out) the ingredients of an item for you, then **they probably don't make it fresh in house,** which means it could have unnecessary additives like sweeteners and preservatives.
- **If the restaurant staff doesn't know where the meat came from,** then I promise you it's standard factory-farmed fare. I choose to go vegetarian in this case.

- For children, **avoid the kids' menu,** which is usually filled with highly processed items (such as pasta from white flour, factory-made chicken nuggets, corn dogs, and French fries). Instead, put together a plate of adult side items that you think your child would eat (like a baked potato, fruit, vegetable, and nuts or cheese you see offered on a salad) and supplement with things you brought along (like a fruit and nut bar if you have one).

- **Don't be afraid to ask questions,** especially when it comes to things like sauces, dressings, marinades, and even soups. Is it made in-house? Can they tell you what's in it? These types of items are very often made off-site and are full of preservatives, sugar, and artificial ingredients. For salads, opt for extra-virgin olive oil and vinegar (unless they can confirm the dressings are made in house with a simple list of ingredients).

- If time allows, **look at menus in advance** to help you choose restaurants that care about quality and source local ingredients to find the best items at those restaurants.

We learned so much about restaurant food when our 100 Days pledge "forced" us to ask certain questions and be more aware. Now that our strict real-food pledge is over, we're a little more relaxed these days when it comes to eating at restaurants, in part because we don't eat out very often, and in part because when we do eat out we are sure to select restaurants that use high-quality and preferably local ingredients. We do still try to avoid highly processed junk, including those junky kids' menus (except as an occasional "treat")!

Tips for Trips

Our family is no stranger to travel, especially with our extended family members being so spread out. Here are tactics we use to ensure we get our fill of real food while we are away from home.

Plan Ahead

Think through the location of your upcoming trip. Are you staying with family? Renting a beach house? Staying in a hotel? The first two options are a little easier to plan for, because you'll most likely have access to a full kitchen. Hotels can be a little trickier, but did you know most hotels offer small refrigerators by request? This is a pretty important feature for guests who need to keep certain medications or their baby's milk cold . . . oh, and for us high-maintenance real-foodies, too. Sure, there's usually a fee, but think how much money you'll save on the breakfast buffet if you bring along your own cereal to eat with milk that you can buy near the hotel. Now it won't be the local non-homogenized milk you might be used to home, but don't forget: flexibility.

No matter where my travels take me, I like to take a little food along, even if it's just a bag of granola. I'll also sometimes take along some whole-wheat sandwich bread or tortillas and plenty of snacks, such as homemade trail mix (nuts, seeds, dried fruit, and popcorn), Spiced Nut Mix (page 202), prepackaged fruit and nut bars, and maybe some homemade whole-grain muffins. Even if I'm hopping on a plane I always leave room for these things in my suitcase. If you're driving you'll have the luxury of taking a cooler, possibly with a packed lunch and some perishable foods, including whole-grain pasta salads, green salads, and fresh-cut vegetables and fruit.

Airport Travel

We fly a lot, and I have one hard and fast rule: Never spend a dime at the airport. This is good advice from a budget perspective, and it also allows you to avoid a lot of low-quality food and expensive bottles of water. As long as you don't take liquids or sauces, you're allowed to pack and take your own lunch through security, so we actually take empty water bottles with us and fill them up after security at a coffee shop or drinking fountain. I pack items such as sandwiches, apple slices, popcorn, raisins, nuts, and crackers to eat on the airplane. If you take something that's somewhat perishable like cheese, just pack some frozen peas to go along with it! Avoid items like applesauce or yogurt that might be questioned as a liquid.

SUMMARY OF SIMPLE CHANGES

- When revamping your (and your family's) diet, start by tackling one meal of the day at a time. Don't move on to lunch or snacks until breakfast is cleaned up first.
- Increase your consumption of whole foods in general—especially vegetables and fruits. This will help to displace some of the processed foods in your diet.
- Don't order off the kids' menu, because more often than not the selections are highly processed; try assembling a plate from various side items or sharing an adult entrée instead.
- Always plan ahead, because eating this way is much better for your body and mind, but it takes attention and planning even for those of us veterans (more on this in Chapter 5).
- Don't reward or bribe your children with junk food.
- Pack balanced, real-food lunches for your children to take to school.

5. Food Budget Tips and Meal Plans

Real-Food Tip: The key to avoiding processed food is planning ahead (and it can help you save money, too)!

How do you take advantage of all this real-food goodness without breaking the bank? To start the conversation, let's take a look at an interesting statistic cited by Michael Pollan in *In Defense of Food.*

> In 1960 Americans spent 17.5 percent of their income on food and 5.2 percent of national income on health care. Since then, those numbers have flipped: Spending on food has fallen to 9.9 percent, while spending on health care has climbed to 16 percent of national income. It's hard to argue that these figures aren't at all related.[1]

Is this due to correlation or causation? Either way, we all have to choose our spending priorities; but whether you have cash to spare or can't pinch another penny, here are some budgeting tips that will make your real-food lifestyle as pocket-friendly as possible.

12 Tips for Real Food on a Budget

1. **Set a specific budget.** This tip may sound basic, but simply thinking about "not spending a lot of money" *does not* work! Also, if you don't already know how much you're spending on groceries, that would be a great place to start. Here's how to structure a budget:

   Pick a realistic budget amount that you will adhere to each week or month. I personally think a weekly budget is easier to follow because you can't go too far over budget before you realize you're in trouble.

Consider shopping with cash in an envelope, so going over budget isn't even possible. Also, make a commitment that if you do go over budget you'll deduct that amount from the following week or month.

Define what will and won't be included in the budget. Will it just be for food, or for household items, too? What about "extras" like alcohol, entertaining, and going out to eat?

Keep track of all your expenses on paper, whether you use cash or not. It is important to see where your money goes.

Share and discuss the running budget total with the other adults and older kids in your household. Accountability is where it's at!

2. **Be organized and plan out your meals for the week.** Last-minute purchases that you haven't put a lot of thought into can add up fast.
3. **Minimize waste** by planning ways to use leftovers, such as using vegetable scraps to make stock, and teaching your family to take only as much food as they'll eat (they can always get seconds).
4. **Know and use what you have on hand,** especially if it's perishable. Consider keeping an inventory list of food on your fridge or freezer so different family members can check off items as they use them. I know my husband is more likely to eat some perishable item in the fridge before it goes bad if I leave a note telling him it's there (don't ask me why)!
5. **Make substitutions in recipes** (such as dried herbs instead of fresh) to reduce how many things you have to buy . . . or even leave out a noncritical ingredient altogether.
6. **Build a base of recipes around the use of inexpensive foods** like bananas, beans, root vegetables, and pasta. Some of our favorite inexpensive real-food recipes are Easy Slow-Cooker Refried Beans (page 155), Cinnamon Apple Chips (page 198), Popcorn (page 192), Carrots with Rosemary (page 225), Veggie Pancakes (page 226), and Slow-Cooker Potato Soup (page 276).
7. When making inexpensive meals like soups and pasta dishes, **double the recipe and freeze the leftovers** for when you just don't have time to plan a good dinner and want to avoid unexpected expenses.
8. **Choose to drink water** instead of milk and skip juice and other flavored beverages altogether. If you really have trouble kicking the juice habit, at least water it down a little so the juice lasts longer.
9. **Reduce your consumption of meat and desserts.** Humanely raised meat can be a big-ticket item; experiment with stretching your ground meat dishes by mixing in diced veggies, mushrooms, and/or beans. Make sweets a special-occasion treat rather than a daily indulgence; your family will learn to appreciate it, not expect it.

10. **Buy produce that's in season** and if you frequent your local farmers' market, try going just before closing time to get some great deals on items the vendors won't want to haul back to the farm.

11. Go strategic with your organic purchases; **Consult the Dirty Dozen list and the list of high-risk GMO crops** (see page 51) to help you prioritize.

12. **Check your receipt** after you get home to make sure your money was spent wisely (most grocery stores accept returns!). One time when I was distracted by my kids I accidentally bought a very expensive bag of rice that I didn't desperately need at the time. I had no problem returning the unopened rice for some much-needed cash—especially because I'm a loyal customer and returns are part of their policy!

After our family's initial 100 Days of Real Food pledge we decided, based on feedback from readers of my blog, to do it again—except on a tight budget, to prove that it really could be done. We let our readers vote on the weekly budget amount for groceries for our family of four, and it ended up being $125 (with a $20 weekly eating-out budget that we honestly didn't always utilize). To some that may sound like a lot of money, and to others it may sound like a little. It's certainly all relative; but it's worth noting that—on a cost-comparison basis only—if our family of four were on *full* food stamp (SNAP) benefits we would have had $167 per week to spend on food. We of course have access to many wonderful resources including a plethora of kitchen tools, cooking experience, and multiple grocery stores that I know some on food stamps might not be able to utilize, but either way, it's certainly an eye-opening comparison.[2]

The whole budget series is chronicled on our blog, and I'm here to tell you that it wasn't always easy! I'm a spender at heart, and also one to appreciate some expensive foods, such as goat cheese, avocados, fresh mozzarella, and olives. At one point during our pledge period I had to post a picture of our fridge because it looked so empty, even though I'd just completed my grocery shopping for the week! We just had to be creative with the items we had on hand, and in the end we always had plenty to eat and never had to succumb to buying highly processed food. I just had to get used to eating foods that I could afford as opposed to foods I happened to be craving at the time, which is certainly a first-world problem no matter how you look at it. So once again, I truly believe with some planning and discipline that eating real food on a budget can be done!

THE IMPORTANCE OF MEAL PLANNING

Not only does meal planning keep things on track financially, but I personally think it keeps things interesting as well. If I actually dedicate a little time to planning out our dinners for the upcoming week, we'll avoid the dinnertime scramble, and there's a much better chance we'll have an exciting, and possibly new recipe or two to look forward to.

8 Meal-Planning Tips

1. Scour your fridge, pantry, and freezer and **make note of ingredients you have on hand** that should be used before they spoil. Also, list any staples you could incorporate (such as rice or beans) to reduce your overall grocery purchases.
2. Ask your local farmers' market if they have an e-mail list or newsletter so you can be notified of what they expect to offer at the next market. If not, **figure out what will be in season so you can plan meals around those items** before you go.
3. Check out your favorite **supermarket's weekly sales ad** to see if there's any interesting real food you could incorporate in your meal plan.
4. Sit down and **spend at least fifteen to twenty minutes planning out your dinners** and grocery list for the week ahead based on the food you have on hand, potential farmers' market finds, and grocery store sales.
5. **If you have kids, get them involved in helping you think of meal ideas** for the upcoming week. Pull out some cookbooks, sit down together, and ask for their input. My older daughter doesn't always know it, but she's best at motivating me to try those recipes I'd never have picked on my own!
6. In between your weekly meal planning sessions, **always be on the lookout for new and inspiring** recipes and meal ideas. Keep those recipes handy in a (physical or electronic) folder or other reliable spot so you can reference them easily for inspiration.
7. **Plan to make only four to five different dinners each week**—again, one of which is a new recipe. You can have leftovers, scrounge (breakfast for dinner, anyone?), or be spontaneous on the other nights.
8. Most important: **Be flexible.** If something unexpected comes up one evening (like laziness!), just move the planned dinner to the next night.

PLANNING AHEAD

The key to not being unexpectedly stuck with a processed-food choice—such as a drive-through burger—is planning ahead, whether it's planning out your dinners for the week (see page 122 for a template), having some whole-food snacks in your car, or just mentally running through when and what you'll eat for the upcoming day.

Making Your Own Convenience Food

Making dinners in advance and freezing them for a rainy day is no new concept. Some call it batch cooking or freezer cooking, but it doesn't have to stop with what you can store in your freezer. Making enough dinner to ensure you have leftovers the following night, or even doing some quick weekend prep work like peeling carrots, boiling eggs, and whipping up some homemade salad dressing, can make weeknight dinners, lunches, and snacks much more manageable.

10 Great Make-and-Freeze Recipe Options

1. Jason's Grass-Fed Burgers (page 238) or Quinoa Veggie "Burgers" (page 254)
2. Whole-Wheat Pizza (page 250)
3. Homemade Chicken Nuggets (page 244)
4. Meatballs (see page 256)
5. Veggie Corn Chowder (page 271)
6. Slow-Cooker Flank Steak Fajitas (page 282)
7. Breakfast Tacos (page 147)
8. Super-Easy Whole-Wheat Biscuits (page 222)
9. Slow-Cooker Potato Soup (page 276)
10. Whole-Grain Pumpkin Muffins (page 165)

And when life gets in the way and you can't prepare a homemade dish in advance, there are also some super-fast real-food meals that can be whipped up in no time. Plan ahead by having the right staples on hand to help you avoid highly processed fast food and packaged meals.

5 Super-Quick Wholesome Meals (No Recipe Needed)

1. Whole-wheat spaghetti noodles with store-bought organic tomato sauce, sautéed veggies, and (optional) ground meat.
2. Scrambled eggs (pureed with greens if you have them, to make Green Eggs, page 118) with a side of fruit and (optional) bacon or sausage.
3. Cooked whole-wheat elbow pasta mixed with Basic Cheese Sauce (page 324) and frozen peas with a salad on the side.
4. Whole-wheat pizza toast (add sauce and cheese and melt) with a side of crunchy raw veggies and hummus or another dip.
5. Grilled cheese sandwiches with an add-in such as pesto, tomato, avocado, roasted veggies, and/or leftover meat, with a baked potato and a side of fresh fruit.

MEAL PLANS

The following pages contain four suggested dinner plans organized by season, as well as some blank templates that you can photocopy and use to make your very own. Here's what you can expect from these meal plans:

- Four seven-day practical real-food dinner menu plans designed for busy families.
- Complete meals listed for dinner, with leftovers incorporated when appropriate.
- Food quantities calculated for a family of four (two adults, two young children).
- Corresponding complete grocery list showing what to buy organized by store departments.
- All recipes are doable for working moms/dads, or for anyone who deals with busy weeknights.
- Every meal suggested follows our real-food rules on page 10!

Happy planning!

MEAL PLAN: WINTER

7-day real-food dinner plan for family of 4 and shopping list

MENU

Sunday: Simple Seafood (page 263) with Carrots with Rosemary (page 225) and Super-Easy Whole-Wheat Biscuits (page 222)

Monday: The Best Whole Chicken in the Slow Cooker (page 278) with Cheesy Broccoli Rice Casserole (page 230), then make Overnight Chicken Stock (page 322) with bones

Tuesday: Homemade Chicken Noodle Soup (page 260) made with the leftover chicken and broth, leftover Whole-Wheat Biscuits

Wednesday: Whole-Wheat Spaghetti and Meatballs (page 256) with a spinach side salad drizzled with olive oil and nuts or cheese

Thursday: Slow-Cooker Potato Soup (page 276) with Spinach Salad with Warm Bacon Dressing (page 214)

Friday: Polenta with Mushroom Bordelaise Sauce (page 266) and sautéed green beans

Saturday: Quinoa and Sausage-Stuffed Peppers (page 242) and baked potatoes

LISA'S TIP: Pack dinner leftovers for lunch or make an additional weeknight meal out of them (so the plan will give you eight nights instead of seven). Or consider freezing leftover soup in individual portions for a rainy day.

SHOPPING LIST

PRODUCE

2 pounds fresh spinach (need 7 to 8 cups)
5 pounds carrots
1 bunch celery
¾ pound broccoli
4 large bell peppers, any color
¾ pound green beans
1 lemon
Two 8-ounce packs sliced mushrooms, any variety
1 garlic head
6 large baking potatoes
3 large onions
3 shallots
1 bunch thyme
1 bunch flat-leaf parsley
1 bunch fresh rosemary

DAIRY / EGGS

½ pound (2 sticks) butter
½ gallon milk
1 cup heavy cream
One 8-ounce block cheddar cheese (need 1½ cups grated)
1 container crumbled blue cheese (need ¼ cup)
11 ounces Parmesan cheese (need 2⅔ cups grated)
½ dozen eggs (need 4)

MEAT / SEAFOOD

1 pound mild white fish (such as flounder, cod, or tilapia), wild-caught preferred
1 whole chicken, about 4 pounds
1 link mild Italian sausage
1 pound grass-fed ground beef
One 8-ounce pack bacon (need 6 pieces)

INTERIOR AISLES: DRY / CANNED / GRAINS

One 2-pound bag whole-wheat flour (need 2¾ cups)
One 24-ounce bag coarsely ground whole-grain cornmeal (need 1 cup)
One 14-ounce bag quinoa (need ⅔ cup)
1 small bag/box brown rice (need 1 cup)
1 small bag/canister whole-wheat breadcrumbs (need just under 1 cup)
1 bag/box small whole-grain pasta, such as penne or macaroni (need 3 cups)
1 pound whole-grain spaghetti
One 25.5-ounce jar organic red pasta sauce
One 32-ounce box organic chicken broth (need 4 cups)
One 14.5-ounce can organic beef broth (need 1¼ cups)
¼ cup pine nuts (optional)

FROZEN / OTHER

1 bottle white wine (need ⅓ cup)
1 bottle red wine (need ¾ cup)

PANTRY CHECKLIST

Apple cider vinegar
Baking powder
Bay leaf
Cayenne pepper
Crushed red pepper flakes
Dried Italian seasoning
Garlic powder
Honey
Olive oil
Onion powder
Paprika
Pepper (ground black pepper)
Red wine vinegar
Salt
Soy sauce, low sodium recommended
Thyme (dried)
Yellow (prepared) mustard

MEAL PLAN: SPRING

7-day real-food dinner plan for family of 4 and shopping list

MENU

Sunday: Grilled Teriyaki Salmon (page 272) with Asian-Inspired Rice (page 220) and grilled asparagus

Monday: Cajun Alfredo with Shrimp (page 268) and a side salad

Tuesday: Macaroni Casserole (page 252) with steamed broccoli added

Wednesday: The Best Pulled Pork in the Slow Cooker! (page 286) with baked sweet potatoes and sautéed collard greens (or other greens such as kale or spinach)

Thursday: Whole-Wheat Pizza (page 250, double the recipe) topped with Homemade Tomato Sauce (page 320), grated mozzarella, leftover pulled pork, Sweet and Tangy BBQ Sauce (page 316), and fresh cilantro (added after the pizza is done baking), with a side salad

Friday: Leftover Whole-Wheat Pizza with raw or steamed carrots

Saturday: Jason's Grass-Fed Burgers (page 238) with whole-wheat buns and Grilled Veggie Kabobs (page 218)

SHOPPING LIST

PRODUCE

1 avocado (for Sunday)
One 1-pound bag carrots
1 zucchini
1 bunch asparagus
2 red bell peppers
1 small head broccoli
1 bunch spinach
1 head (or bag or box) lettuce greens
1 bunch collard (or other) greens
2 bunches cilantro
4-inch piece fresh ginger
2 to 3 sweet potatoes
2 garlic heads
1 red onion
3 yellow onions
One 8-ounce pack whole Baby Bella mushrooms

DAIRY / EGGS

¼ pound (1 stick) butter (need 5 tablespoons)
1 quart milk (need 2 cups)
½ pint heavy cream (need 1 cup)
One 1-pound container sour cream
2 ounces Parmesan cheese (need ½ cup grated)
1 pound (16 ounces) cheddar cheese
1 pound (16 ounces) mozzarella cheese

MEAT / SEAFOOD

1 pound salmon, wild-caught preferred
1 pound shrimp
One 3- to 3½-pound pork shoulder
1 pound grass-fed ground beef

"Now, lady, I want to eat my lunch!" —SIENNA, WHEN I WAS TRYING TO TAKE PICTURES OF HER EATING, AGE 7

INTERIOR AISLES: DRY / CANNED / GRAINS

One 2-pound bag whole-wheat flour
1 small canister/bag whole-grain breadcrumbs
1 small box/bag brown rice (need 4 servings)
1 pound box/bag whole-wheat fettuccine
1 pound whole-grain macaroni
1 pack whole-wheat hamburger buns or English muffins (need 4)
Two ¼-ounce packets active dry yeast (need 4½ teaspoons)
1 bottle Paul Prudhomme's Blackened Redfish Magic
Two 24-ounce jars organic pizza (or pasta) sauce
One 8-ounce can plain tomato sauce
1 small container roasted peanuts (need ⅓ cup)

PANTRY CHECKLIST

Apple cider vinegar
Balsamic vinegar
Cayenne pepper
Chili powder
Dijon mustard
Garlic powder
Honey
Mustard powder
Olive oil
Onion powder
Oregano
Paprika
Pepper (ground black pepper)
Pure maple syrup
Red wine vinegar
Rice wine vinegar
Salt
Soy sauce (more than ½ cup needed), low sodium recommended
Thyme (dried)
Toasted sesame oil

MEAL PLAN: SUMMER

7-day real-food dinner plan for family of 4 and shopping list

MENU

Sunday: Grilled shrimp kabobs (brushed with melted butter, minced garlic, and lemon juice), grilled zucchini, and quinoa

Monday: Veggie Corn Chowder (page 271, double the recipe) with Super-Easy Whole-Wheat Biscuits (page 222)

Tuesday: Shortcut Eggplant Parmesan (page 240) over whole-wheat noodles

Wednesday: Leftover Veggie Corn Chowder with baked sweet potatoes

Thursday: Tomato Bisque (page 177), grilled cheese sandwiches on whole-wheat, and a side salad

Friday: Green Eggs (see sidebar) with cantaloupe, the rest of the bacon, and whole-wheat toast

Saturday: Teriyaki Flank Steak Salad (page 258) with quinoa on the side (if desired)

GREEN EGGS
(one of our favorite ways to eat eggs)!

In a blender, combine 6 eggs, 1 tablespoon milk, 2 tablespoons onion, 1 cup fresh kale or spinach leaves (big stems removed), salt, and pepper and puree until smooth. Melt some butter in a skillet over medium-low heat and cook the egg mixture until it's done to your liking. This dish is good with a little cheese sprinkled on top as well.

SHOPPING LIST

PRODUCE

1 lemon
1 lime
1 pound zucchini
One 1-pound bag carrots
1 head celery
1 red bell pepper
8 large ears corn (or 6 cups frozen corn kernels)
1 large or 2 medium eggplants (about 1 pound total)
5 or 6 medium fresh tomatoes
1 cantaloupe
1 bunch spinach
1 head (or box or bag) lettuce greens
1 head lettuce (Boston, Bibb, or butter)
1 bunch cilantro
1 bunch flat-leaf parsley
1 bunch thyme
2 or 3 sweet potatoes
2- or 3-inch piece fresh ginger
1 bunch green onions
3 yellow onions
1 garlic head

DAIRY / EGGS

½ pound (2 sticks) butter
½ gallon milk
1 cup heavy cream
One 8-ounce block mozzarella cheese (need 1½ cups grated)
One 4-ounce block Parmesan cheese (need ¼ cup grated)
One 8-ounce block cheddar cheese (for grilled cheese)
½ dozen eggs (need 6)

MEAT / SEAFOOD

1 pound shrimp
One 8-ounce pack bacon
1 pound flank steak

INTERIOR AISLES: DRY / CANNED / GRAINS

One 2-pound bag whole-wheat flour
1 bag/box quinoa (enough for 8 servings)
One 1-pound box/bag whole-wheat spaghetti
1 loaf good-quality whole-wheat bread
Two 32-ounce cartons plus one 14-ounce can organic chicken (or vegetable) stock
One 24-ounce jar organic red pasta sauce

PANTRY CHECKLIST

Baking powder
Bay leaf
Cayenne pepper
Honey
Olive oil
Pepper (ground black pepper)
Rice wine vinegar
Salt
Soy sauce, low sodium recommended
Toasted sesame oil

MEAL PLAN: FALL

7-day real-food dinner plan for family of 4 and shopping list

MENU

Sunday: Fish Cakes with Dipping Sauce (page 237), roasted Brussels sprouts, and baked potatoes

Monday: Slow-Cooker Flank Steak Fajitas (page 282) with Whole-Wheat Tortillas (page 326), grated Monterey Jack cheese, sour cream, and shredded lettuce

Tuesday: Vegetable Chili (page 248, double the recipe) with leftover fajita steak mixed in and cheese quesadillas on the side (using leftover Whole-Wheat Tortillas and Monterey Jack cheese)

Wednesday: Leftover Vegetable Chili and a spinach side salad

Thursday: Grilled Caprese Paninis (page 181) with sliced apples and whole-wheat pasta salad (mix together cooled cooked pasta, raw diced carrots, grated Parmesan cheese, and Mustard Vinaigrette, page 312)

Friday: The Perfect Omelet (page 131, double the recipe) with Veggie Pancakes (page 226; use potatoes, carrots, and zucchini) and leftover pasta salad

Saturday: Asian Lettuce Wraps (page 206) with brown rice on the side

LISA'S TIP: When meal planning on your own, pick out one brand-new recipe to try each week to keep things interesting! C'mon, be adventurous.

SHOPPING LIST

PRODUCE

2 apples
1 pound Brussels sprouts
2 medium tomatoes
2 pounds carrots
2 zucchini
6 or 7 bell peppers, any color
1 jalapeño
2 large corn cobs (or 1½ cups frozen corn kernels)
2 lemons
1 head lettuce (shredded for fajitas)
1 head lettuce leaves (large leaves such as Bibb, for lettuce wraps)
1 bunch spinach, for side salads
1 bunch basil
1 bunch cilantro
3 to 4 russet potatoes
1 shallot
1 garlic head
2-inch piece fresh ginger
2 onions
1 bunch green onions

DAIRY / EGGS

¼ pound (1 stick) butter (need 4 teaspoons)
1 quart milk (need 2 tablespoons)
One 8-ounce block Monterey Jack cheese (for fajitas)
One 4-ounce block Parmesan cheese (need ⅔ cup grated)
One 8-ounce block Havarti or mozzarella cheese (for paninis)
One 1-pound container sour cream
1½ dozen eggs (need 13)

MEAT / SEAFOOD

1 pound white fish (such as cod, flounder, or sole), wild-caught preferred
1½ pounds flank steak
1 pound ground pork

INTERIOR AISLES: DRY / CANNED / GRAINS

One 2-pound bag whole-wheat flour
1 canister/bag whole-grain breadcrumbs (need 1 cup)
1 bag medium whole-wheat pitas (need 4)
1 pound small pasta such as penne or macaroni (for the pasta salad)
1 box/bag brown rice (need 4 servings)
¼ cup pine nuts
Two 28-ounce cans diced tomatoes
Two 15-ounce cans kidney beans
One 8-ounce can diced water chestnuts

PANTRY CHECKLIST

Baking powder
Bay leaves
Cayenne pepper
Chili powder
Coconut oil
Coriander (ground)
Cumin (ground)
Dijon mustard
Ghee/clarified butter (optional)
Olive oil
Pepper (ground black pepper)
Salt
Soy Sauce, low sodium recommended
Toasted sesame oil
White wine vinegar
Yellow mustard

Full Meal Plan Template

DAY	BREAKFAST	LUNCH	SNACK	DINNER
Sunday				
Monday				
Tuesday				
Wednesday				
Thursday				
Friday				
Saturday				

Recipes that should be made in advance over the weekend for the upcoming week:

Recipe 1:

Recipe 2:

Recipe 3:

Shopping List Template

PRODUCE

Qty.	Item

INTERIOR AISLES: DRY / CANNED / GRAINS

Qty.	Item

MEAT / SEAFOOD

Qty.	Item

FROZEN

Qty.	Item

BULK / MISC / OTHER

Qty.	Item

DAIRY / EGGS

Qty.	Item

PANTRY CHECKLIST (ITEMS YOU HAVE ON HAND)

Item	Item
☐	☐
☐	☐
☐	☐
☐	☐
☐	☐
☐	☐
☐	☐
☐	☐

PART TWO

THE RECIPES

BREAKFAST

Whole-Wheat Banana Pancakes (or Waffles!)

This recipe is a long-standing favorite with both my family and our blog readers. If you are trying to convince your family to switch over to whole grains, then this is the dish to start with. The sweetness of the extra-ripe bananas magically transforms these pancakes into something amazing. And here's the bonus: The batter can be used for pancakes or waffles!

Difficulty: Easy
Prep and Cook Time: Less than 30 minutes
Makes 5 to 6 servings

VEGETARIAN
FREEZER FRIENDLY

2 cups whole-wheat flour (I use King Arthur organic white whole-wheat flour)

2 teaspoons baking powder

1½ teaspoons baking soda

½ teaspoon salt

1 tablespoon honey

2 large eggs, lightly beaten

1¾ cups milk

2 tablespoons butter, melted, plus extra for frying

2 ripe bananas, mashed

100% pure maple syrup, for serving

1. In a large bowl, whisk together the flour, baking powder, baking soda, and salt.

2. Make a well, or hole, in the center of the flour mixture and pour in the honey, eggs, milk, and melted butter. Whisk together thoroughly until just combined, but do not overmix.

3. Gently fold the mashed bananas into the batter with a spatula.

4. For the pancakes, heat a griddle to 350°F or a sauté pan over medium heat. Swirl enough butter around the griddle/pan until it is well coated. Using a soup ladle, add one ladleful of batter per pancake. After several minutes, when the pancakes have begun browning on the bottom, flip and cook the other side for several more minutes. Transfer the pancakes to a plate and repeat until no batter remains. While the pancakes are cooking, heat the maple syrup on the stove or in the microwave until warm.

FREEZING BREAD ITEMS

You have two options:

1. Freeze them in one layer on a baking sheet, then transfer them to a big freezer-safe bag or other container.
2. Simply separate the layers of food with pieces of wax paper in a freezer-safe container or bag.

5. Serve with warm maple syrup and a side of fruit. And don't forget to freeze the leftovers for another day!

> **LISA'S TIP:** For waffles, pour the batter into a waffle iron and cook according to the manufacturer's directions.

The Perfect Omelet

If you're tired of eggs that stick to the pan or omelets that never take shape, then you'll appreciate this shortcut method for making the perfect omelet. Keep in mind this recipe doesn't have to be made only for breakfast; with the right fixings this makes a great main dish for a quick and easy weeknight dinner as well.

Difficulty: Easy
Prep and Cook Time: Less than 10 minutes
Makes 2 servings

GLUTEN-FREE
VEGETARIAN

4 eggs

1 tablespoon milk

Salt and ground black pepper, to taste

2 teaspoons butter

Optional: Fillings such as shredded cheese, sautéed onions, bell peppers, cooked sausage, diced tomatoes, mushrooms, and/or leftover diced Grilled Veggie Kabobs (page 218)

1. In a medium bowl, thoroughly whisk together the eggs, milk, salt, and pepper.

2. Melt the butter in a 10-inch sauté pan over medium-high heat.

3. Once the butter has melted, but not yet browned, add the egg mixture to the pan. After about 30 seconds, tilt the pan while simultaneously using a spatula to push the edges of the omelet inward (toward the center of the pan). Tilting the pan will force the runny egg mixture to fill in around the edges. Repeat while rotating the pan for 2 to 3 more minutes until the egg is set and cooked all the way through.

4. Sprinkle fillings (if using) over half of the omelet, fold the other half of the omelet over the top, and serve immediately.

Grandma Esther's (Whole-Wheat) Crepes

Difficulty: Advanced
Prep and Cook Time: Less than 45 minutes
Makes 16 to 18 thin crepes (3 to 4 servings)
Special tools needed: Blender

VEGETARIAN
FREEZER FRIENDLY

My ninety-year-old grandmother is famous for her amazing breakfast crepes. Even though her family has grown over the years from just twelve of us to now twenty-six altogether (including her nine great-grandchildren!), that doesn't stop her from offering a continuous supply of homemade crepes at every single family get-together. This family recipe was one of my very first attempts at subbing whole-wheat flour for white refined flour, and let me tell you the outcome is a real winner! Thank you, Grandma, for all of the wonderful inspiration.

3 eggs

1 cup whole-wheat flour

1 cup milk

¾ cup water

1 tablespoon honey

1 teaspoon Pure Vanilla Extract (page 337) or store-bought vanilla extract

¼ teaspoon salt

1 tablespoon butter, melted, plus extra for cooking

100% pure maple syrup, for serving

Fresh fruit, for serving

1. Put all the ingredients except the maple syrup and fruit in a blender and mix until well blended, 1 to 2 minutes, pausing to scrape the sides if necessary. Let the batter rest for 5 to 10 minutes.

2. In an 8- to 10-inch frying pan, melt a small pat of butter over medium heat.

3. Tilt the pan at an angle and pour in enough batter on one side to thinly and evenly cover the pan. Quickly rotate the pan to swirl the batter and produce one thin, even layer.

4. Immediately use a spatula to slightly push the thin edges of the crepe batter around the perimeter down and toward the center (to avoid burning).

5. After about 1 minute, when the crepe is golden brown on the bottom, use the spatula to carefully flip it over without tearing the crepe, and cook on the other side.

6. Cook for 1 more minute until the bottom is golden brown. Remove from the pan. Starting at one edge, use your fingers to fold up the crepe. Transfer to a platter and keep warm. Continue cooking in batches until all the batter is gone. Once you get really good, you can get 2 pans going at once.

7. Serve warm with warm pure maple syrup and fresh fruit. To freeze, separate layers of plain crepes with wax paper and seal in a zip-top bag. Crepes can be frozen for several months and reheated in the microwave.

LISA'S TIP: Leftover crepes could be turned into a fun dessert by rolling them up with a fruit filling inside (such as berries or bananas) and topping them off with Simple Chocolate Sauce (page 338)! Also, I've found that store-bought flour works better than freshly ground in this recipe.

"I love crepes because they're homemade and awesome with syrup." —SYDNEY, AGE 9

Homemade Granola Cereal

Difficulty: Easy
Prep Time: Less than 20 minutes
Bake Time: 75 minutes
Makes 3 pounds
Special tools needed: Parchment paper, large baking sheet

GLUTEN-FREE (IF GLUTEN-FREE OATS ARE USED)
VEGETARIAN
DAIRY-FREE (IF COCONUT OIL IS USED IN PLACE OF BUTTER)
FREEZER FRIENDLY

I originally came across this recipe on the Anson Mills website, a great source for organically milled grains, although their recipe called for steel-cut oats, which yielded more of a granola bar rather than a cereal. My family likes steel-cut oats, but they can also be very chewy, so I was excited when my friend Valerie (who at the time was much more experienced with cooking whole foods than I was) suggested using rolled oats instead. This was one of the very first "real food" recipes I ever made, and I fell in love with it. I had never even cooked with rolled oats before! It's amazing how time flies and how recipes change over time. After lots of tweaking over the last few years, this version is now our favorite breakfast cereal.

3½ cups rolled oats

2 cups raw mixed chopped nuts (my favorite combo is 1 cup almonds, 1 cup cashews, and an extra handful of pecans or walnuts for good measure)

1 cup raw sunflower or pumpkin seeds (I usually do half and half)

1 cup unsweetened shredded coconut

2 teaspoons ground cinnamon

1½ teaspoons ground ginger

½ teaspoon ground nutmeg

½ teaspoon salt

6 tablespoons butter (¾ stick) or coconut oil

½ cup honey

2 teaspoons Pure Vanilla Extract (see page 337) or store-bought vanilla extract

1. Preheat the oven to 250°F. Line a 13 x 18-inch rimmed baking sheet with parchment paper and set aside.

2. In a large bowl, mix together the oats, nuts, seeds, shredded coconut, spices, and salt until well combined.

3. In a small pot over low heat, combine the butter and honey. Simmer until the butter is completely melted and then add the vanilla extract.

4. Pour the wet ingredients over the dry ingredients and mix together thoroughly.

5. Using a rubber spatula, spread the granola mixture onto the baking sheet so it's evenly distributed and bake for 75 minutes.

6. Let the baked granola cool completely before crumbling it into cereal. Serve with milk or yogurt or store in an airtight container at room temperature for up to 2 weeks.

LISA'S TIP: The raw, assembled granola can be refrigerated for up to 24 hours before baking. When you're ready to bake, it can go straight from the fridge to the oven. Also, for a budget-friendly version use all sliced almonds for the nuts and all sunflower seeds for the seeds.

Fruit Salad with Orange Zest

This is a quick and easy way to switch up plain old diced fruit, and the result is surprisingly delicious. Serve as a breakfast side or add it to a brunch buffet. This is best if served within a few hours after mixing the fruit with the yogurt.

Difficulty: Easy
Prep Time: Less than 20 minutes
Seasonal Note: Use locally grown berries and melon in the summer and locally grown apples in the fall.
Makes 4 to 5 servings
Special tools needed: Microplane zester/grater or lemon zester

GLUTEN-FREE
VEGETARIAN

4 cups diced fruit (like melon, apples, bananas, kiwi, and/or berries)

½ cup plain yogurt

2 teaspoons pure maple syrup

½ teaspoon Pure Vanilla Extract (page 337) or store-bought vanilla extract

½ teaspoon chopped orange zest

1. Place the diced fruit in a large serving bowl and set aside.

2. In a small bowl, combine the yogurt, maple syrup, vanilla, and orange zest. Mix thoroughly.

3. Pour the yogurt mixture into the fruit bowl and carefully combine until well blended. Serve immediately or within a few hours.

Oatmeal

Difficulty: Easy
Prep and Cook Time: Less than 10 minutes
Makes 4 servings

GLUTEN-FREE (IF GLUTEN-FREE OATS ARE USED)
DAIRY-FREE (IF WATER IS USED IN PLACE OF MILK)
VEGETARIAN

2½ cups milk

2 cups rolled oats

¼ cup raisins

1 teaspoon honey

¼ teaspoon ground cinnamon

½ teaspoon Pure Vanilla Extract (page 337), or store-bought vanilla extract (optional)

Optional toppings: Pecans, walnuts, berries, diced apples

It's amazing how the food industry can mess up something as simple as oatmeal, from adding artificial dye in the fast food version to disguising artificially flavored dried apple bits as strawberries in the preflavored boxed packets. No wonder it's really hard to trust the "big food" companies these days. Whether it's oatmeal, yogurt, or even cream cheese, it's always best to buy plain and flavor it yourself. My daughters love this simple version of oatmeal, and they enjoy taking it warm in a thermos for their morning snack at school.

1. Combine all the ingredients in a small pot, bring the mixture to a boil, and stir.

2. Turn the heat down to a low simmer and stir occasionally until almost all the milk is absorbed, about 5 minutes.

Eggs in a Basket

My daughters absolutely love this dish . . . and not just for breakfast. They would happily eat Eggs in a Basket any meal of the day, even as their after-school snack. Feel free to use any shape cookie cutter you'd like to cut out the middle of the bread. I think a ghost shape around Halloween time would be especially fun!

Difficulty: Easy
Prep and Cook Time: Less than 10 minutes
Makes 4 servings
Special tools needed: Any shape cookie cutter approximately 3 inches in diameter

VEGETARIAN
DAIRY-FREE (IF COCONUT OIL IS USED IN PLACE OF BUTTER)

- 4 slices Everyday Whole-Wheat Bread (page 332) or good-quality store-bought whole-wheat bread
- 2 tablespoons butter, divided
- 4 eggs
- Salt and ground black pepper, to taste

1. Cut out the center of each slice of bread using a cookie cutter (set the cutouts aside but do not discard).

2. Melt 1 tablespoon of the butter in a medium sauté pan over medium-low heat, or on a griddle set at 350°F.

3. Add 2 pieces of bread to the pan and crack an egg into each bread hole. If there's room in the pan, add the bread cutouts to toast. Season with salt and pepper and cook for several minutes until the eggs are mostly set. Carefully flip over all the pieces and cook for another 1 to 2 minutes. Add more butter to the pan if necessary.

4. Repeat with the remaining 2 sets of bread and 2 eggs and serve warm.

Breakfast Sausage Casserole

This is one of those dishes that's fancy-looking enough to be served on Christmas morning and easy enough to throw together for a weeknight dinner. You can prepare part of this casserole the night before to make for a smooth morning. Serve with the Fruit Salad with Orange Zest (page 137) and the Super-Easy Whole-Wheat Biscuits (page 222) and you have yourself a wholesome meal.

Difficulty: Medium
Prep Time: Less than 20 minutes
Bake Time: Less than 30 minutes
Seasonal Note: Use locally grown bell peppers in the summer and fall months.
Makes 6 to 7 servings
Special tools needed: 13 x 9-inch casserole dish

GLUTEN-FREE

- 1 tablespoon olive oil
- 1 pound breakfast sausage, casings removed
- 1 green or red bell pepper, cored, seeded, and diced
- ½ cup grated cheddar or Swiss cheese
- 12 eggs
- ⅛ to ¼ teaspoon salt
- Ground black pepper, to taste

1. Preheat the oven to 350°F.

2. In a medium sauté pan, heat the olive oil over medium heat. Add the sausage and cook while breaking up the meat with a spatula.

3. When the sausage is almost brown, throw the diced bell pepper into the pan and continue to cook while breaking up the sausage for another 2 to 3 minutes, or until it is cooked all the way through and no longer pink. Drain the oil from the pan and discard.

4. Transfer the mixture to the bottom of an ungreased casserole dish. Be sure to spread out the sausage mixture for even coverage. Sprinkle with the grated cheese.

5. Crack the 12 whole eggs (not beaten) into two rows on top of the sausage mixture and season with the salt and pepper.

6. Bake for about 25 minutes or until the eggs are cooked to the desired consistency. Serve warm.

MAKE-AHEAD NOTE: The sausage, bell peppers, and cheese can be assembled and stored in the fridge the night before. The next morning, simply crack the 12 eggs on top, season with salt and pepper, and add an extra 5 to 10 minutes to the baking time.

Potato Hash (for Breakfast or Dinner!)

Difficulty: Easy
Prep and Cook Time: Less than 30 minutes
Makes 4 to 5 servings
Special tools needed: Cast-iron skillet (12 to 14 inches in diameter)

GLUTEN-FREE
DAIRY-FREE (IF COCONUT OIL IS USED IN PLACE OF GHEE)
VEGETARIAN

3 tablespoons ghee (aka clarified butter, see below) or other high-temperature cooking fat (see page 29 for suggestions)

2 white potatoes with the skin on (about 1½ pounds total), cut into ½-inch dice

⅓ cup diced onion

½ teaspoon salt

2 garlic cloves, minced

1 tablespoon fresh thyme leaves (optional)

This is both a simple and delicious side dish that would be great with anything from an egg breakfast to a steak dinner. Dicing the potato into small pieces helps to cut down the cooking time, so in no time at all this dish can be ready to hit the table.

1. In a cast-iron skillet over medium-high heat, melt the clarified butter.

2. Add the diced potatoes and cook, stirring occasionally, for 5 to 6 minutes.

3. Stir in the diced onion and salt and cook for another 2 minutes. Add the garlic and thyme (if using) and cook for another minute or until the potatoes are soft when pierced with a fork. Remove from the heat and serve warm.

HOW TO MAKE GHEE (CLARIFIED BUTTER)

Melt chunks of unsalted butter in a small saucepan over low heat. Skim the white milk solids off the top and discard (or save for another dish). Set a piece of cheesecloth in a strainer or sieve and place it over a bowl. When the butter stops bubbling, pour it through the cheesecloth in order to remove any remaining milk solids. Store in the fridge and follow the expiration date for original butter.

LISA'S TIP: Since "clarifying" butter removes the milk solids, it can be cooked longer and at a higher temperature without burning (unlike regular butter). It can also sometimes be tolerated by those with an intolerance to milk!

Breakfast Tacos

These may be called Breakfast Tacos, but to be honest, my family would happily devour them at any time of day. This recipe is versatile and can easily be modified depending on the ingredients you have on hand. Feel free to top them off with everything from sour cream to sautéed peppers or even Easy Slow-Cooker Refried Beans (page 155).

Difficulty: Easy
Prep and Cook Time: Less than 20 minutes
Makes 4 servings

GLUTEN-FREE
VEGETARIAN
FREEZER-FRIENDLY

7 eggs

1 tablespoon milk

1/8 teaspoon salt

Ground black pepper, to taste

2 tablespoons butter

1/2 cup diced onion

1/2 jalapeño, cored, seeded, and minced

3/4 cup diced tomato (1 large tomato)

Lime wedge (optional)

Ten 5- to 6-inch soft Corn Tortillas (page 329), or store-bought whole-grain corn tortillas, warmed by wrapping the stack in foil and putting them in the oven on low heat (for store-bought I like Food for Life brand in the freezer section)

1 3/4 cups grated Monterey Jack cheese

Optional toppings: Sour cream, avocado, sautéed bell or poblano peppers, cilantro, and/or salsa

1. In a large bowl, whisk together the eggs, milk, salt, and pepper. Set aside.

2. Melt the butter in a sauté pan over medium heat. Add the onion and jalapeño and, while stirring, cook until the onion becomes soft, about 2 minutes. Add the diced tomato and cook for 1 more minute.

3. Pour in the egg mixture and cook without stirring for 1 minute, then start scrambling the eggs with a spatula until they are cooked all the way through and no longer runny, 2 to 3 more minutes. Squeeze juice from a lime wedge onto the cooked eggs (if using).

4. Spread the warm tortillas out on a large cutting board or serving platter. Divide the scrambled eggs, cheese, and optional toppings evenly among the tortillas. Fold the tacos in half and serve warm.

FREEZING INSTRUCTIONS

These can also be wrapped up and frozen individually so they can be defrosted for a quick weekday breakfast. Defrost overnight in the fridge and warm up in the oven or microwave.

Sunday Brunch: Eggs Benedict with Kale

Difficulty: Advanced
Prep and Cook Time: 30 minutes
Seasonal Note: Use locally grown kale in the winter and spring months.
Makes 4 servings
Special tools needed: Electric mixer, steamer basket, small round cookie cutter (or glass turned upside down)

GLUTEN-FREE (IF GLUTEN-FREE BREAD IS SUBSTITUTED)
VEGETARIAN

1 tablespoon white vinegar

1½ cups loosely packed kale leaves, stems removed

8 eggs, plus 2 egg yolks, divided

4 slices Everyday Whole-Wheat Bread (page 332) or good-quality store-bought whole-wheat bread or English muffins

4 tablespoons (½ stick) unsalted butter

1 tablespoon freshly squeezed lemon juice

⅛ teaspoon salt

This is definitely not your weekday "on-the-go" type of breakfast dish, but rather a tasty special-occasion meal that would be perfect for Sunday brunch, Father's Day, or a surprise birthday breakfast in bed.

1. Fill a large pot with water and set it over high heat. Add the vinegar to the water.

2. Pour ½ inch of water into a medium saucepan, top with a steamer basket and a tight-fitting lid, and set over high heat. Once the water in the saucepan starts to boil, add the kale to the steamer basket. After 1 minute, remove the pan from the heat, drain the water, and set the pan, with the kale still in the basket, aside to keep warm.

3. Once the large pot of water is boiling, turn the heat down to a soft boil. Carefully crack each egg into a separate little prep bowl and drop into the water one by one. You may need to turn the temperature up slightly so the water comes back up to a soft boil. Set the timer for 5 minutes.

4. Cut each piece of bread into two smaller round pieces using a cookie cutter or glass turned upside down. Toast the bread rounds in a toaster or toaster oven, until golden.

5. To make Hollandaise sauce, melt the butter in a small pot over medium-low heat. Meanwhile, place the 2 egg yolks in the bowl of an electric mixer. Once the butter has completely melted, stir in the lemon juice and salt and let it come to a light bubbling simmer. Start simultaneously beating the egg yolks on high (still in a separate mixing bowl) for approximately 1 minute. While the mixer is still running pour the simmering butter into the egg yolks and keep the mixer on high for 1 more minute, until the sauce is a creamy consistency.

6. Once the eggs have boiled for the full 5 minutes, transfer them to a large bowl using a slotted spoon to drain.

7. Divide the toasted rounds evenly among 4 plates. Top with equal amounts of steamed kale, eggs, and then sauce. Serve warm with a side of fruit.

> **LISA'S TIP:** Making a Hollandaise sauce the right consistency can be tricky, so be sure to follow the recipe closely.

LUNCH

* Lunch Box Section

Grilled Cheese with Apples and Bacon

This sandwich brings together three of my younger daughter's most favorite foods of all time: cheese, apples, and bacon. Oh, and I guess the bread should count, too. This girl of mine loves her bread products (thankfully she likes the whole-grain variety)! So the first time I made this recipe it was quite a kick to witness her reaction. We've done our best to teach our daughters to savor and enjoy their food and to also notice the different, tasty flavors of a dish. As she was taking her first few bites of this sandwich it became apparent that she actually remembered to think about these things. She excitedly exclaimed, "Mmm . . . yummy! This is the best sandwich in the whole entire universe! Thank you for making it with all of my favorite foods!"

This is a rich, filling sandwich, so at my house, four half-sandwiches will feed four people (with a variety of sides, of course).

Difficulty: Easy
Prep Time: Less than 20 minutes
Makes 4 sandwich halves

GLUTEN-FREE (IF GLUTEN-FREE BREAD IS SUBSTITUTED AND BACON IS LABELED AS GLUTEN-FREE)
VEGETARIAN (IF BACON IS OMITTED)

2 tablespoons butter

4 slices Everyday Whole-Wheat Bread (page 332) or good-quality store-bought whole-wheat bread

4 slices cheese (such as cheddar, Havarti, or Monterey Jack), about 1 ounce per slice

4 slices cooked bacon, broken in half to make 8 pieces

½ unpeeled green apple, cut into ¼-inch-thick slices

1 tablespoon freshly grated Parmesan cheese (optional)

1. Melt 1 tablespoon of the butter in a large sauté pan over medium heat. Carefully rub one side of each slice of bread in the melted butter to coat and set aside. Turn off the heat.

2. Assemble the sandwiches by starting with a single slice of bread, butter side down, then topping it with 1 cheese slice, half of the bacon, half of the apple, and another slice of cheese. Top with

COOKING BACON

Stovetop Method: Set a sauté pan over medium heat. Add the bacon without overcrowding the pan (no cooking oil is necessary). Cook for several minutes, or until the bacon starts to curl up and darken on the bottom. Flip and cook for several minutes longer, until cooked all the way through or to your desired doneness. I like my bacon crispy, so I cook it until both sides are dark brown.

Oven Method: Preheat the oven to 400°F. Set a metal cooling rack on top of a baking sheet. Lay the bacon across the rack in a single layer. Bake for 15 to 20 minutes, depending on the thickness of the bacon and how crispy you like it.

another slice of bread (butter side up this time). Repeat with the remaining ingredients.

3. Melt the rest of the butter in the same pan over medium-low heat. Add the assembled sandwiches to the pan and cook until the bottoms are lightly toasted, 3 to 4 minutes.

4. Flip over and, if using, evenly sprinkle half of the grated Parmesan over the tops of the two sandwiches. When the bottoms are lightly toasted, flip again and cook for a minute or so, just long enough for the Parmesan to melt into the bread. Be careful not to burn the Parmesan. Sprinkle the remaining Parmesan on top of the other side and repeat. Slice and serve warm.

LISA'S TIP: I avoid pregrated cheese from the store because a powdery anticaking agent has been added to prevent the cheese from clumping together. But packets of quality presliced cheese have no unwanted additives, so I do buy those for convenience on occasion, especially since I find it hard to make such perfect slices myself at home.

Easy Slow-Cooker Refried Beans

I went from practically hating all beans to being borderline obsessed with this recipe. I don't know if it's the texture or the flavor, but something about these beans is just short of amazing. You pop them in the slow cooker after dinner and just like that . . . you wake up craving breakfast tacos. But if you can hold off for a few hours (just turn the slow cooker down to low) they make an incredibly quick and appetizing lunch as well. I freeze this dish in individual portions for a quick and easy lunch.

Difficulty: Easy
Prep Time: Less than 15 minutes
Cook Time: 8 to 10 hours
Makes just under 4 cups cooked beans
Special tools needed: Slow cooker and potato masher

GLUTEN-FREE
DAIRY-FREE
VEGETARIAN
FREEZER FRIENDLY

2 cups dried pinto beans, rinsed

1 onion, peeled and halved

½ (or whole) jalapeño or other hot pepper, cored, seeded, and diced

2 garlic cloves, peeled and crushed

1¼ teaspoons salt

½ teaspoon ground black pepper

⅛ teaspoon ground cumin

Optional toppings: Shredded Monterey Jack or Havarti cheese, sour cream, cilantro, and/or salsa

1. Combine all the ingredients plus 6 cups water in a slow cooker and cook on high for 8 to 10 hours.

2. Remove the onion chunks from the cooked beans and discard, drain out most (but not all) of the liquid, and smash the beans with a potato masher until smooth. (The first time you make this recipe, you may want to reserve some of the liquid just in case you need to add some back to get the right consistency.) Serve warm topped with cheese, salsa, sour cream, and cilantro or freeze for another day.

Black Bean Tostada

Difficulty: Easy
Prep and Cook Time: Less than 30 minutes
Makes 3 to 4 servings
Special tools needed: Large baking sheet

GLUTEN-FREE (IF CORN TORTILLAS ARE SUBSTITUTED)
VEGETARIAN

- One 15-ounce can black beans, drained and rinsed
- 1 tablespoon freshly squeezed lime juice
- ¼ cup chopped fresh cilantro
- ½ teaspoon ground cumin
- ⅛ teaspoon salt (unless the canned beans already contain salt)
- Big pinch of cayenne pepper
- 3 Whole-Wheat Tortillas (page 326) or store-bought whole-wheat tortillas
- 1¼ cups grated Monterey Jack cheese
- Suggested toppings: Sour cream, avocado, shredded lettuce, and/or diced tomato

It's funny how when I first let my daughters try a bite of this black bean mixture, they were not big fans. But then I spread it on some tortillas, topped it with cheese, and baked it in the oven, and suddenly they couldn't get enough. They were literally stealing pieces off my plate. I just thought I would share in case you weren't already drooling over the picture!

1. Preheat the oven to 400°F.

2. In a medium bowl, combine the beans with the lime juice and 1 tablespoon water, then mash until smooth with the back of a fork. Stir in the cilantro, cumin, salt, and cayenne until mixed together thoroughly.

3. Lay out the tortillas on a large baking sheet. Evenly divide and spread the black bean mixture onto the tortillas in a thin layer and top with the grated cheese. Bake until the cheese is melted and begins to brown, about 8 minutes.

4. Top with sour cream, avocado, or desired toppings and serve warm.

LISA'S TIP: The black bean mixture can be prepared in advance and refrigerated.

Greek Stuffed Pitas

This meal could pass as lunch or even a quick and easy dinner. Couscous takes only about five minutes to cook, which could make this a great go-to dish when it comes to those busy weeknight meals! And these stuffed pitas are surprisingly good left over the next day. If you want to try them on picky kids, consider holding the vinegar and garlic.

Difficulty: Easy
Prep Time: Less than 20 minutes
Seasonal Note: Use locally grown cucumbers and tomatoes (and dill!) in the summer months.
Makes 4 servings

VEGETARIAN

4 small whole-wheat pita pockets

½ cup dry whole-wheat couscous, cooked according to the package directions

½ cup plain yogurt

½ unpeeled cucumber, grated

½ cup crumbled feta cheese

12 cherry tomatoes, sliced in half

½ teaspoon dried dill

½ teaspoon red wine vinegar

⅛ teaspoon salt

Cayenne pepper, to taste

1 garlic clove, minced

8 lettuce leaves, for serving (Bibb or romaine will work well)

1. Using kitchen shears, cut each pita pocket in half down the middle. Set aside.

2. In a medium bowl, combine the couscous, yogurt, cucumber, feta, tomatoes, dill, vinegar, salt, cayenne, and garlic.

3. Stuff each pita pocket with a piece of lettuce and some of the couscous mixture. Serve immediately or wrap up for later.

Southwest Chicken Wraps

Difficulty: Easy
Prep Time: Less than 30 minutes
Makes 6 servings

SOUTHWEST SAUCE

¾ cup sour cream

⅓ cup chopped fresh cilantro

Juice of ½ lime

½ teaspoon chili powder

½ teaspoon ground cumin

¼ teaspoon cayenne pepper

¼ teaspoon salt

WRAPS

Six or seven 8-inch Whole-Wheat Tortillas (page 326) or store-bought whole-wheat tortillas

3 cups shredded or sliced cooked chicken (such as leftover slow-cooker chicken, see page 278)

3 cups chopped raw spinach

1½ cups grated Monterey Jack cheese

1 avocado, sliced

Optional wrap fillings: Diced tomato, black beans, sliced red onion (use what you have on hand!)

This recipe will definitely kick up your lunch a few notches! I often scrounge the fridge for leftovers when lunchtime rolls around, so when I take a little extra time to put together something like this it's a treat the whole family enjoys.

1. To make the Southwest Sauce, thoroughly mix all the ingredients in a small bowl. Set aside.

2. To assemble the wraps, lay out the tortillas on a large cutting board or platter next to an assembly line of the filling ingredients, including the sauce. Evenly distribute the chicken, spinach, cheese, avocado, and sauce in a strip down the middle of each tortilla. Fold up the wraps on both sides and serve.

MAKE-AHEAD TIP: If you're making these in advance, store the wraps rolled up in foil in the fridge and serve with the sauce on the side, to prevent sogginess.

LUNCH BOX

Pizza Bites

When my kids love a dish as much as they love pizza, they don't care if it's warm or cold. This certainly makes things easy for me when I want to pack pizza in their lunch on Fridays . . . which just happens to be the same day the school cafeteria serves it. I have to thank my friend Natalie for giving me the idea to make this miniature "pizza bite" version, which is easy to make in advance and then freeze. The night before pizza day, all I have to do is pull a few out of the freezer, let them defrost in the fridge overnight, and voilà! Lunch is done.

Difficulty: Easy
Prep and Cook Time: Less than 20 minutes
Makes 14 pizza bites
Special tools needed: Large baking sheet

VEGETARIAN
FREEZER FRIENDLY

14 mini whole-wheat pita pockets (about 2½ inches across; we buy ours from Trader Joe's)

½ cup Homemade Tomato Sauce (page 320) or store-bought organic sauce

¾ cup grated mozzarella cheese

1. Preheat the oven to 425°F.

2. Lay the whole pitas out on a baking sheet. Spread a small spoonful of the tomato sauce on top of each pita, then divide the cheese evenly among them.

3. Bake for 8 to 10 minutes, or until the cheese is melted and starts to turn golden brown. Serve the pizzas warm, refrigerate them for up to several days, or freeze them in a large freezer-safe container or bag separated with wax paper.

LUNCH BOX

Whole-Grain Pumpkin Muffins

This recipe was my first experience using spelt flour, and let me tell you . . . I'm a fan! Spelt is an ancient grain that's part of the wheat family. Its flour gives a more cake-like texture than whole-wheat flour and the taste is also a little milder. I had you at "cake," right? Trust me, you won't be disappointed, but even if you aren't in the mood to experiment you can easily make these with whole-wheat flour instead.

Difficulty: Easy
Prep Time: Less than 15 minutes
Cook Time: Less than 20 minutes
Seasonal Note: Make your own homemade puree from locally grown pumpkins in the fall months.
Makes 12 standard-size muffins
Special tools needed: Muffin pan, paper or silicone muffin liners

VEGETARIAN
FREEZER FRIENDLY

- 1½ cups whole-spelt or whole-wheat flour
- 1 tablespoon pumpkin pie spice blend (sold in the spice aisle)
- 1 teaspoon baking soda
- ½ teaspoon salt
- ¼ teaspoon baking powder
- 2 eggs
- ½ cup honey
- ⅓ cup melted butter
- 1 cup canned pumpkin puree (not pie filling)

1. Preheat the oven to 350°F. Line a muffin pan with liners and set aside.

2. In a large bowl, whisk together the flour, pumpkin pie spice, baking soda, salt, and baking powder.

3. Make a well (hole) in the center of the flour mixture and drop in the eggs, honey, and melted butter. Mix together until smooth, but don't overmix. Fold in the pumpkin puree just until combined.

4. Divide the batter among 12 muffin cups (each cup should be about three-quarters full). Bake until golden brown and a toothpick comes out clean, 18 to 20 minutes. Store at room temperature or freeze for a rainy day!

"I always beg my mom to make these pumpkin muffins because they're so tasty."—SYDNEY, AGE 9

Apple Sandwich

If you're looking for a way to make over your kid's lunch (or your own!), here's the answer. Sandwiches are no longer a bore if you just switch out the regular bread and use Cinnamon-Raisin Quick Bread (page 173), waffles (see page 129), or even apples! Apple sandwiches are easier than they look, plus you can mix things up by using any small cookie cutter shape to cut out the core. A heart on Valentine's Day would be adorable! Check out 100daysofrealfood.com/applesandwich for step-by-step pictures.

Difficulty: Easy
Prep Time: Less than 10 minutes
Seasonal Note: Use locally grown apples in the fall months.
Makes 2 sandwiches
Special tools needed: 1-inch cookie cutter (round or other shape), wooden toothpicks (to keep the sandwich together in a lunch box)

GLUTEN-FREE
DAIRY-FREE
VEGETARIAN

1 large unpeeled apple, any variety

1 teaspoon freshly squeezed lemon juice (optional; keeps the apple from turning brown)

2 tablespoons nut or seed butter (such as peanut butter, almond butter, or sunflower butter)

2 teaspoons raisins (optional)

1. Turn the apple on its side and slice off the top inch of the apple and discard (or eat what's around the stem!).

2. Carefully make four (or more, depending on the size of your apple) ½- or ¾-inch-thick slices that will become the "bread" of the sandwiches. Stop about an inch before the bottom. Either eat or discard the very bottom piece of apple.

3. Lay the slices flat on a cutting board and use the small cookie cutter to cut the core out of the middle. Alternatively, core it with a paring knife, but it won't be nearly as pretty.

4. To prevent the apples from turning brown, mix the lemon juice with ¼ cup water in a small bowl and douse the apple slices in the lemon mixture. (I've also found that some varieties of apples, such as Honeycrisp and Gala, don't brown nearly as quickly as the common Red Delicious variety so that's what I usually buy instead of using lemon juice.)

5. Spread 1 tablespoon of nut or seed butter on top of 2 apple slices. Evenly distribute the raisins on top of the nut or seed butter (if using) and top with another apple slice. Secure with 2 wooden toothpicks (not plastic, because they can break off in the apple) if you anticipate that the sandwich will get tossed around in the lunch box, but instruct your little ones to take toothpicks out before taking a bite!

LISA'S TIP: One time when I wanted to make apple sandwiches at my parents' place without a small cookie cutter, I figured out that the small round top from their milk carton was the perfect substitute!

Hummus Sandwiches Three Ways

If you're in a PB&J sandwich rut, this combination will be a welcome alternative. If your children are turned off by anything green, start by leaving the spinach off the sandwich altogether. Once they decide they love the sandwich, slowly work your way to adding small amounts of the green stuff . . . even if that means one leaf at a time.

Four of these hearty half-sandwiches (along with a variety of sides) will feed four people at my house.

Difficulty: Easy
Prep Time: Less than 10 minutes
Makes 4 sandwich halves

GLUTEN-FREE (IF GLUTEN-FREE BREAD IS SUBSTITUTED)
DAIRY-FREE (IF CHEESE IS NOT USED)
VEGETARIAN

6 tablespoons plain hummus

4 slices Everyday Whole-Wheat Bread (page 332) or good-quality store-bought whole-wheat bread

2 ounces cheese, sliced (Havarti or sharp Cheddar recommended)

1⅓ cups fresh spinach leaves, washed and trimmed (or tomato or avocado slices)

1. Spread the hummus evenly over 2 bread slices. Top each with cheese and spinach (or tomato or avocado slices).

2. Top with the other bread slices to make sandwiches, then use a bread knife to slice each in half. Serve or refrigerate, covered, and eat within a couple of days.

LUNCH BOX

Mini Lunch-Box Quiches

Packing school lunches can be quick and easy if you cook and freeze items ahead of time. Quiche is traditionally served warm, but it's actually pretty good cold as well and makes the perfect main dish for any child's lunch. My girls always gobble this one up when I pack it for them.

Difficulty: Medium
Prep Time: Less than 20 minutes
Bake Time: Less than 20 minutes
Makes 12 mini quiches
Special tools needed: 12 silicone muffin liners (paper liners not recommended) or twelve 5-inch parchment paper squares

VEGETARIAN
FREEZER FRIENDLY

1 cup whole-wheat flour

½ teaspoon salt

6 tablespoons (¾ stick) butter, melted

4 eggs

1½ cups milk

⅛ teaspoon ground black pepper, or to taste

⅓ cup grated cheese, such as cheddar, Monterey Jack, or Havarti

1. Preheat the oven to 400°F. Line a muffin pan with either 12 silicone muffin liners or 5-inch parchment squares.

2. In a medium bowl, blend the flour and ¼ teaspoon of the salt. Stir in the melted butter until the flour is completely moistened and then set aside.

3. In a large glass measuring cup or bowl with a spout (if you have one), whisk together the eggs, milk, remaining ¼ teaspoon salt, and pepper.

4. Put 1 tablespoon of the flour mixture in the bottom of each lined muffin cup. Push it down flat with your fingers so it covers the bottom from edge to edge. If you're using the parchment paper liners, this is your chance to really shove each piece down into its hole.

5. Sprinkle the cheese evenly on top of the little crusts, then carefully pour the egg mixture on top, filling the cups two-thirds full.

6. Bake until the eggs are set and lightly browned on top, 18 to 20 minutes. Eat warm, refrigerate for later in the week, or freeze for another day!

Cinnamon-Raisin Quick Bread

This bread is divine. I'd be lying if I told you otherwise. No bread machine or fancy equipment needed . . . all it takes is a little bit of time and a few wholesome ingredients, and you'll be incredibly pleased with the outcome. Toast a slice and top it with butter for breakfast, create a sandwich with some softened cream cheese in the middle for lunch, or eat it plain as a snack. You won't be disappointed!

Difficulty: Easy
Prep Time: Less than 20 minutes
Bake Time: Less than 1 hour
Makes 1 loaf
Special tools needed: 5 x 9-inch loaf pan

VEGETARIAN
FREEZER FRIENDLY

½ cup (1 stick) butter, melted, plus more for greasing the pan
1½ cups whole-wheat flour
1½ teaspoons ground cinnamon
1 teaspoon baking soda
¼ teaspoon baking powder
½ teaspoon salt
2 eggs
1 cup unsweetened applesauce
⅓ cup pure maple syrup
¾ cup raisins

1. Preheat the oven to 325°F. Grease a loaf pan with butter and set aside.

2. In a large mixing bowl, whisk together the flour, cinnamon, baking soda, baking powder, and salt.

3. Using a fork, mix in the eggs, applesauce, melted butter, and syrup until well combined, taking care not to overmix. Gently fold in the raisins.

4. Spoon the batter into the prepared loaf pan. Bake until a skewer inserted into the center comes out clean, 45 to 55 minutes.

LISA'S TIP: For an extra-special weekend breakfast, use this bread to make French toast!

LUNCH BOX

Guacamole with Bell Pepper "Chips"

Tortilla chips are a rare sight at our house since they're usually deep-fried in refined oil, but that doesn't mean we have to miss out on one of our favorite dips: guacamole! A blog reader actually gave me the idea to use bell pepper strips instead of traditional chips. Not only does the combo taste good together, but it's a super-easy way to ensure you get in your fair share of veggies for the day! And if your kids are into avocado (like mine), it's a great lunch-box addition as well.

Difficulty: Easy
Prep Time: Less than 15 minutes
Seasonal Note: Use locally grown bell peppers in the summer and fall months.
Makes 3 or 4 appetizer servings

GLUTEN-FREE
DAIRY-FREE
VEGETARIAN

- 2 ripe avocados (not too soft to the touch!)
- 2 tablespoons freshly squeezed lime juice
- 2 tablespoons chopped fresh cilantro
- ½ jalapeño, seeded and diced (optional)
- 2 tablespoons diced white or red onion (optional)
- 1 garlic clove, minced
- ½ teaspoon salt
- 2 bell peppers, any color, cored, seeded, and cut into ½-inch-thick slices

1. Slice the avocados in half and remove the pits. Scoop out the flesh into a medium bowl and mash with the back of a fork.

2. Add the lime juice, cilantro, jalapeño (if using), onion, garlic, and salt and mix thoroughly. Serve with bell pepper "chips" or cover and refrigerate and eat within 24 hours.

LUNCH BOX

Tomato Bisque

This is my older daughter's favorite soup of all time. I make big double batches, freeze it in individual jelly jars (with room left at the top for the soup to expand), and then send some warm bisque in an insulated thermos for her school lunch. With whole-wheat noodles floating in the soup and complementary side items (such as a cold grilled cheese sandwich and fruit), I have one happy girl come lunchtime.

Difficulty: Medium
Prep and Cook Time: Less than 1 hour
Makes 6 to 8 servings
Special tools needed: Countertop blender or handheld immersion blender

VEGETARIAN (IF BACON IS OMITTED AND VEGETABLE BROTH IS USED)
FREEZER FRIENDLY

4 tablespoons (½ stick) butter

1 small yellow onion, diced

2 slices uncooked bacon (or prosciutto, pancetta, or ham), chopped

4 garlic cloves, minced

¼ cup plus 1 tablespoon whole-wheat flour

5 cups homemade chicken stock (page 322) or good-quality store-bought broth

5 to 6 medium fresh tomatoes, boiled for 1 minute and then peeled, top of tomato core discarded, and roughly chopped (or one 28-ounce can whole peeled tomatoes, chopped, with liquid)

3 flat-leaf parsley sprigs

3 thyme sprigs

1 bay leaf

1 cup heavy cream (or less if desired)

1 teaspoon salt (or more if you're using unsalted homemade broth)

Ground black pepper, to taste

1. Heat the butter in a large soup pot over medium-high heat. Add the onion and cook for 5 or 6 minutes, or until soft.

2. Add the bacon and garlic and cook, stirring, for another 2 to 3 minutes, or until the meat is cooked through.

3. Add the flour and whisk vigorously for 2 to 3 minutes.

4. Pour in the broth and tomatoes and bring to a boil while whisking constantly.

5. Turn the heat to low, throw in the herbs, and simmer, uncovered, for 30 minutes.

6. Remove the herbs and puree the soup either in a blender (in batches) or with a handheld immersion blender.

7. Stir in the desired amount of heavy cream, salt, and pepper. Serve warm and freeze the leftovers.

PB&J Smoothie

Inspired by a drink that's served at our local Earth Fare cafe, I bring you . . . the PB&J Smoothie! This is by far one of my girls' favorite smoothie recipes, and if I'm being honest, mine as well. These are great to pack in reusable Norpro silicone ice pop molds (pictured) and found easily online, for school lunches. Just be sure to wait until the morning of school before you safely wedge the completely frozen mold into your child's lunch container. Then transfer your divided container to an insulated lunch bag along with several ice packs. It should be almost thawed by lunchtime and will quite possibly be the envy of the lunchroom!

Difficulty: Easy
Prep Time: Less than 10 minutes
Makes 2 to 3 servings
Special tools needed: Blender and ice pop molds (optional)

GLUTEN-FREE
VEGETARIAN
FREEZER FRIENDLY

1/3 cup milk

1/3 cup apple juice

1/3 cup natural peanut butter

1 to 2 ripe bananas (the riper, the sweeter)

1 cup frozen or fresh berries (if using fresh, add a handful of ice cubes as well)

Optional (but highly recommended!): 1 cup loosely packed spinach, kale, or Swiss chard leaves, big stems removed

Combine all the ingredients in a blender and puree until smooth. Serve cold or freeze in an ice cube tray or ice pop molds.

LISA'S TIP: If your school has banned peanut products, substitute sunflower seed butter for the peanut butter or leave it out altogether.

LUNCH BOX

Grilled Caprese Paninis

This is another dish that's great either warm or cold. Of course if we're at home we usually scarf these down right off the panini grill, but on a whim one day I decided to pack up a bunch in a cooler and take them up to the pool. That's when I realized how perfect they would be as a lunch-box sandwich as well. I'd take the cold version in my lunch over a regular sandwich any day!

Difficulty: Medium
Prep and Cook Time: Less than 20 minutes
Seasonal Note: Use locally grown tomatoes and basil in the summer months.
Makes 4 servings
Special tools needed: Small or large food processor and a panini grill (optional, see note)

GLUTEN-FREE (IF GLUTEN-FREE BREAD OR PITAS ARE SUBSTITUTED)
VEGETARIAN

PESTO SAUCE

½ cup fresh basil leaves

½ cup fresh spinach leaves

⅓ cup freshly grated Parmesan cheese

¼ cup pine nuts

1 garlic clove

2 tablespoons olive oil

SANDWICHES

4 medium whole-wheat pita pockets (we get ours from Trader Joe's)

4 ounces Havarti or mozzarella cheese, cut into 8 slices

2 medium tomatoes, cut into 8 slices

Olive oil, for coating the panini grill

1. Preheat the panini grill.

2. To make the pesto, combine the basil, spinach, Parmesan cheese, pine nuts, garlic, and olive oil in a small food processor. Puree until the mixture becomes a thick paste.

3. To assemble the sandwiches, cut each pita in half. Open the pita pockets and smear pesto in each, then load up each pita pocket with 1 cheese slice and 1 tomato slice.

4. Grease the top and bottom of the panini grill with olive oil, add the sandwiches, and close the lid. (Depending on the size of your grill, you may need to work in batches.) Cook the sandwiches for 3 to 4 minutes, or until golden brown on top. Serve warm or cold.

LISA'S TIPS:

If you don't have a panini maker, a George Foreman grill would work, or you can cook them in a pan or on a griddle like a grilled cheese sandwich (page 153).

Pesto can be made in advance and frozen in ice cube trays, then transferred to a large bag or other freezer-safe container. The oil content helps them defrost rather quickly.

Let the sandwich cool completely before boxing it up so the steam doesn't cause sogginess.

More School Lunch Ideas: Lunch-Box Packing Chart

Pick 1 Main	Pick 1 or 2 Produce	Pick 1 Grain or Other Snack
Apple Sandwich (page 167)	Apple	100% whole-grain crackers
My Dad's (Brown Rice) Risotto (page 246) with Vegetables*	Applesauce	100% whole-wheat pretzels***
Cheese quesadillas (cooked in advance and served cold)	Carrots***	Cashews
Homemade Chicken Noodle Soup* (page 260)	Blueberries	Almonds
Homemade Chicken Nuggets (page 244), served cold	Celery*** (plain or with peanut butter and raisins, aka Ants on a Log)	Cheese (cubes or sticks, with or without crackers)
Vegetable Chili* (page 248)	Canned fruit such as mandarin oranges (packed in orange juice, not sugary syrup)	Asian-Inspired Rice (page 220)
Cinnamon-Raisin Quick Bread sandwich with cream cheese (see page 173)	Cantaloupe	Brown rice cakes or crackers
Egg salad	Cherries	Cold Whole-Wheat Crepes (page 132) or Pancakes (page 129)
Greek Stuffed Pita (page 159)	Cooked green beans	Spiced Nut Mix (page 202)
Grilled Caprese Paninis (page 181)	Cucumber slices***	Granola chunks (see page 134)
Grilled Cheese (page 153), cold	Cinnamon Apple Chips (page 198)	Hard-boiled or deviled eggs
Hummus sandwich (see page 169)	Organic edamame (good with soy sauce)	Kit's Organic Fruit & Nut Bars or Lärabars
Leftover The Best Whole Chicken in the Slow Cooker (page 278)	Figs	Organic and/or local bacon
Macaroni Casserole* (page 252)	Dried or freeze-dried fruit (such as mango, banana, blueberries, or strawberries)	Peanuts
Mini Lunch-Box Quiches (page 171)	Frozen peas (no cooking necessary!)	Pecans

Pick 1 Main	Pick 1 or 2 Produce	Pick 1 Grain or Other Snack
Oatmeal*	Fruit kabob (see page 205)	Pine nuts (good lightly toasted)
Whole-Wheat Pasta with Kale-Pesto Cream Sauce* (page 274)	Fruit Salad with Orange Zest (page 137)	Pistachios (shelled)
PB&J** sandwich (on bread, pita, or crackers)	Grapefruit slices	Plain yogurt (flavored with a little honey or maple syrup and vanilla extract or Berry Sauce, page 334)
PB&J** Smoothie (page 179)	Grapes	Popcorn (page 192)
Peanut butter** and honey sandwich	Honeydew melon	Pumpkin seeds
Pizza Bites (page 163), leftover Whole-Wheat Pizza (page 250), toast pizza, or make-your-own pizza (with sauce, grated cheese, and pizza crust or pita triangles), served cold	Kiwi	Sunflower seeds
Slow-Cooker Potato Soup* (page 276)	Mango	Toasted whole-grain pita triangles***
Easy Slow-Cooker Refried Beans* (page 155)	Olives	Trail mix (nuts, seeds, and dried fruit)
Sienna's Purple Potion Smoothie (page 201)	Oranges	Walnuts
Tomato Bisque* (page 177)	Peaches	Whole-Grain Pumpkin Muffins (page 165), or a variation
Veggie Corn Chowder* (page 271)	Organic papaya (a high-risk GMO crop; buy organic for non-GMO)	
Waffle (see page 129), cream cheese, and jelly sandwich	Pear	
Whole-grain crackers and cheese slices	Pineapple	
Grandma Esther's (Whole-Wheat) Crepes (page 132) filled with berries or bananas	Plums	

Pick 1 Main	Pick 1 or 2 Produce	Pick 1 Grain or Other Snack
Whole-Wheat Spaghetti and Meatballs* (page 256)	Pomegranate seeds (good mixed in yogurt)	
Whole-Wheat Banana Pancakes (page 129), plain or as a cream cheese sandwich	Radish slices	
	Cherry tomatoes***	
	Raisins (unsweetened)	
	Raspberries	
	Broccoli (raw or cooked)***	
	Bell peppers, sliced***	
	Sugar snap peas***	
	Salad with olive oil or homemade dressing (on side, if desired)	
	Star fruit	
	Strawberries	
	Watermelon	

**Send warm in an insulated container such as a thermos.*
***Or substitute almond butter or sunflower seed butter*
****Good with a dip such as hummus or onion dip (see page 189).*

SNACKS AND APPETIZERS

Onion Dip with Veggie Sticks

It's a fact. My kids (and I) will eat at least twice as many veggies if they are accompanied by some sort of dip. And even though this "individual cup" serving idea is fancy enough to serve at a party, it's actually ideal to have on hand in your fridge all week long. Whether your kids are hungry for a snack after school or your spouse is home and dinner isn't quite ready yet, the family can help themselves to a (healthy) little snack that's ready and waiting! This dip would also be great with sliced bell pepper or broccoli florets.

Difficulty: Easy
Prep Time: Less than 15 minutes
Makes 8 servings

GLUTEN-FREE
VEGETARIAN

One 16-ounce container sour cream

1 recipe Homemade Dried Onion Soup Mix (page 317)

4 carrots, peeled and trimmed

3 celery stalks, trimmed

1 cucumber

1. In a medium bowl, mix the sour cream and dried soup mix thoroughly. Divide the dip evenly among 8 small serving cups (about 4½ tablespoons per cup). Set aside.

2. Cut the vegetables into sticks about 3 inches long and ½ inch thick. Evenly distribute the veggies among the cups (about 7 sticks per cup). Serve or refrigerate for later.

OTHER USES FOR THIS DIP

My daughters love this dip so much I figured out some other great uses for it:

- Thin the dip with 1 or 2 tablespoons of milk and use it as a salad dressing.
- Top off your Vegetable Chili (page 248) with it instead of plain sour cream.
- Mix it with leftover chicken for a sour cream and onion chicken salad.

Pimento Cheese Crackers

Difficulty: Easy
Prep and Cook Time: Less than 15 minutes
Makes 6 servings
Special tools needed: Large baking sheet

GLUTEN-FREE (IF GLUTEN-FREE CRACKERS ARE USED)
VEGETARIAN

- 2 cups shredded sharp cheddar cheese
- ½ cup cream cheese, softened
- 3 tablespoons diced jarred pimentos, with juice
- 2 garlic cloves, minced
- ½ teaspoon Dijon mustard
- ¼ teaspoon paprika
- ⅛ teaspoon ground black pepper
- 1 or 2 drops hot sauce
- Whole-grain crackers, for serving (such as Ak-Mak brand)

The day I tried pimento cheese warm instead of cold, it changed everything. Whether it's in a grilled cheese sandwich, stuffed inside halved jalapeños and baked (to make poppers), or melted on crackers, warm pimento cheese is definitely the way to go!

1. Preheat the oven to 350°F.

2. In a medium bowl, blend all the ingredients except the crackers with a fork.

3. Spread a thin layer of the pimento cheese on top of the crackers and lay them out on a baking sheet. Bake until the cheese is melted, 5 to 7 minutes. Serve warm.

Popcorn: Microwave or Stovetop

Difficulty: Easy
Prep and Cook Time: Less than 10 minutes
Makes 3 to 4 servings

GLUTEN-FREE
DAIRY-FREE (IF OLIVE OIL IS USED IN PLACE OF BUTTER)
VEGETARIAN

I'd heard about the "popcorn in a brown paper bag" trick from my blog readers for months. Could it really be that easy? Would my microwave blow up? I must admit I was skeptical, but this "popcorn trick" really is that simple and easy, and it keeps you away from those junky store-bought bags that are often full of unwanted additives and chemicals.

I'm also including instructions for making popcorn on the stove, which can be a fun activity if you have a little more time on your hands. I think it tastes extra good that way, too.

Homemade Microwave Popcorn

Special tools needed: Brown paper lunch bag

⅓ cup popcorn kernels
Melted butter, to taste
Salt, to taste

1. Pour the popcorn kernels into the bottom of a standard brown paper lunch bag. Secure the bag by simply folding down the top 2 or 3 times. Pinch the entire crease between your fingers.

2. Lay the bag on its side in the microwave and cook for 3 to 3½ minutes, or until the popping slows to 2 to 3 seconds between pops. For us that happens after about 3 minutes and 15 seconds.

3. Pour the popcorn into a large bowl and season with melted butter and salt. Or, alternatively, just drizzle butter and sprinkle salt right into the bag and shake!

WHY GHEE?

Ghee is basically just clarified butter, which means the milk fats have been boiled and skimmed off, giving it the ability to be cooked at a high temperature without burning. It can be purchased at some stores or made at home, as on page 144.

Stovetop Popcorn

1 tablespoon ghee (clarified butter; see page 144), olive oil, or coconut oil

⅓ cup popcorn kernels

Salt, to taste

1. In a medium pot with a tight-fitting lid, combine the ghee and popcorn kernels. Cover the pot and turn the heat to medium.

2. As soon as you hear the first pop, hold the lid down with one hand and give the pot a little shake every 10 to 20 seconds to keep the popcorn from burning. Once the popping slows down to 2 to 3 seconds between pops, pour the popcorn into a large bowl and season with salt.

White Bean Dip

I am a fair-weather bean fan . . . I either love them or hate them, depending on how they're prepared. I have to thank my friend Holly for introducing me to the idea of a white bean dip, one of the few ways I truly enjoy eating beans. And even my daughters, who normally despise balsamic vinegar, chowed down on this dip without even realizing it was in there. Serve with crusty whole-grain bread or toasted pita triangles for a sure crowd-pleaser. Plus the best part is how incredibly simple this dish is to throw together!

Difficulty: Easy
Prep Time: Less than 15 minutes
Makes 4 servings

GLUTEN-FREE
DAIRY-FREE
VEGETARIAN

One 15-ounce can white cannellini beans, drained and rinsed

1/3 cup diced red onion

1 tomato, diced

3 tablespoons extra-virgin olive oil

2 tablespoons good-quality balsamic vinegar

2 garlic cloves, minced

1/2 teaspoon salt (if needed; it depends on the sodium content of your beans)

1/4 teaspoon ground black pepper

Place all the ingredients in a medium bowl and gently mix together. Serve with good-quality whole-grain bread, toast, pitas, or crackers; or cover and refrigerate for up to 5 days.

LISA'S TIP: If you're using canned beans that already contain sodium, taste this dish before adding the salt.

How to Make the Perfect Juice—Three Ways

GUEST RECIPE BY VANI HARI

Difficulty: Easy
Prep Time: Less than 15 minutes (each)
Makes 2 servings
Special tools needed: Juicer or high-powered blender

GLUTEN-FREE
DAIRY-FREE
VEGETARIAN

This is a guest recipe by my friend Vani Hari, aka the Food Babe (foodbabe.com). After struggling with her health and weight as a young adult as well as suffering from a serious case of appendicitis, she finally woke up and found the answer to all her troubles: eating real food! Vani voraciously learned about the best healing foods available—especially the power of vegetables. One of her favorite ways to supplement her diet with lots of extra veggies is to juice them. Vani says the beauty of juicing is that you can juice just about any vegetable or fruit you like.

1. Pick one vegetable or fruit from each category:

Base neutral ingredients: Cucumber, celery, fennel, romaine lettuce

Dark greens: Spinach, kale, collards, chard, flat-leaf parsley, cilantro

Sweet additions: Apple, carrot, beet, orange, pineapple

Optional flavorings: Lemon, ginger, garlic (if you're really daring!)

2. Thoroughly wash all ingredients (unless noted otherwise, there's no need to peel).

WHY I PERSONALLY DON'T JUICE

I asked Vani to share her favorite juicing recipes with you because it has helped her so much and because, after a brief juicing stint, I've found that juicing just isn't really for me. Per her advice, I borrowed a friend's juicer and tried it for a week (which is a great idea for anyone who's considering giving it a go)! While juicing is a great way to consume extra vegetables, I learned the fiber of the vegetables is not actually retained. The machine basically spits the pulp out the side; you either use it in another recipe or discard it. For me this meant spending money on fresh veggies that made just a single serving of juice that didn't fill me up enough to replace a meal. Plus it took time to make the juice and hand-wash the machine afterward. So, while by the end of my test week I really started to enjoy the taste of my green juice every day, I just knew it wasn't something I could personally fit into my schedule or budget on a regular basis.

3. Juice according to your juicer's instructions. Alternatively, you can blend the fruit and vegetables in a high-powered blender and strain the pulp through a cheesecloth. You can keep the juice in the fridge for 24 hours in an airtight container.

"Here are three juice combos that I personally make all the time. All of them have carrot juice in them, which I swear has made my eyelashes grow longer and my eyes brighter. I love juicing. It's here to stay!" —FOOD BABE

Green Punch

1 cucumber

4 celery stalks

1 bunch kale

4 carrots, tops removed

1 green apple, cored

1 orange, peeled

1 lemon, peeled

Ravishing Red

1 cucumber

½ bunch kale

4 celery stalks

1 handful flat-leaf parsley

5 carrots, tops removed

1 beet, peeled, greens removed

1 green apple, cored

1 piece ginger, about 2 inches long

Spicy Rabbit

1 cucumber

6 carrots, tops removed

1 red apple, cored

1 piece ginger, about 2 inches long

Cinnamon Apple Chips

Difficulty: Easy
Prep Time: Less than 15 minutes
Bake Time: More than 1 hour
Makes 2 to 4 servings
Special tools needed: Large rectangular baking sheet and 1-inch cookie cutter (any shape, like circle, heart, flower, or star)

GLUTEN-FREE
DAIRY-FREE
VEGETARIAN

Butter, for greasing the pan

2 apples, any variety

¼ teaspoon ground cinnamon

After making my first batch of apple chips I couldn't believe I'd waited so long to try them. These are a super-easy, tasty, and fun snack for both little and big ones! They do take a while to bake, but the prep time is minimal.

1. Preheat the oven to 250°F. Generously grease the baking sheet with butter.

2. On a cutting board, turn an apple on its side and cut it into very thin slices (right through the core), about ⅛ inch to ¼ inch thick. (Or use a mandoline for easy slicing.) Using a small cookie cutter, cut the core/center out of each apple slice and discard. Repeat with the second apple.

3. Spread the slices out in one layer on the baking sheet. Sprinkle with cinnamon. Bake for 30 minutes, flip the apple pieces over, and then bake for another 30 to 50 minutes, or until crisp. Depending on how evenly you sliced the apples, some may be done sooner than others. If so, remove the thinner ones when they are brown and crisp and allow the thicker ones additional time in the oven.

Sienna's Purple Potion Smoothie

My kids love to help me in the kitchen, and even the littlest of children can handle adding ingredients to the "smoothie maker" (as my girls call our blender). Plus smoothies are such an easy way to get your kids to actually eat some leafy greens. Just make sure they know what they're drinking (either during or afterward) so they understand that those big green veggies aren't so horrible after all. I had to coax Sienna into letting me add kale to this blueberry smoothie recipe, but once I did she could barely even tell it was in there. As a result we have some healthy, tasty purple potion to share! And most days (depending on how the wind blows), purple also happens to be her favorite color.

Difficulty: Easy
Prep Time: Less than 10 minutes
Makes 2 to 3 servings
Special tools needed: Blender, straws (optional)

GLUTEN-FREE
VEGETARIAN
FREEZER FRIENDLY

1 cup blueberries, fresh or frozen

1 ripe banana (the riper, the sweeter)

1 cup loosely packed fresh kale leaves, big stems removed (or substitute fresh spinach, which has a milder flavor)

1 teaspoon honey

⅔ cup milk

⅓ cup plain yogurt

Place all the ingredients in a blender. If using fresh blueberries, add a few ice cubes as well. Puree until smooth. Straws are recommended for serving.

Spiced Nut Mix

Difficulty: Easy
Prep and Cook Time: Less than 10 minutes
Makes 3 to 4 servings
Special tools needed: Parchment paper, small baking sheet

GLUTEN-FREE
DAIRY-FREE
VEGETARIAN

½ cup raw pecans
½ cup raw cashews
1 tablespoon honey
¾ teaspoon chili powder
¼ teaspoon salt
Dash of cayenne pepper

If you're looking for a quick and easy snack that's a break from the norm, then you'll love this recipe. It takes less than ten minutes to make and will please snackers of all ages. These nuts would also be a great addition to salads if you want to spice things up a bit.

1. Preheat the oven to 375°F. Line a rimmed baking sheet with parchment paper.

2. Combine the pecans and cashews in a medium mixing bowl. Mix in the honey, chili powder, salt, and cayenne pepper and stir until thoroughly combined.

3. Transfer the mixture to the prepared baking sheet and bake for 5 minutes. Stir the nuts to help prevent burning and bake for 3 to 5 minutes more.

4. Allow the nuts to harden in clumps as they cool, then break them apart with your hands.

Fruit Kabobs with Yogurt Dip

Everything's more fun on a stick, right? Especially when you're a kid. Use your child's favorite fruit on these kabobs and throw in one new one that they don't normally eat. The key to getting your child to eat something new is repeated exposure, and this is a great way to start.

Difficulty: Easy
Prep Time: Less than 15 minutes
Makes 12 small kabobs
Special tools needed: Small kabob sticks, about 6 inches long

GLUTEN-FREE
VEGETARIAN

½ cup plain yogurt

1 teaspoon pure maple syrup

¼ teaspoon Pure Vanilla Extract (page 337) or store bought vanilla extract

3 cups bite-size fruit pieces (such as cubed melon, sliced banana, grapes, cubed apples, and berries)

1. Combine the yogurt, syrup, and vanilla in a small bowl. Set aside.

2. Assemble the kabobs by adding colorful cubes of fruit to each kabob stick. Serve with the yogurt dip on the side.

Asian Lettuce Wraps

Difficulty: Medium
Prep and Cook Time: 30 to 40 minutes
Makes 4 to 5 servings
Optional tool: Mini-chopper or food processor, to help mince the veggies

GLUTEN-FREE (IF GLUTEN-FREE SOY SAUCE IS USED)
DAIRY-FREE
FREEZER FRIENDLY (MEAT MIXTURE ONLY)

1 teaspoon coconut oil (or olive oil)

2/3 cup chopped green onions (white and green parts)

1 cup peeled and minced carrots (about 4 carrots)

2 tablespoons peeled and minced fresh ginger

1 pound ground pork

One 8-ounce can (about 1 cup) diced water chestnuts, drained

1/4 cup soy sauce (preferably low sodium)

2 tablespoons toasted sesame oil

Big pinch of crushed red pepper flakes

1/3 cup chopped fresh cilantro

Large lettuce leaves (we prefer Bibb lettuce), for serving

The filling for these lettuce wraps was inspired by my boss, Bruce Goldberg, at my very first job out of college. I graduated aspiring to be an event planner and got as close as I could by taking a job as the office manager of a small event planning and catering company in Portland, Oregon. I walked into that job making casseroles out of canned cream of mushroom soup and left making homemade pot stickers and egg rolls (and never looked back!).

These can be served as an appetizer or as a main course with a side of brown rice. Either way—delicious!

1. Heat the oil in a medium sauté pan over medium heat.

2. Add the chopped green onions and cook for 2 to 3 minutes, until they begin to soften, but do not brown. Add the carrots and ginger and sauté for another 1 or 2 minutes.

3. Turn the heat up to medium high and add the ground pork. Cook, breaking up the meat as needed, until the meat is fully browned, 6 to 8 minutes.

4. Add the water chestnuts, soy sauce, toasted sesame oil, and red pepper flakes to the meat mixture and stir until well combined. Cook until the liquid is mostly evaporated, about 2 to 3 minutes. Remove from the heat and fold in the cilantro.

5. Use a slotted spoon to drain and scoop the filling into lettuce cups. Serve warm.

OTHER SIMPLE REAL-FOOD SNACK IDEAS

FRUITS AND VEGETABLES

Apple (good with peanut butter)
Applesauce
Avocado (good with a little soy sauce)
Banana (good with peanut butter)
Blueberries (good with yogurt dip, see page 205)
Canned fruit, such as mandarin oranges (look for brands that use orange juice instead of sugary syrup)
Cantaloupe
Carrots (cooked or raw, good with hummus or onion dip, see page 189)
Celery (good with peanut butter and raisins, aka Ants on a Log)
Cherries
Cherry tomatoes (good with hummus or onion dip, see page 189)
Cooked green beans
Cooked snow peas
Cucumber slices (good with hummus or onion dip, see page 189)
Dried apple rings (available in the produce section of some supermarkets)
Dried or freeze-dried fruit (such as mango, banana, blueberries, or strawberries)
Edamame (good with soy sauce)
Figs (good smeared with a little goat cheese)
Frozen peas (frozen . . . no cooking necessary!)
Fruit leathers
Grapefruit
Grapes
Honeydew melon
Jicama
Kiwi
Mango
Mashed sweet potato (good with butter and cinnamon)
Olives
Oranges
Papaya
Peaches (good with Yogurt dip, see page 205)
Pear
Pineapple
Plums
Pomegranate seeds (good in yogurt)
Raspberries (good with yogurt dip, see page 205)
Raw broccoli (good with hummus or onion dip, see page 189)
Raw cauliflower
Raw sliced bell peppers (good with hummus or onion dip, see page 189)
Raw sugar snap peas (good with hummus)
Star fruit
Strawberries (good with yogurt dip, see page 205)
Unsweetened raisins
Watermelon

WHOLE-GRAIN

100% whole-grain crackers (good topped with cheese, peanut butter, or a cream cheese and jelly combo)
100% whole-wheat pretzels
Brown rice cakes or crackers
Oatmeal (served warm in a thermos if sending to school)
Popcorn (page 192)
Puffed whole-grain cereal (corn, brown rice, wheat, or millet variety)
Shredded wheat (look for brands that contain one ingredient)
Small cooked whole-grain noodles
Whole-grain toast
Whole-grain muffins or quick bread

NUTS AND SEEDS

Almonds
Cashews
Kit's Organic Fruit & Nut Bars
Lärabars
Nut trail mix, including dried fruit
Peanuts
Pecans
Pine nuts (lightly toasted)
Pistachios
Pumpkin seeds
Sesame seeds
Walnuts

OTHER

Cheese (cubes or sticks, with or without crackers)
Garbanzo beans (chickpeas)
Hard-boiled or deviled eggs
Organic and/or local bacon
Plain yogurt (flavored with a little honey or maple syrup and vanilla extract)
Smoked salmon (good with cream cheese and crackers)

SALADS AND SIDES

Goat Cheese, Pear, and Pecan Salad

If you're looking for a super-quick and easy salad recipe and don't want to bother with homemade dressing, here's your answer. I've never been a huge salad person, but this is one of my favorite combinations. If I'm going to like a salad it's got to have lots of yummy "accessories" on top of the lettuce, and this recipe totally fits the bill. This dish would be a great addition to your November or December holiday table.

Difficulty: Easy
Prep Time: Less than 15 minutes
Seasonal Note: Use locally grown pears in the fall months.
Makes 4 servings

GLUTEN-FREE
DAIRY-FREE (IF CHEESE IS OMITTED)
VEGETARIAN

½ cup raw pecans, chopped

8 cups cut, torn, or baby lettuce leaves, such as Bibb, mixed greens, and/or spinach

½ unpeeled pear, cored and diced

Salt and ground black pepper, to taste

1 tablespoon olive oil

2 teaspoons good-quality balsamic vinegar

⅓ cup crumbled goat cheese

1. In a dry skillet over medium-high heat, toast the pecans, stirring occasionally, until fragrant, about 5 minutes. Alternatively, preheat the oven or toaster oven to 350°F and toast the pecans on a rimmed baking sheet for 5 to 8 minutes. Set aside to cool.

2. In a large bowl, combine the lettuce, pecans, pear, salt, and pepper. Drizzle the oil and vinegar over the lettuce mixture and toss until thoroughly combined. Sprinkle the goat cheese on top and serve.

LISA'S TIP: Switch up this recipe by using blue cheese instead of goat cheese and apple instead of pear!

Spinach Salad with Warm Bacon Dressing

Difficulty: Medium
Prep and Cook Time: Less than 30 minutes
Seasonal Note: Use locally grown spinach in the winter and spring months.
Makes 3 to 4 servings
Special tools needed: Electric mixer

GLUTEN-FREE (IF BACON IS LABELED AS GLUTEN-FREE)
DAIRY-FREE (IF CHEESE IS OMITTED)

When it comes to salads, this one has been a longtime favorite of ours. You have to admit, it's hard to turn down the combination of bacon, blue cheese, and hard-boiled eggs, especially when topped with this quick and simple homemade dressing. No more excuses for not eating your greens!

SALAD

7 to 8 cups fresh spinach (about 5 ounces), washed

¼ cup crumbled blue cheese

2 hard-boiled eggs, diced (see Note)

6 cooked bacon slices (see page 153), crumbled, with grease reserved

3 tablespoons diced shallot (or red onion)

WARM BACON DRESSING

2 to 3 tablespoons bacon grease, reserved from the cooked bacon (depending on how much you get)

1 tablespoon apple cider vinegar

2 teaspoons honey

Pinch of salt

1 egg

1. Toss all the salad ingredients together in a large bowl and set aside. Keep in mind that if little ones are involved you may want to serve the "stinky" blue cheese on the side!

2. For the dressing, combine the bacon grease, vinegar, honey, salt, and 1 tablespoon water in a small saucepan over medium heat and bring to a low boil. Right next to the stove, set up an electric mixer with the egg in a medium bowl. Beat the egg for about 1 minute with the electric mixer on high. Turn the mixer down to low, pour the bacon grease mixture into the bowl with the egg, and turn the setting back up to high for another 30 seconds or so.

3. Pour the dressing back into the saucepan over low heat while whisking constantly for about a minute, or until the dressing thickens. The goal is to slightly cook the egg in the dressing without forming any solid clumps. Feel free to add a splash or two of water to thin out the dressing a little if desired.

4. Plate the salad and drizzle the dressing on top, or serve it on the side.

LISA'S TIP: When measuring both a cooking fat, like bacon grease or oil, and honey, always measure the fat first so the honey will slide right out of the spoon.

HOW TO MAKE HARD-BOILED EGGS

Making hard-boiled eggs is easy: Simply bring a small pot of water to a boil, turn the heat down to medium, add eggs, and cook for 15 minutes. Drain and cover with ice water. Once cool, remove the shells.

NOTE: When consuming undercooked eggs, the FDA recommends pasteurized eggs to reduce the chance of infection in the elderly, very young, or anyone with a compromised immune system.

Shortcut Caesar Salad

What would a Caesar salad be without yummy, crunchy croutons? Making your own croutons at home is much easier than you think, and it allows you to control both the quality of the bread used and the seasonings. Get your kids to help you make this dish and maybe they'll even take a bite. Once mine did they were fans!

Difficulty: Medium
Prep and Cook Time: Less than 30 minutes
Makes 5 to 6 servings
Special tools needed: Small baking sheet

GLUTEN-FREE (IF GLUTEN-FREE BREAD IS SUBSTITUTED)
VEGETARIAN

WHOLE-WHEAT CROUTONS

2 tablespoons plus 1 teaspoon olive oil

1¼ teaspoons dried Italian seasoning

½ teaspoon garlic powder

¼ teaspoon salt

3 slices Everyday Whole-Wheat Bread (page 332) or store-bought whole-wheat bread, cut into 1-inch cubes

DRESSING

⅓ cup olive oil

1 tablespoon freshly squeezed lemon juice

2 garlic cloves, minced

¼ teaspoon ground black pepper, plus more for serving

¼ teaspoon salt

2 tablespoons freshly grated Parmesan cheese

SALAD

2 romaine lettuce hearts, washed, trimmed, and cut into 1-inch-wide strips

½ cup freshly grated Parmesan cheese

1. To make the croutons, preheat the oven to 350°F.

2. Mix together the olive oil and seasonings in a medium bowl. Drop in the bread cubes and use a spoon or your hands to mix until evenly coated. Transfer to a small rimmed baking sheet and bake, stirring occasionally, until golden brown, 15 to 18 minutes.

3. Meanwhile, make the dressing. In a medium measuring cup with a spout (or a medium bowl), combine the olive oil, lemon juice, garlic, pepper, salt, and Parmesan cheese. Whisk thoroughly to emulsify the dressing, or better yet, use an immersion blender (for easy cleanup) or countertop blender if available. You could also shake it up in a jar with a tight-fitting lid.

4. To assemble the salad, toss the dressing with the lettuce in a large salad bowl. Top with the croutons, the ½ cup Parmesan cheese, and more pepper if desired. Serve immediately.

Grilled Veggie Kabobs

GUEST RECIPE BY JASON LEAKE

Difficulty: Easy
Prep and Cook Time:
Less than 30 minutes
Seasonal Note: Use locally grown peppers and zucchini in the summer months.
Makes five 12-inch skewers
Special tools needed:
Five 12-inch wood or metal skewers (if using wood, soaking them in water first will prevent burning), grill
Optional tools:
Handheld immersion blender or countertop blender, for the marinade

GLUTEN-FREE
DAIRY-FREE
VEGETARIAN

1 medium yellow onion

1 red bell pepper, halved, cored, and seeded

1 medium zucchini

One 8-ounce package Baby Bella mushrooms, brushed clean and stems removed

¼ cup extra-virgin olive oil

¼ cup soy sauce (preferably low sodium)

3 tablespoons balsamic vinegar

4 garlic cloves, minced

1 teaspoon dried oregano

½ teaspoon ground black pepper

When the afternoon yard work stretches into the evening, I enjoy catching whiffs of my neighbors' grilled food as the scent travels through the cul-de-sac. Sometimes I'm pleasantly surprised that the source is in fact my house.

Here's a basic recipe for the grill that can be adapted as you see fit. Try different veggies or herbs, kick it up with some red pepper, or try marinating meat or seafood as well. This recipe can be served as a side item or as the main dish over rice. The leftovers are also great chopped up in anything from pizza to quesadillas to omelets to pasta.

1. Cut the onion and bell pepper into 1- to 1½-inch square pieces and slice the zucchini into ½-inch-thick rounds. Place the vegetables and mushrooms onto the skewers, alternating ingredients to make 5 mixed skewers. Place them flat in a large rectangular baking dish and set aside.

2. Vigorously whisk the remaining ingredients in a medium bowl (or large glass measuring cup with a spout) to emulsify the marinade, or use your hand immersion blender if you have one.

3. Brush or pour the marinade onto the vegetable skewers, drizzling any remaining liquid over the top. Cover and marinate for 20 minutes or overnight, turning once halfway through.

4. Preheat a gas grill to medium-high heat, around 425°F (or prepare a charcoal fire) and place the skewers on the grill. Continue to brush the skewers with any extra marinade that dripped off in the bottom of the baking dish.

5. After about 6 minutes, turn the skewers and brush again with any remaining marinade. Cook for another 6 minutes, or to desired doneness. Serve warm.

Asian-Inspired Rice

Difficulty: Easy
Prep Time: Less than 15 minutes (if rice is precooked)
Makes 4 to 5 servings

GLUTEN-FREE (IF GLUTEN-FREE SOY SAUCE IS USED)
DAIRY-FREE
VEGETARIAN

- 4 servings brown rice (3 cups cooked), cooked according to the package directions
- 1 avocado, diced
- ½ cup chopped fresh cilantro
- ⅓ cup roasted peanuts, chopped
- 2 tablespoons soy sauce (preferably low sodium)

Let's face it . . . plain rice can be pretty boring. But luckily it's pretty easy to switch things up by mixing in different herbs, nuts, seeds, sauces, or even dried fruit. This simple side dish pairs perfectly with the Grilled Teriyaki Salmon on page 272 or the Asian Lettuce Wraps on page 206.

Mix all the ingredients in a large bowl. Serve warm or cold.

LISA'S TIP: If making this dish in advance, wait to add the peanuts just before serving.

Super-Easy Whole-Wheat Biscuits

Recipe Difficulty: Easy
Prep and Cook Time:
Less than 20 minutes
Makes 8 to 10 biscuits
Special tools needed:
Cookie cutter (any shape) or a drinking glass turned upside down for cutting out the biscuits, large baking sheet

VEGETARIAN
FREEZER FRIENDLY

2 cups whole-wheat flour

4 teaspoons baking powder

½ teaspoon salt

4 tablespoons (½ stick) cold butter

1 cup cold milk

These biscuits are so easy my nine-year-old can make them by herself! Biscuits are a great addition to breakfast or dinner, and if you bake extra they freeze beautifully for another day. So leave behind the canned dough versions made with refined flour, refined sugar, and partially hydrogenated oil (i.e., trans fat).

1. Preheat the oven to 450°F.

2. In a medium bowl, combine the flour, baking powder, and salt. Mix well with a whisk or a fork.

3. Cut the butter into little pea-size pieces and scatter them over the flour mixture.

4. Mix the flour and butter together, using the back of a fork to mash the butter pieces into the flour until the mixture resembles coarse crumbs. (You can also just forget the fork and use your fingers to mash the butter into the flour. It's okay if the outcome just looks like pea-size pieces of butter covered with flour.)

5. Add the milk and mix together thoroughly without overmixing. Knead the dough with your hands 8 to 10 times, then turn the dough out onto a floured counter or cutting board.

6. Pat the dough out flat with your hands until it's about ¾ inch thick. If the dough sticks to your fingers, sprinkle a little flour on the top and bottom. If it's too dry (not holding together), add a splash or two of milk or water.

7. Using a cookie cutter (any shape) or upside-down drinking glass, cut out biscuit rounds. Gently press together the scrap dough and cut another biscuit or two, taking care not to over-handle the dough.

8. Place the biscuits on an ungreased baking sheet and bake for 10 to 12 minutes, or until lightly browned.

Carrots with Rosemary

Oddly enough, my younger daughter will hardly take a bite of a raw carrot, yet she'll gobble down cooked carrots all day long. I guess beggars can't be choosers when it comes to getting kids to eat veggies! This is a remarkably simple dish that takes less than ten minutes to cook, and you can do all the peeling and chopping in advance.

Difficulty: Easy
Prep and Cook Time: Less than 15 minutes
Seasonal Note: Use locally grown carrots in the winter and spring months.
Makes 6 side servings

GLUTEN-FREE
DAIRY-FREE
VEGETARIAN

- 2 pounds fresh carrots, washed, peeled, and trimmed
- 1 tablespoon olive oil
- Pinch of salt
- 1 teaspoon chopped fresh rosemary

1. Cut the carrots into ½-inch pieces. To make this dish "fancy," cut the carrots at an angle. Pat the carrots dry to allow them to sear in the pan instead of steam.

2. In a medium sauté pan over medium-high heat, heat the olive oil. When the oil is hot, add the carrots and a big pinch of salt. Stir and cook for 6 to 7 minutes, then sprinkle in the fresh rosemary. Cook for another 1 to 2 minutes, or until the carrots are somewhat tender (but not mushy) when pierced with a fork. Serve warm.

LISA'S TIP: Rosemary is a very easy herb to grow year round. I am told this dish is also lovely with tarragon!

Veggie Pancakes

Difficulty: Medium
Prep and Cook Time: Less than 30 minutes
Makes 4 to 5 servings

DAIRY-FREE
VEGETARIAN
FREEZER FRIENDLY

3 cups grated veggies (white potato and/or sweet potato, with skin on, plus zucchini, yellow squash, and/or peeled carrots)

3 eggs

2 tablespoons whole-wheat flour

¾ teaspoon salt

Olive oil, for cooking

Sour cream, applesauce, or freshly grated Parmesan cheese, for serving

This side dish provides a fabulous way to use up the vegetables you have on hand and introduce your children to new ones as well. Start with something familiar, like white or sweet potatoes, then mix in some zucchini, carrot, or something else unexpected. Just be sure to tell your little ones about it afterward so they know that new foods aren't so scary after all!

1. In a large bowl, mix together the grated veggies, eggs, flour, and salt until thoroughly combined.

2. Heat a thin layer of olive oil in a sauté pan over medium heat. It's important that the heat not be too hot or too cool, because you want the pancakes to cook all the way through the middle by the time they're brown on the outside. When the oil is hot, drop pancake-size dollops of the veggie mixture into the pan, without overcrowding. Cook for 3 to 4 minutes, or until the bottom starts to brown. Flip and cook until browned on both sides, then repeat until the batter is gone.

3. Transfer cooked pancakes to a plate lined with paper towels and keep warm by tenting with foil or placing in the oven on the lowest setting.

4. Serve warm with a topping of sour cream and applesauce or Parmesan cheese.

Zucchini with Almonds and Parmesan

Difficulty: Easy
Prep and Cook Time: Less than 15 minutes
Seasonal Note: Use locally grown zucchini in the summer months.
Makes 4 to 5 side servings

GLUTEN-FREE
VEGETARIAN

1 pound zucchini (about 2)

⅓ cup sliced almonds

2 ounces Parmesan or Romano cheese

1 tablespoon olive oil

Salt, to taste

Recipes don't get much simpler than this, and when you're using fresh, in-season produce, simple can go a long way. This recipe was inspired by a dish my dad loves at Alchemy restaurant on Martha's Vineyard and has since adopted as his own signature zucchini side dish. Thankfully my daughters like the flavors of the cheese and toasted almonds so much they barely notice they're consuming some zucchini along the way.

1. Julienne the zucchini using a knife or mandoline until you have about 4 cups, loosely packed.

2. Preheat the oven to 350°F, or set a toaster oven on the "toast" setting. Place the almonds on a rimmed baking sheet and toast them until golden brown, about 5 minutes. Stir and check them regularly, because thinly sliced almonds will burn quickly.

3. Use a vegetable peeler to shave the cheese into long, thin slices. (Alternatively, you could finely grate the cheese, but shaving makes a nice presentation.) Set aside.

4. Heat the oil in a large sauté pan over medium heat. Add the zucchini and sauté, stirring constantly, until the zucchini begins to turn translucent, 1 to 2 minutes.

5. Transfer to a serving platter, sprinkle with salt, and top with the toasted almonds and shaved cheese. Serve immediately.

Cheesy Broccoli Rice Casserole

Difficulty: Medium
Prep and Bake Time: Less than 30 minutes
Seasonal Note: Use locally grown broccoli in the winter and spring months.
Makes 4 or 5 servings
Special tools needed: 8 x 8-inch square baking dish

VEGETARIAN

1 cup uncooked brown rice, cooked according to the package directions

¾ pound broccoli, roughly chopped (4 or 5 cups) and steamed for about 5 minutes (see box)

2 tablespoons butter

¼ cup diced onion

2 tablespoons whole-wheat flour

1½ cups milk

1½ cups grated sharp cheddar cheese

¾ teaspoon salt

½ teaspoon yellow mustard

Ground black pepper, to taste

½ cup Whole-Wheat Breadcrumbs (page 331) or good-quality store-bought whole-wheat breadcrumbs

Extra-virgin olive oil

It's easy to get tired of eating plain old steamed broccoli, but how can you pass on something covered in yummy melted cheese? This casserole is relatively quick to throw together and would complement almost any main dish. It's also great left over the next day.

1. Preheat the oven to 400°F.

2. Combine the cooked rice and broccoli in a large mixing bowl and set aside.

3. Melt the butter in a medium sauté pan over medium heat. Add the onion and cook, stirring, until softened, about 2 minutes. Sprinkle in the flour and cook for 1 or 2 minutes, until the flour begins to brown but doesn't burn, whisking almost continuously.

4. Whisk in the milk, watching for lumps. Sprinkle in the cheese, salt, mustard, and pepper and stir until well combined. Bring to a simmer and cook, stirring, until the mixture is the consistency of very thick gravy, less than 5 minutes.

5. Pour the cheese sauce over the broccoli and rice. Mix thoroughly and spread evenly in an 8 x 8-inch baking dish.

6. Sprinkle the casserole with the breadcrumbs and then drizzle (or spray) enough olive oil over the top to coat the breadcrumbs.

7. Bake for 12 to 14 minutes, or until the breadcrumbs are nicely browned. Serve warm.

STEAMING VEGETABLES

Steamed veggies are a quick and easy side dish. Fill a medium pot with 1 or 2 inches of water, place a mesh steamer basket inside, and set it over high heat. As soon as the water starts boiling, turn it down to low, add the vegetables to the basket, and cover with a lid. Steam until the veggies can easily be pierced with a fork, 5 to 10 minutes, depending on the veggie and how fresh they are.

"Mom, I love this broccoli casserole . . . you should put it in your cookbook."

—SIENNA, AGE 7

SIMPLE DINNERS

★ Weeknight Meal Section

BBQ Chicken Quesadillas

Barbecue sauce and quesadillas make a stellar combination. Our family may be biased because we live in North Carolina, the barbecue capital of the country (according to Google!), but this dish is a crowd-pleaser no matter where you live. And it can be whipped up fairly quickly if your tortillas are prepared in advance. If you decide to purchase them rather than making your own, Ezekiel brand, found in the frozen section, is recommended.

Difficulty: Medium
Prep and Cook Time: Less than 30 minutes
Makes 6 servings

GLUTEN-FREE (IF CORN TORTILLAS ARE SUBSTITUTED)

- 1 tablespoon olive oil
- ¾ cup chopped onion
- 1 green bell pepper, cored, seeded, and diced
- ½ jalapeño, seeded and diced (optional)
- 1 boneless, skinless chicken breast, patted dry and cut into ¼-inch cubes (or 1 cup leftover cooked chicken)
- ½ teaspoon paprika
- ¼ teaspoon salt
- Cayenne pepper, to taste
- 3 cups freshly grated Monterey Jack cheese (about one and a half 7-ounce blocks)
- Twelve 6-inch Whole-Wheat Tortillas (page 326) or store-bought whole-wheat tortillas
- Butter, for cooking
- 1 recipe Sweet and Tangy BBQ Sauce (page 316)

Other recommended toppings: Sour cream, fresh cilantro, lime wedges, and seeded, minced hot peppers

1. In a large skillet over medium-high heat, heat the olive oil. Add the onion, bell pepper, and jalapeño (if using) and cook for 3 or 4 minutes, or until they begin to soften. Add the chicken and season with the paprika, salt, and cayenne. Cook until slightly browned and cooked all the way through (if using already cooked leftover chicken, add the chicken and cook just until warmed through). Remove from the heat.

2. Stir the grated cheese into the chicken mixture until well combined.

3. Lay out 6 of the tortillas on a large cutting board. Evenly distribute the chicken and cheese mixture on top of the tortillas and top with the remaining 6 tortillas.

4. Wipe out the skillet and place it over medium heat (or set a griddle to 350°F). Melt a big pat of butter in the pan. Working in batches, place the quesadillas in the pan. Smear another small pat of butter on top of each tortilla to help grease the pan when you flip the quesadillas over. Cook until the tortillas are golden brown, 3 to 5 minutes on each side.

5. Transfer the cooked quesadillas back to the large cutting board to cool while you cook the remaining quesadillas. When the cheese is slightly cooled and set, cut each quesadilla into 4 or 6 slices. A pizza cutter makes this job easy. Serve warm with BBQ sauce, sour cream, cilantro, lime wedges, and minced hot peppers (if desired).

Fish Cakes with Dipping Sauce

I love crab cakes, but it's hard for me to find fresh crab that isn't fishy-tasting, and it's awfully expensive for a family dinner anyway. Mild white fish cooks quickly, and I've found it to be the perfect substitute in this crab cake–like recipe! This dish is my favorite way to use leftover fish. (For a simple recipe for pan-seared fish, see page 263.)

Difficulty: Medium
Prep and Cook Time: Less than 30 minutes (if fish is already cooked)
Makes about eight 2¼-inch cakes

DIPPING SAUCE

½ cup sour cream

2 teaspoons freshly squeezed lemon juice

½ teaspoon yellow mustard

FISH CAKES

1 cup Whole-Wheat Breadcrumbs (page 331) or good-quality store-bought whole-wheat breadcrumbs

1 pound white fish, such as cod or flounder, cooked and shredded

2 eggs, lightly beaten

1 tablespoon minced fresh onion

2 tablespoons sour cream

2 teaspoons freshly squeezed lemon juice

½ teaspoon yellow mustard

½ teaspoon salt

Dash of cayenne pepper

Ghee (clarified butter; see page 144) or olive oil, for cooking

1. To make the dipping sauce, combine all the sauce ingredients in a small bowl. Cover and refrigerate.

2. To make the fish cakes, spread ½ cup of the breadcrumbs on a plate and set out another empty plate.

3. In a medium bowl, thoroughly combine the fish, eggs, onion, sour cream, lemon juice, mustard, salt, cayenne pepper, and the remaining ½ cup of breadcrumbs.

4. To form the cakes, grab a golf ball–size handful of the fish mixture and squeeze it together with your hands just enough for it to come together (discard any excess liquid). Slightly flatten the ball, coat the outside with a light layer of breadcrumbs, and place it on the empty plate. Repeat with the rest of the fish mixture.

5. Set a large sauté pan over medium-low heat and add a thin layer of ghee or olive oil to cover the bottom. When the oil is hot, cook the fish cakes (in batches if necessary) until golden brown, 3 to 5 minutes per side. Serve warm with the dipping sauce.

Jason's Grass-Fed Burgers

Difficulty: Easy
Prep and Cook Time:
Less than 30 minutes
Makes 4 burgers
Special tools needed: grill

GLUTEN-FREE (IF GLUTEN-FREE SOY SAUCE AND BUNS ARE USED)
FREEZER FRIENDLY (FREEZE BUNS AND MEAT SEPARATELY)

1 tablespoon soy sauce

1 teaspoon mustard powder

½ teaspoon garlic powder

¼ teaspoon ground black pepper

½ cup diced onion

¼ cup grated white cheddar cheese, plus 4 slices to top the burgers

1 pound ground grass-fed beef

4 good-quality whole-wheat hamburger buns

Optional garnishes: Lettuce, thinly sliced onion, and tomato

After some trial and error, my husband, Jason, officially has his own signature burger recipe. Sure, plain grilled burger patties can be satisfactory, but why not kick them up a notch with some added flavor? We especially love to take these burgers along on camping trips because they're extra tasty grilled over a charcoal flame. But any outdoor grill will do when you're in the mood for a good grass-fed burger!

These go well with the Grilled Veggie Kabobs on page 218.

1. Preheat a gas grill to 425°F (or prepare a charcoal fire).

2. In a medium bowl, mix together the soy sauce, mustard powder, garlic powder, and black pepper. Add the onion, grated cheese, and beef and mix thoroughly with your hands.

3. Divide the meat mixture into 4 equal portions and form them into patties. Press down on the centers of the patties so they're thicker around the edge than in the middle. This will help keep the burgers flat on the grill.

4. Place the burgers on the grill and cook for 6 minutes, then flip. After about 3 more minutes, place the cheese slices on the burgers

KNOW YOUR BURGER

Why buy grass-fed meat? Cows are meant to eat grass, not corn, and as a cost-saving measure big factory (feedlot) farms often provide a diet of corn (that's likely GMO) instead. And if cows aren't eating their natural diet in their natural environment—given room to roam on green pastures—then they won't be very healthy animals and in turn won't be providing you with the most nutritious animal products.

Aren't turkey burgers "better"? My belief is if both meat products are humanely raised (pastured and organic), one is not better than the other. They're just different.

and place the buns on the grill to toast for several minutes. Remove from the grill when the cheese is melted and the burgers are cooked to the desired temperature (red = rare, reddish/pink = medium rare, pink = medium, brown = medium well). The USDA recommends cooking burgers to a minimum internal temperature of 160°F. At our house we prefer our burgers cooked medium.

5. Place the burgers on the buns and top with garnishes as desired.

"Daddy, did you make that? It looks so good, it looks like Mommy made it."—SIENNA, AGE 7

Shortcut Eggplant Parmesan

Difficulty: Medium
Prep and Cook Time: Less than 30 minutes
Seasonal Note: Use locally grown eggplant in the summer months.
Makes 4 servings

VEGETARIAN

1 large or 2 medium eggplant (about 1 pound total)

2/3 cup whole-wheat flour

Olive oil, for cooking

Salt and ground black pepper, to taste

1 cup Homemade Tomato Sauce (page 320) or store-bought tomato sauce, warmed

1½ cups grated (or thinly sliced) mozzarella cheese

¼ cup freshly grated Parmesan cheese

Recommended accompaniments: Cooked whole-wheat pasta noodles with tomato sauce and/or a salad

When my younger daughter was five she could never remember what to call an eggplant (is it a squash? a zucchini?), but whatever the name, she loves the outcome of this quick and easy eggplant Parmesan dish! With this shortcut recipe you can forget the egg, forget the breadcrumbs, and even forget the oven, which means you have yourself a super-simple (and delicious) weeknight dinner.

1. Preheat the oven to 200°F.

2. Cut the eggplant into even round slices about ¼ inch thick.

3. Place two clean plates side by side and pour the flour onto one of the plates. Coat both sides of the eggplant slices with flour and lay them on the other plate.

4. Put a large sauté pan with a tight-fitting lid on the stove over medium heat. Pour in a thin layer of olive oil. When the oil is hot, add the eggplant slices, working in batches so as not to overcrowd them.

5. Cook until the bottoms are golden brown, 2 to 3 minutes. If the eggplant soaks up all the oil, drizzle a little more into the pan before flipping them. Flip the eggplant slices over and immediately sprinkle with plenty of salt (and pepper if desired).

6. Working very quickly, add a dollop of tomato sauce on top of each eggplant disk and then sprinkle each piece with about 1 tablespoon of grated mozzarella. Cover the pan for 30 to 60 seconds, or until the cheese is melted and the bottom is golden brown.

7. Transfer the eggplant slices to a baking sheet, pat the excess oil off the bottom with a paper towel if desired, and place the baking sheet in the oven to keep the eggplant warm while you finish the rest of the eggplant slices. (It's helpful to rinse and wipe out the pan and add fresh olive oil with each batch.)

8. To serve, sprinkle the warm eggplant slices with Parmesan cheese. Serve over whole-wheat noodles tossed with tomato sauce or on top of a big salad.

Quinoa and Sausage–Stuffed Peppers

Difficulty: Medium
Prep and Cook Time: Less than 45 minutes
Seasonal Note: Use locally grown bell peppers in the summer and fall months.
Makes 4 servings
Special tools needed: 9 x 13-inch baking dish

GLUTEN-FREE

- 1 tablespoon butter
- ½ cup chopped onion
- ⅔ cup uncooked quinoa, rinsed
- 4 large bell peppers, any color
- 1 link (3 to 4 ounces) mild Italian sausage, casing removed
- 1 garlic clove, minced
- 1 cup diced mushrooms, any variety
- ¼ cup pine nuts (optional but recommended)
- ¾ teaspoon salt
- ½ cup heavy cream
- 1 cup freshly grated Parmesan cheese

This elegant dish is great for entertaining guests or even for an upscale family dinner at home. Who wouldn't feel special having their dinner served in a beautiful, edible "cup"? Serve this savory dish with some soup, salad, grilled seafood, or other side item and enjoy!

1. Preheat the oven to 400°F.

2. In a medium sauté pan, melt the butter over very low heat. Add the onion and cook, stirring occasionally, for 10 to 15 minutes, while you prepare the rest of the ingredients.

3. In a small saucepan with a tight-fitting lid, combine the quinoa and 1⅓ cups water over high heat. When the water comes to a boil, cover the pan and reduce the heat to low. Cook until the water is completely absorbed, 15 to 20 minutes. Remove from the heat.

4. While the quinoa is cooking, cut the bell peppers in half lengthwise. Scoop the cores and seeds out of the middle and discard. Place the peppers in a 9 x 13-inch baking dish with the cut side facing up and bake until tender when pierced by a fork, 15 to 20 minutes.

5. While the peppers are roasting, turn the heat under the onion up to medium. Add the sausage to the pan. Crumble the sausage using a spatula while it cooks.

6. When the sausage is almost brown all the way through, add the garlic, mushrooms, and pine nuts. Cook for 3 or 4 more minutes, until the pine nuts have begun to turn brown.

7. Stir in the salt, cream, and ½ cup of the Parmesan and cook until the mixture thickens, 1 or 2 minutes. Turn off the heat and stir in the cooked quinoa.

8. If cooking liquid has accumulated inside the peppers, use tongs to drain the peppers into the sink. Divide the quinoa filling evenly among the pepper cavities. Sprinkle with the remaining ½ cup Parmesan cheese and bake the peppers for 10 minutes. Turn the oven to broil and broil for 3 to 5 minutes, or until the cheese on top turns a golden brown. Take care that it doesn't burn; the broiler works quickly! Serve warm.

Homemade Chicken Nuggets

Difficulty: Medium
Prep and Cook Time: Less than 30 minutes
Makes 4 servings

FREEZER FRIENDLY

1 pound boneless, skinless chicken breasts

Salt and ground black pepper, to taste

1 egg

1 cup Whole-Wheat Breadcrumbs (page 331) or good-quality store-bought whole-wheat breadcrumbs

¼ cup freshly grated Parmesan cheese

½ teaspoon paprika

½ teaspoon garlic powder

Olive oil (or ghee, see page 144), for cooking

Optional: Sydney's Honey Mustard Sauce (page 319), for dipping

Making chicken nuggets at home is a bit more work than just buying the frozen variety, but the outcome is so much better tasting and better for you! As with anything that's homemade, you have the ability to control the ingredients, including humanely raised pastured chicken, whole-grain breadcrumbs, and good-quality cooking oil. Cook a double batch and you can have dinner-ready nuggets in the freezer any time!

Leftover cooked nuggets are great for lunch boxes; my kids love them even when I serve them cold.

1. Cut the chicken into 1½-inch chunks and season with salt and pepper.

2. Lightly beat the egg in a shallow bowl. In another shallow bowl, combine the breadcrumbs, cheese, paprika, and garlic powder and mix with a fork. Set aside a large clean plate for the prepared chicken pieces.

3. Make one of your hands the "wet hand" (touching only the wet ingredients) and the other one the "dry hand" (touching only the dry ingredients). With your wet hand, toss some of the chicken chunks into the egg mixture until they are coated on all sides, then drop them on top of the breadcrumb mixture. With your dry hand, sprinkle some breadcrumbs on top of the chicken and flip the chicken pieces over a few times, until the pieces are evenly coated. Place the coated pieces on the clean plate while you bread the rest of the chicken.

4. Heat a thin layer of oil or ghee in a large sauté pan over medium-low heat. Add the chicken nuggets to the pan in batches and cook until they are golden brown on both sides and cooked all the way through, 5 or 6 minutes on each side. Cut a nugget down the middle to make sure it is fully cooked (no longer pink inside).

5. Transfer the nuggets to a plate lined with a paper towel to absorb any excess oil. Serve warm with Sydney's Honey Mustard Sauce and refrigerate or freeze the leftovers.

My Dad's (Brown Rice) Risotto

Difficulty: Medium
Prep Time: Less than 15 minutes
Cook Time: 45 minutes
Makes 4 servings

GLUTEN-FREE
VEGETARIAN

4 cups homemade chicken stock (see page 322), or good-quality store-bought broth, plus more if needed

1 tablespoon olive oil

2 tablespoons butter

½ cup diced onion

1 garlic clove, minced

1 cup quick-cooking whole-grain brown rice (does not have to be Arborio)

¼ cup dry white wine

½ cup finely grated Parmigiano-Reggiano cheese, plus extra for garnish if desired

1¼ cups cooked diced veggies (such as steamed asparagus, roasted bell peppers, or sautéed mushrooms)

Salt and ground black pepper, to taste

I've got some Italian in me from my dad's side, so it's no surprise that we're lovers of risotto. Ever since I was a little girl I can remember my dad making risotto (at the time he used white Arborio rice) for holidays and special occasions or even just Sunday dinner. These days whenever our family gathers at my parents' house we often find—and look forward to—his risotto on the dinner table. So I was thrilled when my dad agreed to create a whole-grain version! This book wouldn't be complete without it.

1. Heat the chicken stock in a medium saucepan over medium-low heat.

2. In a large skillet over medium heat, heat the olive oil and 1 tablespoon of the butter. Add the onion and sauté for 5 or 6 minutes, or until translucent but not yet brown. Add the garlic and cook for 1 minute, stirring often.

3. Add the brown rice and cook for 3 minutes, stirring often to coat the rice with the oil and butter. The rice will begin to brown.

LISA'S TIP: This dish is simple but it takes some time to cook, so plan on doing a second kitchen project (such as packing lunches or making muffins for breakfast) in between stirring the rice to best utilize your time in the kitchen!

4. Add the wine and stir until almost all the liquid is evaporated (most of the alcohol will cook out), 1 or 2 minutes.

5. Reduce the heat to medium low, add 1 or 2 ladles of hot chicken stock, and cook until it's almost absorbed, stirring often. Repeat with more chicken stock, until the rice is tender but still al dente and the risotto is slightly soupy, 30 to 40 minutes. You may need all the chicken stock; if you need more liquid, you can add more stock or a little water.

6. Stir in the grated Parmigiano-Reggiano and the remaining 1 tablespoon of butter. Mix in the cooked veggies, season with salt and pepper, and serve, garnished with additional cheese if desired.

My parents and their four grandkids.

Vegetable Chili

2 tablespoons olive oil

¾ cup diced onion

1 bell pepper, any color, cored, seeded, and diced

¾ cup fresh or frozen corn kernels (no need to defrost frozen corn)

2 garlic cloves, minced

One 28-ounce can diced tomatoes with juice

One 15-ounce can kidney beans, drained and rinsed

2 bay leaves

2 teaspoons chili powder

1 teaspoon ground cumin

1 teaspoon salt

⅛ teaspoon cayenne pepper, or to taste

Recommended toppings: Grated cheese, sour cream or homemade onion dip (see page 189), avocado, and/or homemade whole-grain corn bread (found on 100daysofrealfood.com)

There's no better way to warm up on a cold winter day than with some homemade chili. And even though it's best to let this one simmer for a while, it takes no time at all to throw the ingredients in the pot to get things started. Once it's done, this recipe is perfect to freeze for another day, so consider doubling the ingredients before you get started!

Difficulty: Easy
Prep Time: Less than 15 minutes
Cook Time: 30 minutes
Seasonal Note: Use locally grown bell peppers and corn in the summer months.
Makes 4 servings

GLUTEN-FREE
DAIRY-FREE
VEGETARIAN
FREEZER FRIENDLY

1. Heat the olive oil in a large saucepan over medium heat. Add the onion and bell pepper and cook until they begin to soften, about 5 minutes. Stir in the corn and garlic and sauté for 1 or 2 minutes.

2. Add the tomatoes, beans, bay leaves, and seasonings and bring to a boil. Lower the heat and simmer uncovered for at least 30 minutes and up to 1 hour. The longer it simmers, the better the chili will be.

3. Remove the bay leaves, ladle the chili into bowls, and serve with the desired toppings.

Whole-Wheat Pizza

Difficulty: Medium
Prep Time:
Less than 30 minutes
Bake Time:
Less than 10 minutes
Makes 4 to 5 servings
Special tools needed:
Food processor (optional), rolling pin, large baking sheet (or pizza stone)

VEGETARIAN
FREEZER FRIENDLY

1 small packet (2 teaspoons) active dry yeast

1 cup warm water

1 teaspoon salt

2 tablespoons olive oil, plus extra for greasing the baking sheet and bowl

3 cups whole-wheat flour

Pizza toppings of your choice (see box for ideas)

I got this recipe from the sister-in-law of my good friend Valerie, and it's one of the first real-food recipes we ever made. It's not that we never made pizza from scratch before . . . we just always did it with white flour! I think this is a great place for anyone to start when it comes to cutting out processed and refined foods, because homemade pizza is always a real winner. With all the yummy toppings, no one will even notice that the crust is slightly different.

1. Add the yeast to the warm water in a large measuring cup with a spout. When the yeast is dissolved and foams up a little, mix in the salt and olive oil.

2. In a food processor fitted with a dough blade, add the flour. Turn the machine on and pour the yeast mixture through the feed tube while the machine is running. (The dough can also be mixed and kneaded by hand in a large bowl; they certainly didn't have food processors in ancient Italy!)

3. In the food processor the dough should turn into a ball chasing itself around the machine. If it's too sticky, add more flour 1 tea-

OUR FAVORITE PIZZA TOPPINGS

- Mozzarella cheese and tomato sauce (classic!)
- Sautéed shallots, mushrooms, and sausage
- Leftover diced Grilled Veggie Kabobs (page 218)
- Leftover filling for Asian Lettuce Wraps (page 206) topped with fresh cilantro*
- Pulled pork (see page 286) with BBQ sauce (see page 316), fresh cilantro,* toasted pine nuts, and red onion
- Pesto (see page 274) and goat cheese, with or without arugula* (no tomato sauce)

**Be sure to add fresh greens after the pizza has come out of the oven.*

spoon at a time, and if it won't hold together add more water 1 teaspoon at a time.

4. Remove the ball of dough and put it into a large bowl that's been lightly greased with olive oil and cover with plastic wrap (or a greased plastic bag). Place the dough on the counter at room temperature for a couple of hours, or overnight in the refrigerator, to allow it to rise (or if you're in a pinch, you can use it right away—not ideal, but it's better than not having pizza).

5. When you're ready to bake the pizza, preheat the oven to 500°F and lightly oil a baking sheet. To make one large pizza, leave the dough in a big ball, or divide it into 4 equal portions to make personal pizzas—our family favorite because it allows for personalized toppings, and the kids love to make their own.

6. Using a rolling pin on a lightly floured surface, roll out the dough into circles about ¼ inch thick. Move the dough to the prepared baking sheet and fold over the edges by pinching down with the back of a fork to make the crust. Add your desired toppings (minus the fresh herbs) and bake for 8 to 10 minutes, or until the crust and cheese are golden brown. Garnish with fresh herbs as desired.

Macaroni Casserole

Difficulty: Medium
Prep and Bake Time: Less than 40 minutes
Makes 5 to 6 servings
Special tools needed: 8- or 9-inch square or round baking dish

VEGETARIAN

I used to buy macaroni and cheese in the blue box. Now that I know that the noodles are made with refined grains and the powdery "sauce" is sometimes made with artificial dye (for more info on dyes, see page 23) among other things, I always prefer it homemade. If you make macaroni and cheese from scratch you can control the ingredients and include whole grains, organic dairy, and even some vegetables. The end result is not just for kids—it can be dinner for the whole family! This casserole recipe was inspired by a dish that my mom used to make for me when I was a kid.

- 2 tablespoons butter
- ¼ cup diced onion
- 2 garlic cloves, minced
- 2 tablespoons whole-wheat flour
- 2 cups milk
- 1 teaspoon salt
- Ground black pepper, to taste
- ½ cup sour cream
- 2½ cups grated cheddar cheese
- 1½ cups uncooked whole-grain pasta, such as elbow macaroni or penne, cooked according to the package directions
- 1 cup add-ins, such as diced cooked green beans, chopped steamed broccoli, frozen peas, or shredded cooked chicken (optional)
- ⅓ cup Whole-Wheat Breadcrumbs (page 331) or good-quality store-bought

1. Preheat the oven to 450°F.

2. In a large saucepan over medium-low heat, melt the butter. Add the onion and cook for 3 to 4 minutes, or until it begins to soften. Add the garlic and sauté for 1 more minute.

3. Sprinkle the flour over the onion and garlic and whisk continuously until the flour mixture begins to brown. Whisk in the milk and cook, stirring, until the mixture begins to boil. Lower the heat to a light simmer and cook until the milk thickens, whisking occasionally.

4. Turn off the heat and whisk in the salt, pepper, sour cream, and cheese. Add the noodles and an "add-in" ingredient (if using) to the sauce and stir until well coated. Don't worry if it seems like a lot of sauce, because it will be absorbed into the pasta while baking.

5. Transfer the mixture to an 8- or 9-inch baking dish, sprinkle with the breadcrumbs, and bake for 14 to 16 minutes, or until golden brown on top. Serve warm. (Refrigerate the leftovers for up to 5 days or freeze for another day.)

LISA'S TIP: To reheat the macaroni casserole, put the leftovers in a small pot on the stove and add a few splashes of milk to bring back the creaminess to the sauce.

Quinoa Veggie "Burgers"

Difficulty: Medium
Prep and Cook Time: 30 to 40 minutes
Makes 8 burgers

VEGETARIAN
FREEZER FRIENDLY

1 cup uncooked quinoa, cooked according to the package directions (about 3 cups cooked)

2/3 cup grated sharp cheddar cheese

3/4 cup minced carrot (about 3 carrots)

1/3 cup minced onion

3 garlic cloves, minced

2 eggs

1/4 cup whole-wheat flour

3/4 teaspoon ground cumin

3/4 teaspoon salt

3 tablespoons raw sunflower seeds (optional)

2 tablespoons olive oil

Recommended accompaniments: Large lettuce leaves, such as Bibb, green leaf, or romaine; hummus; sliced avocado

When I can't make it up to Luna's Living Kitchen (an organic restaurant in Charlotte, North Carolina) for one of their awesome quinoa burgers, I'm thankful to have this homemade substitute. I love to serve these surprisingly filling "burgers" on big lettuce leaves and pair them with hummus and sliced avocado. These are also great left over, so don't hesitate to put some aside for a quick lunch or dinner later in the week, or to freeze them for a rainy day.

1. In large bowl, thoroughly combine all the ingredients except for the oil. With wet hands, form the quinoa mixture into 8 patties about 1 inch thick and place on a clean plate or cutting board.

2. In a large sauté pan with a tight-fitting lid, heat the olive oil over medium-low heat. Add the burgers to the pan, cover, and cook until the bottoms are browned, 6 to 8 minutes. (Covering the pan will ensure the burgers cook all the way through the middle without overcooking on the outside.) Flip and repeat, adding another tablespoon of oil if necessary (the pan should not be dry).

3. Serve warm topped with hummus and avocado and wrapped in big lettuce leaves.

Whole-Wheat Spaghetti and Meatballs

Difficulty: Medium
Prep Time: Less than 20 minutes
Bake Time: Less than 15 minutes
Makes 4 to 5 servings
Special tools needed: Large baking sheet

FREEZER FRIENDLY (COOKED MEATBALLS AND SAUCE)

Who doesn't love spaghetti and meatballs? Here's a definite crowd-pleaser that also provides an easy way to work in a dose of veggies, thanks to the addition of the minced carrot. This is another one of those dishes that would be great left over (stored in the fridge or freezer), so if you're really feeling productive, make some extra for another day. My seven-year-old loves to find this dish in her school lunch thermos.

MEATBALLS

Olive oil, for greasing the baking sheet

1 pound ground beef

1 egg, beaten

⅓ cup Whole-Wheat Breadcrumbs (page 331) or store-bought whole-wheat breadcrumbs

⅓ cup freshly grated Parmesan cheese

½ cup minced carrot (about 2 carrots)

3 garlic cloves, minced

1½ teaspoons red wine vinegar

1½ teaspoons soy sauce (preferably low sodium)

1 teaspoon dried Italian seasoning

¼ teaspoon salt

Crushed red pepper flakes, to taste

SPAGHETTI

1 pound whole-wheat spaghetti, cooked according to the package directions

Homemade Tomato Sauce (page 320) or store-bought tomato sauce, warmed

Freshly grated Parmesan cheese, for serving

1. Preheat the oven to 425°F. Generously grease a baking sheet with olive oil and set aside.

2. In a large bowl, use your hands to combine all the meatball ingredients. Roll the mixture into golf ball–size meatballs and place them in rows on the prepared baking sheet. (This is a fun job for little ones.)

3. Bake for 9 to 11 minutes, or until the meatballs are brown all the way through.

4. Serve the meatballs with the spaghetti and warm tomato sauce. Garnish with Parmesan cheese.

LISA'S TIP: To mince carrots, either grind them in a food processor or grate them and then mince. They need to be uniformly small so that they will cook evenly.

Teriyaki Flank Steak Salad

This salad is so filling and flavorful that you'll forget you're even eating salad. I've never been a big salad person, but this recipe is so tasty I could eat it every week. And if you aren't in the mood for a salad, the teriyaki-marinated flank steak makes a great stand-alone entrée as well!

Difficulty: Medium
Prep and Cook Time: 30 minutes
Makes 3 to 4 servings
Special tools needed: Grill

GLUTEN-FREE (IF GLUTEN-FREE SOY SAUCE IS USED)
DAIRY-FREE

STEAK

Teriyaki Marinade (page 318)

1 pound flank steak, preferably grass fed

DRESSING

¼ cup olive oil

2 tablespoons soy sauce (preferably low sodium)

1 tablespoon rice wine vinegar

1 teaspoon peeled and minced fresh ginger

2 teaspoons honey

2 teaspoons freshly squeezed lime juice

Cayenne pepper, to taste

SALAD

1 head lettuce, preferably Boston, Bibb, or butter lettuce

2 cups fresh spinach leaves

1 carrot, peeled and diced

1 red bell pepper, cored, seeded, and diced

½ cup chopped fresh cilantro

⅓ cup sliced green onions (white and light green parts)

Sesame seeds (optional)

1. To make the steak, pour the teriyaki marinade into a medium shallow dish, such as a square baking dish. Submerge the steak in the marinade, then cover and refrigerate for at least 20 minutes, or up to 24 hours for more intense flavor.

2. For the dressing, blend all the dressing ingredients using a countertop blender or handheld immersion blender. Set aside.

3. Preheat a gas grill to about 400°F (medium-high).

4. To assemble the salad, in a large bowl toss the lettuce, spinach, carrot, bell pepper, cilantro, and green onions.

5. Grill the steak for 5 to 6 minutes on each side, or until light pink in the middle. Let the steak rest for a few minutes, then slice it into thin strips, cutting across the grain.

6. Toss the salad with the desired amount of dressing and the sesame seeds, if desired, and serve immediately with steak slices on top.

Homemade Chicken Noodle Soup

Difficulty: Easy
Prep and Cook Time: Less than 20 minutes
Makes 6 or 7 servings

GLUTEN-FREE (IF GLUTEN-FREE NOODLES ARE USED)
DAIRY-FREE
FREEZER FRIENDLY

9 cups homemade chicken stock (see page 322) or good-quality store-bought broth

3 cups uncooked small whole-grain noodles (such as mini penne, elbow macaroni, or fusilli)

10 carrots, peeled and cut into ½-inch or ¼-inch dice

5 celery stalks, washed and sliced (or 1 sliced green bell pepper, which my younger daughter prefers over celery)

2 cups cooked chicken, shredded or diced

Salt and ground black pepper, to taste

Once you try chicken noodle soup made from homemade chicken stock, you'll never go back to the canned stuff again! Homemade stock is so tasty I could honestly drink it plain, but of course it's even better with some yummy noodles, veggies, and chicken mixed in. If efficiency is your goal, make and serve The Best Whole Chicken in the Slow Cooker (page 278) on day 1 (reserving 2 cups shredded or diced chicken); use the leftover bones to make Overnight Chicken Stock in the Slow Cooker (page 322), and then make and serve this soup on day 2. If you have leftover soup, consider freezing some in individual portions for lunch on a rainy day!

1. In a large pot over high heat, bring the chicken stock to a boil.

2. Add the noodles and cook until done, 7 or 8 minutes.

3. When there are 5 to 6 minutes left in the cooking time, throw in the chopped carrots and celery. Keep the stock boiling.

4. Add the chicken at the end to warm it up. Taste the soup and add salt and pepper as needed. Serve warm or freeze for another day!

Simple Seafood

One great thing about having fish for dinner is that it doesn't take long at all to cook. Served with a couple easy side dishes (such as roasted veggies, a salad, and/or baked potatoes), this dish could quickly be whipped up for a weeknight meal—and if you happen to have any leftovers, be sure to check out the fish cake recipe on page 237!

Difficulty: Easy
Prep and Cook Time: Less than 20 minutes
Makes 4 or 5 servings

DAIRY-FREE (IF OLIVE OIL IS USED IN PLACE OF BUTTER)

½ cup whole-wheat flour

1 pound mild white fish, such as flounder, cod, or sole (wild-caught preferred)

Salt and ground black pepper, to taste

2 tablespoons butter

⅓ cup white wine

Juice of 1 lemon (or less if preferred)

Optional garnish: Chopped fresh flat-leaf parsley or capers

1. Sprinkle the flour onto a large plate.

2. Season the fish with salt and pepper and then dip it in the flour to coat on all sides. Transfer to a clean plate.

3. In a large sauté pan over medium heat, melt the butter. Add the coated fish to the pan and cook for several minutes (depending on the thickness of the fish), until the fish is golden brown on the underside. Flip and cook until it is golden brown on the other side and the center is white, flaky, and cooked all the way through. Transfer the fish to a clean plate and cover it with foil to keep warm.

4. To make the sauce, add the wine to the pan and turn the heat to high. Cook the wine for several minutes, until reduced by half, while scraping the brown bits off the bottom of the pan and incorporating them into the sauce. Pour in the lemon juice and stir to combine. The sauce will remain somewhat thin.

5. Drizzle the sauce over the fish and garnish with fresh parsley or capers, if desired. Serve warm.

Taco Night!

Difficulty: Easy
Prep and Cook Time: Less than 30 minutes
Makes 4 servings

GLUTEN-FREE
DAIRY-FREE
FREEZER FRIENDLY

- 2 tablespoons olive oil
- ⅓ cup chopped onion
- 1 pound ground pork (ground beef can be substituted, but we prefer pork's milder flavor)
- 1 teaspoon chili powder
- ½ teaspoon ground cumin
- ½ teaspoon dried oregano
- ½ teaspoon salt
- Juice of ½ lime
- Recommended accompaniments: Corn Tortillas (page 329), lettuce or sliced cabbage, sour cream, grated cheese, lime wedges, hot peppers, salsa

If eating real food means you can still eat tacos, count me in! In all seriousness, though, I used to buy those handy little packets of taco seasoning to flavor our meat for taco night. Then one day I looked at the ingredients and saw that those packets contain more highly refined additives than actual spices. There's no need for that when it's so easy to mix up your own seasonings and make tacos from scratch.

1. Heat the oil in a sauté pan over medium heat. Add the onion and cook until soft but not browned, 3 to 4 minutes.

2. Add the ground pork and cook while breaking up the meat with a spatula. Continue to cook until the meat has browned all the way through. Drain off the fat (if desired), then season with chili powder, cumin, oregano, and salt.

3. Stir in the lime juice and serve warm with the taco fixings of your choice.

LISA'S TIP: To stretch this recipe even further, add black beans, minced carrot, and/or diced mushrooms to the meat mixture (along with extra seasoning).

TACO SEASONING

Make this taco seasoning in bulk in advance.

1 tablespoon chili powder
1½ teaspoons ground cumin
1½ teaspoons dried oregano
1½ teaspoons salt

Combine all the ingredients and store in an airtight container. Use 2½ teaspoons taco seasoning per 1 pound ground meat.

Polenta with Mushroom Bordelaise Sauce

Difficulty: Easy
Prep and Cook Time:
Less than 30 minutes
Makes 4 servings

VEGETARIAN

This dish may seem fancy, but guess what, it's quick and easy! And delicious, I might add. It would surely impress any dinner guest and may even fool them into thinking you were slaving in the kitchen all day long—yet it's so simple it could easily become one of your weeknight staples. Serve it alongside a salad or top it with steamed green beans and dinner is done!

4 cups milk, plus more as needed

1 cup coarsely ground cornmeal

3⁄4 teaspoon salt

3 tablespoons butter

2 shallots, minced

One 8-ounce package sliced mushrooms (button, cremini, or your favorite gourmet variety)

2 tablespoons whole-wheat flour

3⁄4 cup red wine

1 1⁄4 cups good-quality beef stock (or broth)

1 teaspoon chopped fresh thyme, plus extra sprigs for garnish if desired

1⁄3 cup freshly grated Parmesan cheese

Optional topping: 3⁄4 pound steamed green beans

1. Combine the milk, cornmeal, and ½ teaspoon of the salt in a medium saucepan over high heat. When the mixture comes to a light boil, turn the heat to medium low and simmer for 15 minutes, or until the milk has been almost completely absorbed by the cornmeal, whisking every few minutes so it doesn't stick to the bottom of the pan. Add more milk if necessary to keep the polenta from becoming overly thick.

2. Meanwhile, melt 2 tablespoons of the butter in a medium sauté pan over medium heat. Add the shallots and sauté for 3 or 4 minutes, until they begin to soften but do not turn brown. Add the mushrooms and the remaining 1 tablespoon of butter and cook for about 3 more minutes, or until the mushrooms have soaked up the butter and begun to brown. Sprinkle the flour on the mushrooms and stir until the flour is almost completely absorbed.

3. With the heat still on medium, slowly pour the wine into the mushroom mixture and stir. Be careful to avoid flare-ups; if cooking over a gas flame, you may want to turn off the burner completely for a moment.

4. Simmer to reduce the wine a bit, about 2 minutes. Pour in the beef stock and remaining ¼ teaspoon of salt. Cook and stir until the liquid thickens to the consistency of gravy, about 5 minutes. Remove from the heat and sprinkle in the fresh thyme.

5. Set out 4 large soup bowls and divide the polenta among them. Top the polenta with mushroom bordelaise sauce and Parmesan cheese. Garnish with fresh thyme sprigs or top with steamed green beans.

LISA'S TIP: Some people cook their polenta with broth (or water), but I love how creamy it is when made with milk.

Cajun Alfredo with Shrimp

Difficulty: Medium
Prep and Cook Time: Less than 30 minutes
Makes 4 servings

GLUTEN-FREE (IF GLUTEN-FREE NOODLES ARE USED)

3 tablespoons butter

½ cup diced red onion

1 red bell pepper, cored, seeded, and diced

1 pound peeled and deveined raw medium shrimp, patted dry

1 tablespoon Chef Paul Prudhomme's Blackened Redfish Magic seasoning or other Cajun spice mix

2 garlic cloves, minced

3 cups loosely packed raw spinach leaves

1 cup heavy cream

½ cup freshly grated Parmesan cheese

8 ounces whole-wheat fettuccine noodles, cooked according to the package directions

If you love creamy Alfredo sauce, then you're in for a treat! This is your basic Alfredo kicked up a few notches without being too spicy. We find this dish to be a welcome variation from the norm, and thankfully our kids enjoy these Cajun flavors. I suppose it's hard to go wrong with creamy, cheesy goodness!

1. In a large sauté pan over medium heat, melt the butter. Add the onion and cook for 3 to 4 minutes, or until the onion is softened.

2. Add the bell pepper and shrimp to the pan and sprinkle with the seasoning mix. Cook, stirring occasionally, until the shrimp are pink, curled up, and cooked all the way through, 4 to 5 minutes.

3. Toss the garlic and spinach leaves into the pan and cook for 1 minute. Add the heavy cream and Parmesan to the pan and then reduce the heat to low. Simmer for 3 to 4 more minutes, stirring occasionally, until the sauce just begins to thicken.

4. Mix the noodles into the sauce mixture until well combined, divide into pasta bowls, and serve warm.

Veggie Corn Chowder

This soup is very quick and easy to make, and if you double the recipe you can freeze the leftovers for another day. If you have the space, freezing fresh produce while it's in season is one way to eat local all year round; so during the summer, buy some extra local (organic) corn, parboil it, freeze the kernels in one layer, and then transfer them to a large freezer bag! I do the same with fresh summer berries as well (minus the parboiling, of course).

Difficulty: Easy
Prep and Cook Time: 30 minutes
Seasonal Note: Use (or freeze) locally grown corn in the summer months.
Makes 6 servings
Special tools needed: Countertop blender or handheld immersion blender

VEGETARIAN
FREEZER FRIENDLY

3 tablespoons butter

2 tablespoons whole-wheat flour

1 medium onion, diced

3 large carrots, peeled and diced

3 large celery stalks, diced

3 cups corn kernels (fresh or frozen; no need to defrost)

1 teaspoon salt

Cayenne pepper, to taste

2 cups homemade chicken stock (see page 322) or good-quality store-bought chicken or vegetable broth

2 cups milk

1. In a large soup pot over medium heat, melt the butter. Whisk in the flour and keep whisking until the mixture darkens but does not burn, 4 to 5 minutes. This is called making a roux.

2. Add the onion, carrots, and celery and stir occasionally until the veggies begin to soften, 5 to 6 minutes.

3. Add the corn, salt, and cayenne pepper to the pot and cook, stirring, for another 2 or 3 minutes. (If using frozen corn, add a minute to the cooking time.)

4. Pour in the stock and milk and bring to a boil. Lower the heat and simmer for 10 minutes, until thickened.

5. Partially puree the soup by transferring only half to a countertop blender, then returning the puree to the pot, or by sticking a hand immersion blender in the pot and briefly pureeing for less than a minute. Ladle into soup bowls and serve warm or freeze in individual portions for another day.

LISA'S TIP: Immersion blenders make pureeing soups a breeze. They're a small investment that will save quite a bit of time and mess!

Grilled Teriyaki Salmon

Difficulty: Easy
Prep Time: Less than 20 minutes
Cook Time: Less than 15 minutes
Makes 4 servings
Special tools needed: Gas or charcoal grill

GLUTEN-FREE (IF GLUTEN-FREE SOY SAUCE IS USED IN MARINADE)
DAIRY-FREE

1 pound fresh wild-caught salmon (or try sea bass!)

1 recipe Teriyaki Marinade (page 318)

Olive oil spray, for cooking

Make the teriyaki marinade in advance and enjoy this perfect quick, wholesome dinner on any busy weeknight. Pair it with some brown rice and something green and call it a day!

1. Place the salmon in a shallow baking dish. Pour the teriyaki marinade over the fish and marinate in the refrigerator for no more than 30 minutes.

2. Preheat a gas grill on high for several minutes (or prepare a charcoal fire). Spray the grates of the grill with a light coating of olive oil, place the salmon on the grill, and cook for 4 to 6 minutes (depending on thickness), then carefully flip the salmon.

3. Pour some of the remaining marinade over the fish if desired. Grill for another 4 to 6 minutes, or until cooked all the way through. Serve warm.

Whole-Wheat Pasta with Kale-Pesto Cream Sauce

Difficulty: Medium
Prep and Cook Time: Less than 30 minutes
Seasonal Note: Use locally grown kale in the winter and spring and locally grown basil in the summer.
Makes 4 servings

GLUTEN-FREE (IF GLUTEN-FREE NOODLES ARE USED)
VEGETARIAN

- 8 ounces uncooked whole-wheat pasta
- 1¼ cups loosely packed shredded stemmed kale leaves
- 1¾ cups loosely packed fresh basil leaves, plus extra for garnish
- ¾ cup freshly grated Parmesan cheese
- ½ cup pine nuts (or substitute walnuts for a budget-friendly version)
- 3 peeled garlic cloves
- ⅓ cup extra-virgin olive oil
- 2 tablespoons butter
- ¾ cup heavy whipping cream
- Salt and ground black pepper, to taste

This pasta dish is so good and rich you'll completely forget that you're eating one of the most nutrient-dense greens available, kale. And this versatile spinoff on traditional pesto can be used in many other ways: Try it on pizza, paninis, crackers, salads, and even cheese. The pesto can also be frozen in ice cube trays so you can enjoy its fresh flavor when you are short on time.

1. Cook the pasta according to the package directions.

2. Meanwhile, in a food processor, combine the kale, basil, Parmesan, pine nuts, garlic, and olive oil. Pulse the mixture a few times until it's well blended but not overly smooth (I personally like it when my pesto has a little crunch). Set aside.

3. In a large sauté pan over medium heat, melt the butter. Add the cream and stir until well combined. Cook and stir until the mixture begins to thicken, 3 to 5 minutes. Add the pesto and stir to combine. Season with salt and pepper.

4. Drain the pasta and add to the pan with the cream sauce. Mix well to coat. Divide among 4 pasta bowls, garnish with fresh basil leaves, and serve immediately.

LISA'S TIP: For a plain pesto that can be used elsewhere, complete only step 2 of this recipe.

Slow-Cooker Potato Soup

3 to 4 large potatoes or 9 small potatoes (about 2¼ pounds russet or other similar potatoes), unskinned, scrubbed and cut into 1-inch pieces

½ cup diced onion

4 cups homemade chicken stock (see page 322) or good-quality store-bought broth

2 garlic cloves, crushed

1 teaspoon salt

2 tablespoons butter

½ cup heavy cream

Recommended toppings: Shredded cheddar cheese, sour cream, bacon pieces, and sliced green onions

This hearty dish is both simple and delicious. Serve it with a big green salad (the Spinach Salad with Warm Bacon Dressing on page 214 would be perfect) and dinner's done. This soup freezes well for great leftovers; we like to freeze our soups in individual portions for easy use in work or school lunches.

Difficulty: Easy
Prep Time: Less than 20 minutes
Cook Time: 4 hours on high or 7 to 8 hours on low
Seasonal Note: Use locally grown potatoes in the fall and winter months.
Makes 5 or 6 servings
Special tools needed: Slow cooker and countertop blender or handheld immersion blender

GLUTEN-FREE
VEGETARIAN (IF VEGETABLE BROTH IS SUBSTITUTED)
FREEZER FRIENDLY

1. Add the potatoes, onion, stock, garlic, and salt to the slow cooker. Cook on high for 4 hours or low for 7 to 8 hours.

2. Add the butter and puree the soup using a handheld immersion blender or countertop blender. (If you prefer a chunkier soup, reserve a few ladles of the large potato pieces before pureeing.) Stir in the cream.

3. Ladle the soup into bowls, garnish with the toppings of your choice, and serve immediately.

The Best Whole Chicken in the Slow Cooker

2 teaspoons paprika

1 teaspoon salt

1 teaspoon onion powder

1 teaspoon dried thyme

½ teaspoon garlic powder

¼ teaspoon cayenne pepper

¼ teaspoon ground black pepper

1 onion, peeled and cut into large pieces

1 large whole chicken (about 4 pounds)

This is by far the most popular recipe on my blog, so it just wouldn't be right if I didn't include it here as well. Inspired by my neighbor Elizabeth, who first turned me on to the idea of cooking meat in a slow cooker without adding water, this is an easy yet tasty dinner, or great for any recipe that calls for cooked chicken.

Difficulty: Easy
Prep Time: Less than 15 minutes
Cook Time: 4 hours on high or 7 hours on low
Makes 5 or 6 servings, depending on the size of the chicken
Special tools needed: Slow cooker

GLUTEN-FREE
DAIRY-FREE
FREEZER FRIENDLY (COOKED CHICKEN OFF THE BONE)

1. Combine all the spices in a small bowl and set aside.

2. Place the onion in the bottom of the slow cooker.

3. Remove any giblets from the chicken (or leave them if you wish, but be sure to remove any plastic or paper bags), then rub the spice mixture all over the outside of the chicken. You can even put some of the spices inside the cavity and under the skin covering the breasts.

4. Put the chicken breast-side down on top of the onions and cover the slow cooker. There's no need to add any liquid.

5. Cook on high for about 4 hours or on low for 7 hours, or until the chicken is falling off the bone. Remove the edible chicken pieces from the slow cooker and serve.

LISA'S TIP: When dinner is over, don't forget to save the leftover bones and cooking juices to make homemade stock (see page 322) overnight!

Slow-Cooker BBQ Ribs

Barbecued ribs are a great excuse to eat with your hands and just get downright messy, and thankfully eating real food doesn't mean you have to miss out on this summer favorite! This recipe is especially easy if you have some leftover Sweet and Tangy BBQ Sauce on hand.

Difficulty: Easy
Prep Time: Less than 15 minutes
Cook Time: 4 to 5 hours on high
Makes 3 to 4 servings
Special tools needed:
Slow cooker

GLUTEN-FREE
DAIRY-FREE

2 tablespoons paprika

1 teaspoon salt

½ teaspoon garlic powder

½ teaspoon cayenne pepper

½ teaspoon ground black pepper

2½ to 3 pounds pork ribs (spareribs or baby back)

1 onion, peeled and halved

1 recipe Sweet and Tangy BBQ Sauce (page 316)

1. In a small bowl, combine the paprika, salt, garlic powder, cayenne pepper, and black pepper.

2. Cut the rack of ribs into 4 or 5 smaller pieces and sprinkle the spice mixture onto all sides of the raw meat. Use your hands if necessary to get a good even coating.

3. Place the onion in the slow cooker. Add the ribs and cover. There's no need to add any water or other liquid.

4. Cook on high for 4 to 5 hours, or until the meat is tender and almost falling off the bone. Top the cooked ribs with the BBQ sauce and serve warm.

Slow-Cooker Flank Steak Fajitas

1½ teaspoons chili powder

1 teaspoon ground cumin

1 teaspoon ground coriander

½ teaspoon salt

¼ teaspoon ground black pepper

1½ pounds grass-fed flank steak

2 tablespoons soy sauce (preferably low sodium)

1 jalapeño, seeded and chopped

2 garlic cloves, minced

4 or 5 bell peppers, any color, cored, seeded, and sliced

1 onion, sliced

Recommended accompaniments: Whole-Wheat Tortillas (page 326), freshly grated Monterey Jack cheese, sliced avocado, fresh cilantro, lime wedges, fresh chopped lettuce, sour cream, and/or diced jalapeño

If you're looking for some easy and delicious comfort food, here you go. This dish is great for entertaining guests or even just for a cold winter day at home. It's hard to go wrong when slow-cooked steak, tortillas, and cheese are involved! Or if you don't have time to make homemade tortillas I love the suggestion from a blog reader to just serve this dish over brown rice.

Difficulty: Easy
Prep Time: Less than 20 minutes
Cook Time: 5 to 6 hours on high or 9 hours on low
Makes 5 to 6 servings
Special tools needed: Slow cooker

GLUTEN-FREE (IF GLUTEN-FREE SOY SAUCE IS USED)
DAIRY-FREE

1. In a small bowl, combine the chili powder, cumin, coriander, salt, and pepper.

2. Rub the spice mixture over all sides of the flank steak, place it in the bottom of the slow cooker, and add the soy sauce.

3. Top the flank steak with the jalapeño, garlic, bell peppers, and onion. There's no need to add any water or other liquid.

4. Cook on high for 5 to 6 hours or on low for 9 hours, or until the steak can easily be shredded with two forks.

5. Thoroughly drain the meat and peppers, shred the meat, and serve with the fajita fixings of your choice.

Slow-Cooker Pollo al Disco

1 onion, quartered

4 garlic cloves, peeled and crushed

1 tablespoon olive oil

1 whole chicken, cut into parts (or equal amount of bone-in chicken breasts and thighs)

1 cup homemade chicken stock (page 322) or good-quality store-bought broth

1 cup white wine (Chardonnay recommended)

1½ teaspoons salt

1 teaspoon dried oregano

½ teaspoon ground black pepper

2 bay leaves

1 rosemary sprig

1 pound small new potatoes cut into 2-inch chunks

10 to 12 carrots (depending on the size of your slow cooker), peeled and cut into thirds

With my recipe for The Best Whole Chicken in the Slow Cooker on page 278 as a blog favorite, I felt compelled to come up with a recipe that's even more of a one-pot wonder. You do need to sear the chicken before it goes in the slow cooker, but the reward is worth it: Your entire meal is ready by dinnertime, and it will be fantastic. Unless you want to add a salad or some simple green side, there's nothing left to do!

This dish was inspired by a dinner we had in Argentina. We learned to make a similar recipe at an informal cooking class that turned out to just be me, my husband, the chef, and a translator in the main kitchen of our boutique vineyard hotel! The "disco" came to be in the recipe title because in the olden days they cooked this dish in a makeshift pot made out of a disk off a plow.

Difficulty: Medium
Prep Time: Less than 30 minutes
Cook Time: 4 hours on high or 7 hours on low
Makes 6 servings
Special tools needed: Slow cooker

GLUTEN-FREE
DAIRY-FREE
FREEZER FRIENDLY (COOKED CHICKEN OFF THE BONE)

1. Add the onion and garlic to the slow cooker.

2. In a large sauté pan over medium heat, add the olive oil. Working in batches as needed, sear both sides of the chicken pieces for 3 to 4 minutes on each side, until golden brown. Add the chicken to the slow cooker.

3. Pour the stock and wine into the slow cooker. Sprinkle the salt, oregano, pepper, bay leaves, and rosemary over the chicken, then carefully place the sliced potatoes and carrots on top. You may have to push some down around the chicken for everything to fit.

4. Cook on high for 4 hours or low for 7 hours, or until the chicken is tender and falling off the bone. Discard the bay leaves and rosemary. Serve the chicken warm with the potatoes and carrots.

LISA'S TIP: Drain and discard the juices from the slow cooker and save the bones to make overnight chicken stock (see page 322).

The Best Pulled Pork in the Slow Cooker!

Difficulty: Easy
Prep Time: Less than 15 minutes
Cook Time: 7 to 8 hours on low
Makes 6 servings
Special tools needed:
Slow cooker

GLUTEN-FREE
DAIRY-FREE
FREEZER FRIENDLY

3 tablespoons paprika

1 tablespoon salt

2 teaspoons ground black pepper

½ teaspoon cayenne pepper

1 teaspoon garlic powder

½ teaspoon dried thyme

½ cup honey

¼ cup red wine vinegar

3 tablespoons olive oil

1 onion, peeled and cut in half

3 to 3½ pounds pork shoulder, cut in half

Recommended sides: Homemade cole slaw, garlic toast, hot sauce (optional)

This recipe took me many months to perfect, and it was totally worth the wait. The outcome is some of the best pulled pork I've had and you don't have to succumb to any highly processed ingredients such as refined sugar, corn syrup, or ketchup. Plus my husband says this stuff is so good it doesn't even need barbecue sauce, but, just in case you disagree, you can always use the homemade recipe on page 316. He likes the pork dipped in a little hot sauce, although some blog readers say it has enough heat without adding anything extra.

1. In a medium bowl, combine the first six ingredients with a fork.

2. Pour in the honey, vinegar, and olive oil and stir to form a paste.

3. Place the onion in the bottom of the slow cooker. Top it with the 2 pieces of pork and then pour the honey paste over all sides of the pork pieces. It's okay if some of it (or a lot of it) just drips down to the bottom. There is no need to add any water or other liquid.

4. Turn the slow cooker on to low and cook for 7 to 8 hours or until the meat is tender enough to be easily shredded with a fork.

5. Serve warm with fixings like homemade cole slaw and garlic toast. Refrigerate or freeze the leftovers.

sydney
Sienna

SPECIAL TREATS

Homemade Ice Cream Three Ways

Vanilla, Berry, or Chocolate

Difficulty: Easy
Prep and Make Time:
Less than 30 minutes
Makes 4 to 5 servings
Special tools needed:
Ice cream maker

GLUTEN-FREE
VEGETARIAN
FREEZER FRIENDLY

VANILLA ICE CREAM

1¼ cups milk (whole milk recommended)

1¼ cups heavy cream

¼ cup pure maple syrup

1 teaspoon Pure Vanilla Extract (page 337) or store-bought vanilla extract

BERRY ICE CREAM

Use ¼ cup chilled Berry Sauce (page 334) in place of the maple syrup

CHOCOLATE ICE CREAM

Use ¼ cup Simple Chocolate Sauce (page 338) in place of the maple syrup

Optional garnishes: Chocolate sauce, fresh strawberries, and/or roasted peanuts

A box of Neapolitan ice cream from the store will likely come with a few unwanted extras, including high fructose corn syrup and artificial dye. And even if you're lucky enough to find ice cream made with just sugar and natural ingredients, it will still likely contain way more sweetener than necessary. One thing I like about making my own ice cream at home—aside from how easy it is—is having control over the ingredients. I also enjoy the amazing texture when it's fresh out of the machine!

1. To make each batch of ice cream, combine the milk, cream, syrup (or chocolate sauce or chilled berry sauce, depending on flavor), and vanilla in a large bowl or glass measuring cup with a spout.

2. Process the mixture in an ice cream maker according to the manufacturer's directions.

3. Serve the vanilla ice cream with warm chocolate sauce on top, the berry ice cream with fresh strawberries, and the chocolate ice cream with roasted peanuts, if desired.

LISA'S TIP: When leftover ice cream or sorbet is stored in the freezer, it turns into a solid block. It's best to let it thaw on the counter for at least 15 minutes for it to regain a creamy consistency.

Whole-Wheat Bread Pudding

Talk about a warm, filling, delicious way to end a meal. You can make this dish either as one big casserole for a crowd or as individual soufflés if you're really trying to get fancy. Either way, it will be devoured by all! Try this with Everyday Whole-Wheat Bread (page 332).

Difficulty: Easy
Prep Time: Less than 15 minutes
Bake Time: Less than 1 hour
Makes 6 servings
Special tools needed: 8-inch square baking dish

VEGETARIAN

- 2 cups whole milk
- 3 eggs
- ½ cup pure maple syrup
- 1 teaspoon Pure Vanilla Extract (page 337) or store-bought vanilla extract
- 1 teaspoon ground cinnamon
- ¼ teaspoon ground nutmeg
- 4 cups good-quality whole-wheat bread cubes (½- or ¾-inch dice, about 4 slices sandwich bread)
- ⅓ cup raisins
- Homemade Whipped Cream (page 339)

1. Preheat the oven to 350°F.

2. In a large mixing bowl, thoroughly whisk together the milk, eggs, maple syrup, vanilla, cinnamon, and nutmeg. The spices may not be fully absorbed by the milk mixture, and that's okay.

3. Gently stir in the bread cubes and raisins until all of the bread is completely coated. Pour into an ungreased 8-inch square baking dish and bake until the bread pudding is dark brown on top and the filling is set, 50 minutes to 1 hour. Serve warm topped with homemade whipped cream.

(Extra) Dark Chocolate Peanut Butter Bites

It's fun to re-create better versions of your old favorite treats, especially when your daughter puts a spin on the name and calls them "Lisa's Peanut Butter Cups!" (Get it?)

As Michael Pollan said, "Eat all the junk food you want as long as you cook it yourself." Regardless, I still try to eat these tasty little treats only in moderation.

Difficulty: Easy
Prep Time: Less than 20 minutes
Freezer Time (to set): 25 minutes
Makes 22 mini cups
Special tools needed: Mini muffin pan and liners (or silicone mini muffin pan)

GLUTEN-FREE
DAIRY-FREE (IF COCONUT MILK OR ALMOND MILK IS USED IN PLACE OF COW'S MILK)
VEGETARIAN
FREEZER FRIENDLY

4 ounces unsweetened chocolate baking bar made of 100% cacao

½ cup pure maple syrup

½ cup natural peanut butter (creamy or crunchy)

3 tablespoons milk

1. Line a mini muffin pan with paper liners. Set aside.

2. In a small pot over very low heat, melt the chocolate, maple syrup, peanut butter, and milk together. Stir until well combined.

3. Using a spoon, evenly distribute the chocolate mixture into the mini muffin cups.

4. Freeze until solidified, 20 to 25 minutes. Store in the refrigerator or freezer.

LISA'S TIP: Keep in mind it takes only one ingredient to make truly "natural" peanut butter. And that's peanuts, of course!

Cinnamon-Glazed Popcorn

Difficulty: Medium
Prep and Cook Time: 20 to 30 minutes
Makes 4 to 5 servings
Special tools needed: Parchment paper, large baking sheet

GLUTEN-FREE
VEGETARIAN

- 6 tablespoons (¾ stick) butter
- ¼ cup honey
- 1 teaspoon ground cinnamon
- ½ teaspoon ground ginger
- ½ teaspoon salt
- 1½ cups raw cashews
- 8 cups cooked plain popcorn (from about ½ cup of kernels; see page 192)

Move over, Cracker Jack . . . you've got some competition. Except this version doesn't contain all the refined sugar (and little actual popcorn) like the boxed stuff!

This popcorn treat is so tasty that I love to bag it up and give it out to teachers, friends, and even the mail carrier over the holiday season. I also love to attach little recipe cards so that everyone can dig in without fear of what might be lurking in the ingredients—and hopefully continue to enjoy and share this wholesome recipe with others.

1. Preheat the oven to 325°F. Cover a large rimmed baking sheet with parchment paper.

2. In a small pot over low heat, melt the butter and honey together. Mix in the cinnamon, ginger, and salt.

3. Put the cashews in an extra-large mixing bowl. Coat them with about 2 tablespoons of the honey-butter mixture.

4. Spread the coated nuts onto the prepared baking sheet and toast them for 6 minutes, or until lightly golden.

5. Meanwhile, in the same large bowl evenly coat the plain popcorn—minus any unpopped kernels—with the remaining honey-butter mixture.

6. Add the popcorn to the tray with the cashews. Combine the mixture thoroughly and bake for 4 more minutes. Stir or shake the mixture around and bake for 2 more minutes. Repeat this process 1 or 2 more times, until the mixture is medium brown. The popcorn can burn easily, so it's important to check on it and stir (or shake around) frequently.

7. The popcorn and nuts will be slightly soft right out of the oven but will harden as they cool. Store in an airtight container.

Frozen Yogurt Pops Two Ways

Orange Cream and Mixed Berry

ORANGE CREAM

2 cups plain yogurt

1 cup orange juice

⅓ cup pure maple syrup

1 tablespoon Pure Vanilla Extract (page 337) or store-bought vanilla extract

MIXED BERRY

2 cups plain yogurt

1 cup frozen mixed berries

⅓ cup maple syrup

There's no better way to cool off on a hot summer day than with some homemade yogurt pops! You don't need artificial dyes and an overload of refined sweeteners to enjoy a cool summer treat with friends. Pick your favorite flavor to make or do half and half for a real crowd pleaser. We all know how much little ones like to choose their flavor!

Difficulty: Easy
Prep Time: Less than 20 minutes
Freezing Time: 4 to 5 hours
Each recipe makes 10 or 11 pops (about ¼ cup each)
Special tools needed: Ice pop molds and (wooden) sticks

GLUTEN-FREE
VEGETARIAN
FREEZER FRIENDLY

For the Orange Cream: In a medium bowl, whisk together all the ingredients. Pour into ice pop molds, insert a wooden stick into the center of each, and freeze for 4 to 5 hours or overnight.

For the Mixed Berry: In a blender, combine all the ingredients and puree until smooth. Pour into ice pop molds, insert a wooden stick into the center of each, and freeze for 4 to 5 hours or overnight.

Mango Sorbet

Sorbet is an extremely refreshing dessert, especially when it's made with only a few simple ingredients, including fresh fruit. This is the perfect treat on a hot summer day or as a follow-up dish to a spicy Asian meal. And if you aren't a mango fan, you can easily substitute fresh peaches, strawberries, or raspberries.

Difficulty: Easy
Prep and Make Time: Less than 30 minutes
Makes 4 servings
Special tools needed: Blender and ice cream maker

GLUTEN-FREE
DAIRY-FREE
VEGETARIAN
FREEZER FRIENDLY (SEE TIP ON PAGE 290)

2 ripe mangoes

1 tablespoon pure maple syrup

Fresh mint, for garnish

1. Peel the mangoes using a vegetable peeler and discard the skin. Remove the mango seeds by carefully slicing the flesh off the sides of the seeds. A mango slicer can come in handy for this job.

2. Put the mango flesh in a blender along with the maple syrup and ¼ cup water. Puree until smooth.

3. Pour the mixture into the ice cream maker and process according to the manufacturer's instructions.

4. Use an ice cream scoop to serve the finished sorbet into small bowls. Garnish with fresh mint leaves.

Peanut Butter Cookies

Difficulty: Easy
Prep and Bake Time: Less than 30 minutes
Makes about 20 cookies
Special tools needed: Electric mixer, large baking sheet, and cooling rack (optional)

VEGETARIAN
FREEZER FRIENDLY

1¼ cups whole-wheat flour

½ teaspoon baking soda

½ teaspoon salt

¾ cup natural peanut butter

¾ cup pure maple syrup

½ cup (1 stick) butter, softened slightly and cut into chunks

1 egg

1 teaspoon Pure Vanilla Extract (page 337) or store-bought vanilla extract

½ cup unsalted peanuts

These cake-like cookies are absolutely delicious—one of my favorite recipes of all time. Plus it takes no time at all to mix these up and pop them in the oven. If you have little ones around, I bet you could even find a helper or two!

1. Preheat the oven to 325°F.

2. In a medium bowl, whisk together the flour, baking soda, and salt. Set aside.

3. In the bowl of a stand mixer fitted with a whisk (or in a large bowl and using a handheld electric beater), thoroughly mix the peanut butter, maple syrup, butter, egg, and vanilla. Mix until almost smooth; some small butter chunks may remain in the batter, which is okay.

4. Turn the mixer down to low and slowly add the flour mixture until well combined. Do not overmix. Carefully stir in the peanuts by hand.

5. Drop the cookie dough by the spoonful onto a large ungreased baking sheet and bake (in batches if necessary) until the cookies are light golden brown, about 15 minutes. Transfer to a rack to cool (if you have one).

Mini Chocolate Truffles

Just because you're avoiding processed food doesn't mean you have to give up chocolate. Thank goodness! I'm guilty of having a sweet tooth, and I'm not sure I would have made it through our 100 Days of Real Food pledge without these little truffles (also known as chocolate powerballs). As with any sweets, be sure to enjoy in moderation.

Difficulty: Medium
Prep Time: Less than 15 minutes
Makes 12 to 14 truffles
Special tools needed: Food processor, large baking sheet

GLUTEN-FREE
DAIRY-FREE (IF COCONUT OIL IS USED IN PLACE OF BUTTER)
VEGETARIAN

1 tablespoon butter

1 cup pecans

1 tablespoon honey

1 cup pitted dried dates

1 tablespoon unsweetened powdered cocoa (dark 100% cacao recommended)

Optional: Unsweetened coconut (either plain or toasted), for coating the outside of the truffles

1. In a small sauté pan over medium-low heat, melt the butter. Add the pecans, drizzle in the honey, and cook, stirring, until the nuts start to brown, 3 to 5 minutes. Be very careful: The pecans can go from perfect to burned very quickly.

2. In a food processor, blend together the toasted pecans, dates, and cocoa powder. Add 1 to 2 teaspoons water as needed to help the mixture stick together.

3. Remove the chocolate mixture from the machine and form it into one big piece on a baking sheet. Using your hands, divide the chocolate into 12 or 14 small equal pieces and roll each piece into a little round truffle.

4. Coat the truffles with plain or toasted unsweetened coconut, if desired. Serve or store in an airtight container in the refrigerator.

Mint Chocolate Chunk Ice Cream

Difficulty: Easy
Prep and Make Time: Less than 30 minutes
Makes 5 to 6 servings
Special tools needed: Ice cream maker

GLUTEN-FREE
VEGETARIAN
FREEZER FRIENDLY (SEE TIP ON PAGE 290)

2 ounces unsweetened 100% cacao chocolate baking bars (does not contain sugar)

3 tablespoons plus ¼ cup pure maple syrup, divided

1 teaspoon butter

1¾ teaspoons natural peppermint flavor extract

1½ cups milk (whole milk recommended)

1½ cups heavy cream

7 or 8 fresh mint leaves, cut into thin strips (optional as garnish)

You won't believe how simple and easy it is to make not only your own ice cream but also your own mint chocolate chunks. Homemade ice cream is far superior to the packaged stuff, which frankly I think tastes a little too much like the actual box. Making this recipe is well worth the mere fifteen or twenty minutes of work. Trust me, you won't be disappointed!

1. Place a layer of wax paper on a plate and set aside.

2. In a small saucepan over very low heat, melt the chocolate, 3 tablespoons of the maple syrup, the butter, and ¼ teaspoon of the peppermint extract. Stir constantly until the chocolate is melted and remove from the heat immediately.

3. Using a small rubber spatula, spoon the chocolate mixture onto the wax paper and spread it into a thin, even layer. Place in the freezer.

4. In a large glass measuring cup, combine the milk, cream, the remaining ¼ cup maple syrup, and the remaining 1½ teaspoons peppermint flavor extract. Add to the ice cream maker and follow the manufacturer's instructions to make ice cream, which takes about 10 to 15 minutes in our machine.

5. When the ice cream is almost ready, take the mint chocolate chunk mixture out of the freezer and flip the wax paper over onto a cutting board. Peel off the wax paper and roughly chop or break the chocolate into small chunks.

6. Dump all but a few pieces of chocolate (reserved for garnish) into the ice cream maker. Let it run for about 30 more seconds, just long enough to mix it up, then turn the machine off.

7. Divide the ice cream evenly among 5 or 6 bowls. Garnish with mint leaves if desired, and the reserved chocolate chunks. Serve immediately.

Carrot Cake with Whipped Cream-Cheese Frosting

Difficulty: Medium
Prep and Bake Time: Less than 45 minutes
Makes one 2-layer cake
Special tools needed: Two 9-inch round cake pans, parchment paper, electric mixer, and cooling rack

VEGETARIAN
FREEZER FRIENDLY (CAKE WITHOUT FROSTING)

I never knew how much my older daughter would like carrot cake until one day when I made one for her. It's now hands-down her favorite cake, even over vanilla and chocolate!

Most carrot cakes aren't as healthy as they sound because they're full of white flour and refined sugar (part of what makes them so light and fluffy), but this recipe is a wholesome treat you can feel good about.

CARROT CAKE

1 cup (2 sticks) butter, softened (but not melted), plus extra for greasing the pans

3 cups whole-wheat flour

2 teaspoons baking soda

2 teaspoons ground cinnamon

1 teaspoon ground ginger

1 teaspoon salt

1 cup honey

2 eggs

2 teaspoons Pure Vanilla Extract (page 337) or store-bought vanilla extract

2 cups unsweetened applesauce

1½ cups peeled and grated carrots, about 5 carrots (either a food processor or cheese grater works well for this)

WHIPPED CREAM-CHEESE FROSTING

2 cups heavy cream

One 8-ounce package cream cheese, at room temperature

¼ cup pure maple syrup

1½ teaspoons Pure Vanilla Extract (page 337) or store-bought vanilla extract

1. To make the cakes, preheat the oven to 350°F. Line the bottoms of two 9-inch cake pans with rounds of parchment paper (it helps to trace a pan on top of the paper and cut along the line to make a perfect round). Grease the sides of the pans with a little butter.

2. In a medium bowl, whisk together the flour, baking soda, cinnamon, ginger, and salt. Set aside.

3. Using an electric mixer in a separate bowl, whisk together the butter, honey, eggs, and vanilla. Slowly add the flour mixture with the mixer on low until well combined. The batter will be fairly thick at this point. Carefully fold in the applesauce and carrots by hand.

4. Divide the batter evenly between the 2 cake pans and bake for 22 to 24 minutes, or until a toothpick inserted into the center of a layer comes clean. Let the cakes cool in the pans on a cooling rack.

5. For the frosting, use an electric mixer to combine the heavy cream, cream cheese, maple syrup, and vanilla. Whip for several minutes, until thick and creamy, starting on low and gradually increasing the speed to avoid splatters.

6. When the cakes have cooled to room temperature, loosen them from the sides of the pans with a dull knife and transfer one layer to a cake plate or stand. Spread half the frosting over the top. Place the second layer on top and spread the remaining frosting over the top of the cake. There should be enough frosting to cover the sides, if desired. Serve or refrigerate for later.

PSST . . . DON'T TELL!

Cut this recipe in half, divide it among 12 muffin cups, bake them for the same amount of time, omit the frosting, and you have yourself wholesome Whole-Wheat Carrot Applesauce Muffins for any day of the week! And that's because on the spectrum of baked goods a healthy whole-wheat cake and a healthy whole-wheat muffin can end up meeting somewhere in the middle.

HOMEMADE STAPLES

Salad Dressing Two Ways

Mustard Vinaigrette

Difficulty: Easy
Prep Time: Less than 15 minutes
Makes about 3/4 cup dressing
Special tools needed: Jar with tight-fitting lid

GLUTEN-FREE
DAIRY-FREE
VEGETARIAN

- 1/2 cup olive oil
- 1/4 cup minced shallot (about 1 small shallot)
- 2 tablespoons white wine vinegar
- 1 tablespoon freshly squeezed lemon juice
- 1 teaspoon Dijon mustard
- 1/4 teaspoon salt
- Pinch of ground black pepper

Sure, it takes a little bit of work to throw together your own salad dressing, but if you take just five or ten minutes to do so over the weekend you can have it available in your fridge all week long! Store-bought salad dressings seem innocent at first, but once you take a closer look you'll find all sorts of ingredients (such as high-fructose corn syrup, artificial dyes, propylene glycol alginate, and maltodextrin, just to name a few) that you wouldn't use to make salad dressing at home. It's worth the extra effort . . . especially since the homemade versions taste far superior!

Combine all the ingredients in a jar and secure with the lid. Shake vigorously for a minute, until the dressing is emulsified. Serve or store in the fridge for 1 to 2 weeks.

LISA'S TIP: The dressing will become a solid in the fridge, so bring it to room temperature by briefly heating it up in the microwave or holding the outside of the jar under warm water. Shake before each use.

Tahini Dressing

If your salads are getting a little boring, this creamy dressing is here to help you switch things up. Tahini is ground sesame seed butter that's sometimes found near the international section of grocery stores. It's often used in hummus recipes, but it also makes a smooth, creamy salad dressing.

Difficulty: Easy
Prep Time: Less than 15 minutes
Makes about 1 cup dressing
Special tools needed: Blender or food processer

GLUTEN-FREE (IF GLUTEN-FREE SOY SAUCE IS USED)
DAIRY-FREE
VEGETARIAN

⅓ cup tahini

⅓ cup olive oil

1 tablespoon soy sauce (preferably low sodium)

1 teaspoon honey

1 garlic clove, crushed

Combine all the ingredients and ⅓ cup water in a blender or food processor and combine until smooth. Serve or store in the fridge for 1 to 2 weeks.

In this case—no salad dressing necessary!

Homemade Cream of Mushroom Soup (Condensed)

Difficulty: Medium
Prep and Cook Time: Less than 20 minutes
Makes 1¼ cups (equivalent to one 10¾-ounce can condensed cream of mushroom soup)

VEGETARIAN
FREEZER FRIENDLY

4 tablespoons (½ stick) butter

¼ cup diced onion

1 garlic clove, minced

¾ cup diced button or Baby Bella mushrooms (optional if solely using this recipe as a binding agent in another recipe)

3 tablespoons whole-wheat flour

¼ teaspoon salt

¾ cup homemade chicken stock (see page 322) or store-bought chicken or vegetable broth

½ cup milk

We all have recipes that call for highly processed canned cream of mushroom soup, and with this simple substitution you now have a way to transform those recipes into real-food ones. Phew, that's a relief!

1. In a medium sauté pan, melt the butter over medium heat. Add the onion and cook for 2 minutes, or until the onion begins to soften.

2. Add the garlic and mushrooms and sauté for another minute. Sprinkle the flour and salt on top and cook while stirring until the flour absorbs the mushroom liquid and they begin to brown, but not burn, about 2 more minutes.

3. Pour in the stock and milk, while stirring and scraping the bottom of the pan, then bring to a boil. Turn the heat down to a light boil and stir while cooking until the liquid thickens to a consistency that's similar to very thick gravy, 6 to 7 minutes.

4. Use in place of store-bought cream of mushroom soup or freeze for another day.

Sweet and Tangy BBQ Sauce

Difficulty: Easy
Prep and Cook Time: Less than 15 minutes
Makes 1 cup

GLUTEN-FREE
DAIRY-FREE
VEGETARIAN

What's not to love about barbecue sauce . . . except a load of refined sugar or high-fructose corn syrup? Luckily it's very easy to make your own sauce at home. This allows you to skip the junky ingredients while—just as important—controlling how much sweetener is used. But because this sauce is on the sweeter side, it's still considered an occasional treat at our house. When the time comes, though, we enjoy it on anything from pizza to quesadillas (see page 235) to ribs (see page 281) to chicken.

- **¾ cup tomato sauce**
- **⅓ cup pure maple syrup**
- **4 teaspoons Dijon mustard**
- **4 teaspoons apple cider vinegar**
- **½ teaspoon onion powder**
- **½ teaspoon chili powder**
- **2 garlic cloves, minced**

Combine all the ingredients in a small pot over medium heat. Bring to a boil, then turn the heat down to low and simmer for 5 to 10 minutes. Use the sauce immediately or store in a jar in the refrigerator for 1 to 2 weeks.

Homemade Dried Onion Soup Mix

Yes, the store-bought packets of onion soup mix are convenient, but they also contain lots of undesirable ingredients like corn syrup solids, monosodium glutamate (aka MSG), and artificial coloring. My version is the perfect homemade "better-for-you" replacement!

Difficulty: Easy
Prep Time: Less than 10 minutes
Makes 1½ ounces (equivalent to a 1-ounce store-bought packet)

GLUTEN-FREE
DAIRY-FREE
VEGETARIAN

¼ cup dried minced onion (found in the spice aisle at your grocery store)

1½ teaspoons onion powder

1¼ teaspoons garlic powder

1 teaspoon dried parsley

1 teaspoon salt

1. Mix all the ingredients together in a small bowl.

2. Use in place of store-bought soup mix packets or store in an airtight container for later.

Teriyaki Marinade

Difficulty: Easy
Prep Time: Less than 10 minutes
Makes 1 cup

GLUTEN-FREE (IF GLUTEN-FREE SOY SAUCE IS USED)
DAIRY-FREE
VEGETARIAN

½ cup soy sauce (preferably low sodium)

½ cup chopped fresh cilantro

2 tablespoons peeled and minced fresh ginger

2 tablespoons toasted sesame oil

2 tablespoons rice wine vinegar

3 garlic cloves, minced

Pinch of cayenne pepper

Teriyaki can jazz up just about anything from meat to seafood to rice to vegetables. And now, instead of wasting money on takeout or buying bottled, factory-made marinade, you can make yummy Asian food at home without ingesting any questionable food additives!

1. Combine all the ingredients in a bowl. Use immediately or store in the fridge for up to 3 days.

2. To use, pour over meat or seafood, and let marinate for as little as 20 minutes or (for meat) up to 24 hours. The longer it marinates the stronger the flavor.

Sydney's Honey Mustard Sauce

Whenever we make Homemade Chicken Nuggets (page 244), it's the job of my older daughter, Sydney, to mix up the honey mustard sauce for dipping. Since there are only two ingredients, and it's a rather forgiving recipe, this is a great place for up-and-coming chefs to start in the kitchen! And in addition to chicken nuggets, this dipping sauce is also excellent paired with baked sweet potato fries.

Difficulty: Easy
Prep Time: Less than 5 minutes
Makes ½ cup sauce

GLUTEN-FREE
DAIRY-FREE
VEGETARIAN

¼ cup honey

¼ cup yellow mustard

In a small bowl, mix the honey and mustard together thoroughly. Refrigerate until ready to use.

Homemade Tomato Sauce

Difficulty: Easy
Prep and Cook Time: Less than 1 hour
Makes about 1⅔ cups sauce
Special tools needed: Blender

GLUTEN-FREE
DAIRY-FREE
VEGETARIAN
FREEZER FRIENDLY

If you haven't already noticed, I'm into shortcuts when it comes to a lot of these "from scratch" recipes. While some recipes for tomato sauce go through extra steps that involve boiling and peeling the tomatoes, I think this simpler recipe yields results that are just as good. This sauce can be used on spaghetti (try it with the meatballs on page 256) or Whole-Wheat Pizza (page 250), or it can be saved for another day (in the fridge for two or three days or in the freezer for as long as six months).

- 2 pounds Roma tomatoes, halved
- 2 tablespoons olive oil
- ½ cup diced or minced onion
- 2 garlic cloves, minced
- ½ teaspoon dried Italian seasoning
- ½ teaspoon salt
- Pinch of red pepper flakes

1. Remove the stem and woody part from the top of the tomato core and discard. Combine the whole trimmed tomatoes in a blender and puree to a smooth consistency. Depending on the size of your blender you may have to puree the tomatoes in two batches. Set aside.

2. Heat the olive oil in a large sauté pan over medium-low heat. Add the onion and cook, stirring, until the onion softens, but does not turn brown, 6 to 7 minutes. Add the minced garlic, Italian seasoning, salt, and red pepper flakes and cook for another minute.

3. Pour in the tomato puree and bring to a boil for 1 minute. Turn the heat down to a simmer and cook, stirring occasionally, for a minimum of 30 minutes and as long as 1 hour. The longer you cook the sauce, the better it will taste. Drain excess liquid if desired and serve or store in the fridge or freezer.

All-Clad
All-Clad

Overnight Chicken Stock in the Slow Cooker

Difficulty: Easy
Prep Time: Less than 10 minutes
Cook Time: 8 to 10 hours on low
Makes 4 to 6 quarts (depending on the size of your slow cooker)
Special tools needed: Slow cooker

GLUTEN-FREE
DAIRY-FREE
FREEZER FRIENDLY

- Leftover bones/carcass from a small or medium chicken
- 1 onion, peeled and roughly chopped
- 1 celery rib, roughly chopped
- 1 carrot, roughly chopped (no need to peel)
- 1 bay leaf
- 1 parsley sprig
- 1 thyme sprig
- 1 tablespoon apple cider or white vinegar (optional)
- Salt, to taste

The flavor of homemade chicken stock is far superior to the store-bought version, and with a recipe this simple there's no reason to keep putting it off. This is a basic starter recipe that could easily be modified by adding garlic or substituting different herbs. The finished stock can be used in a variety of dishes including soups (see page 260), risotto (see page 246), rice, gravy, and other sauces. Plus there's no pressure to use it all up right away because it will freeze beautifully for another day. I usually freeze our stock in one- and two-cup portions as well as in ice cube trays (that I later transfer to a freezer-safe container) in case I need just a little at a time.

1. Place the chicken bones or carcass in the slow cooker. If using a leftover carcass from The Best Whole Chicken in the Slow Cooker (page 278), just remove the edible meat and leave everything else, including the skin, cooking juices, and original onion, in the bottom of the slow cooker.

2. Add the onion, celery, carrot, bay leaf, parsley, thyme, vinegar (if using), and salt. Fill the slow cooker almost to the top with water (leaving at least ½ inch headspace).

3. Turn the slow cooker on to low and cook overnight, or alternatively start the slow cooker in the morning and cook on low for 8 to 10 hours during the day.

4. When the stock is done, turn off the heat and, using a soup ladle, pass the stock through a fine sieve to remove all the solids. Season with salt. Refrigerate for 1 week or freeze for up to 6 months. Dilute stock with water (if desired) before using in recipes.

Basic Cheese Sauce

Difficulty: Easy
Prep and Cook Time: Less than 20 minutes
Makes about 1 cup sauce

VEGETARIAN

This creamy cheese sauce is a great way to top off vegetables or even use for a quick "macaroni and cheese" dish. Let's face it: My "pickier" daughter eats twice as much broccoli if it's covered in cheese sauce! You could even get creative and add some chiles and diced tomatoes to transform this recipe into a queso dip.

I realize this cheese sauce will not be the same bright orange as store-bought "processed cheese products," but the orange color is added only for aesthetic purposes and often comes from a natural additive called annatto (or sometimes from artificial food coloring, so don't forget to read your labels).

2 tablespoons butter

2 tablespoons whole-wheat flour

3/4 cup whole milk

1½ cups shredded sharp cheddar cheese (or a combination of different cheeses that you have on hand)

1 tablespoon cream cheese

1/4 teaspoon salt

1. Melt the butter in a medium sauté pan over medium-low heat. Whisk in the flour, working vigorously to prevent lumps, until the mixture (which is called a roux) darkens a little but does not burn, 1 to 2 minutes.

2. Pour in the milk and continue whisking to break up any lumps. When the milk thickens to the consistency of thin gravy, 2 to 3 minutes, turn off the heat and stir in the cheeses and salt. The cheeses will melt beautifully into the sauce. Serve warm over veggies and/or noodles.

LISA'S TIP: Leftover sauce can be stored in the fridge for 2 to 3 days. When reheating, stir in a little milk to bring it back to the right consistency.

Whole-Wheat Tortillas

Difficulty: Advanced
Prep and Cook Time: Less than 45 minutes
Makes 14 tortillas
Special tools needed: Food processor, rolling pin, cast-iron skillet

DAIRY-FREE
VEGETARIAN
FREEZER FRIENDLY

The flavor and texture of homemade tortillas are light-years above the store-bought variety. This recipe takes a little more time than some of the others in this book, but I promise the results are well worth the effort. Plus you can make these tortillas in advance and freeze them for another day. And don't forget that tortillas can be used for more than just Mexican food, including as sandwich wraps or even pizza crust.

3 cups whole-wheat flour, plus extra for rolling out the dough

2 teaspoons baking powder

½ teaspoon salt

5 tablespoons chilled, solid coconut oil (see Note), plus extra for cooking (see page 31 for information on working with coconut oil)

1 cup warm water, plus more as needed

1. In a food processor outfitted with a dough blade, combine the flour, baking powder, and salt. Pulse to combine.

2. Add the cold coconut oil in chunks on top of the flour and process until the mixture resembles coarse crumbs.

3. With the machine running, slowly pour 1 cup warm water through the feed tube. Within about a minute, a dough ball should form and start chasing itself around the bowl. If the dough is too dry (i.e., crumbly and not forming into a ball), add warm water 1 teaspoon at a time. If the dough is too sticky (i.e., sticking to your finger when you touch it), add flour 1 teaspoon at a time.

4. Transfer the dough to a large cutting board. Use your hands to roll the dough into a large log and then cut it into 14 equal pieces (I start by cutting it down the middle). Roll each disk of dough in your hands into a small ball and then partially flatten onto the cutting board (without letting the pieces touch). Cover with plastic wrap or a dish towel to avoid drying them out.

5. Place a 10- or 12-inch seasoned cast-iron skillet over medium-high heat and let it heat up for several minutes. Ensure adequate ventilation.

6. Meanwhile, sprinkle a tiny bit of flour onto a work surface and set one of the dough pieces on top. Sprinkle a little more flour on top of the dough and with a rolling pin, roll the dough into a circular tortilla shape that is about 8 inches in diameter. As you're rolling out the

tortilla, keep adding small bits of flour as needed, but not too much because excess flour will burn in the pan.

7. After rolling out 2 or 3 tortillas it's time to start cooking them one at a time in the pan. Add a small dollop (about ½ teaspoon) of coconut oil to the center of the hot skillet and lay a tortilla on top. Cook until the bottom of the tortilla starts to brown, usually when the top is bubbling up. Flip and cook for another 1 or 2 minutes, until cooked through. Transfer to a tortilla warmer (or a platter, covering the topmost tortilla with a towel) to keep them warm while you finish cooking the rest of the tortillas. After a little bit of practice, you can roll out the next tortilla while one is cooking in the pan.

8. Serve warm or store in a plastic bag in the fridge for 3 to 4 days or the freezer for a few months.

NOTE: You could substitute pastured lard for the coconut oil, which I often do.

TORTILLA-MAKING TEMPERATURE

The right temperature is critical for making both whole-wheat and corn tortillas, and it may take some practice to find just the right setting on your stove. Cast-iron skillets retain a lot of heat and are therefore slow to react to changes in your dial setting. If the tortillas are bubbling up right away, your pan is too hot. If they're taking more than several minutes to cook per side, the heat is too low and the tortillas will be stiff.

Corn Tortillas

This is a basic recipe for corn tortillas right off the Bob's Red Mill bag of masa harina (corn flour), and since it's a staple in our house I felt it should be included here. I find homemade corn tortillas to be much easier and quicker to make than flour tortillas (which I roll out with a rolling pin) because the tortilla press does most of the work for you. And once you've tried these hot off the stove you'll be amazed at how much better they are than the factory-made version! They make our Breakfast Tacos (page 147) and Taco Night! (page 264) just perfect.

Difficulty: Advanced
Prep and Cook Time: 30 minutes
Makes 14 tortillas
Special tools needed: Tortilla press (or rolling pin) and cast-iron skillet

GLUTEN-FREE
DAIRY-FREE (IF COCONUT OIL IS USED IN PLACE OF GHEE)
VEGETARIAN
FREEZER FRIENDLY

2 cups masa harina (whole corn flour, found in the baking aisle—not to be confused with cornmeal)

¾ teaspoon salt

About 1½ cups warm water

Ghee (clarified butter; see page 144), or other high-temperature cooking fat, for cooking

1. In a large mixing bowl, use a fork to whisk together the masa harina and salt.

2. Pour in 1¼ to 1½ cups warm water, or just enough for the dough to come together. Mix thoroughly with a large spoon and if the dough

is too wet (i.e., sticks to your finger after touching it), add 1 or 2 more tablespoons masa harina. If the dough is too dry (i.e., falling apart and crumbly), add a tablespoon or two more water.

3. Squeeze the dough together with your hands and transfer it to a cutting board. Roll the dough into the shape of a log and cut it into 14 equal pieces (I start by cutting it down the middle). Cover with plastic wrap or a clean dish towel to keep from drying out.

4. Set up the tortilla press by placing it on a dish towel and covering both the top and bottom of the press with plastic wrap to avoid sticking. (I like to use two long pieces of plastic wrap so that I can tie knots around the back of the press to keep the plastic in place.)

5. Heat a cast-iron skillet over medium-high heat. It's important to let the pan heat up thoroughly before you start cooking the tortillas. When the pan is ready, it should be smoking a little. Turn on an exhaust fan or open some windows to keep your smoke alarm quiet.

6. Place a single piece of dough onto the tortilla press and press the handle down firmly to flatten the dough. Flip the tortilla over (or rotate it 180 degrees) and press again to ensure even thickness.

7. Add about 1 teaspoon of ghee to the hot cast-iron skillet and toss in the first tortilla. I can fit two tortillas in my skillet at one time. Cook for 1 minute and then flip to the other side. After another 1 or 2 minutes the tortilla should be cooked all the way through and be bound together (no longer look doughy). If it takes longer than that to cook, then turn up the heat slightly (see page 328 for more on cooking tortillas).

8. Repeat for the remaining dough pieces, using an additional teaspoon of ghee for each new tortilla. As you cook, keep the finished tortillas warm in a tortilla warmer or cover them with a towel until finished. Serve immediately or store in a plastic bag in the fridge for 3 to 4 days or the freezer for a few months.

Whole-Wheat Breadcrumbs

Have you ever noticed how many ingredients are in a canister of conventional breadcrumbs at the grocery store? More than thirty! And that usually includes high-fructose corn syrup and partially hydrogenated vegetable oil (aka trans fat). Why do store-bought breadcrumbs contain so many ingredients when it takes only four or five common ingredients to make good-quality bread at home? I say skip the highly processed stuff and instead try out this quick and easy method for making your own homemade breadcrumbs. If you are in need of Italian breadcrumbs, simply add a couple teaspoons of dried Italian seasoning and a few shakes of salt before baking.

Difficulty: Easy
Prep Time: 5 minutes
Bake Time: Less than 25 minutes
Makes 2 to 3 cups breadcrumbs
Special tools needed: Food processor, large baking sheet

GLUTEN-FREE (IF GLUTEN-FREE BREAD IS USED)
DAIRY-FREE
VEGETARIAN
FREEZER FRIENDLY

6 slices Everyday Whole-Wheat Bread (page 332) or good-quality store-bought whole-wheat bread

1. Preheat the oven to 300°F.

2. In a food processor, grind the bread until crumbly. Spread the crumbs in an even layer on a rimmed baking sheet and bake for 20 to 22 minutes, or until golden brown, stirring after about 10 minutes and then again at 15 minutes to ensure that they cook evenly. Cool and store in an airtight container in the freezer for maximum freshness.

Everyday Whole-Wheat Bread

GUEST RECIPE BY CARRIE VITT

Difficulty: Advanced
Prep Time: More than 1 hour
Bake Time: 20 Minutes
Makes 2 loaves (2 pounds each)
Special tools needed: Rolling pin, baking sheet, parchment paper

DAIRY-FREE (IF BUTTER IS OMITTED)
VEGETARIAN
FREEZER FRIENDLY

1/3 cup butter (optional)

2½ cups warm water (not above 120°F)

1/3 cup honey

1 tablespoon plus 1½ teaspoons active-dry yeast

7 cups white whole-wheat flour, divided, plus more if needed

1 tablespoon sea salt (Celtic brand recommended)

This is a guest recipe from Carrie Vitt, author of Deliciously Organic *(deliciouslyorganic.net), also known as my friend and as the food photographer for this beautiful cookbook! Carrie began her journey toward organic, unprocessed foods in 2003 when she discovered that her debilitating migraines were caused by the pesticides, herbicides, and hormones found in the conventional foods she was eating. Through eating organic, unprocessed food, her family was able to overcome severe asthma, eczema, irritable bowel syndrome, and migraines. I knew I wanted to provide a basic sandwich bread recipe that didn't require a bread machine for all those just starting on their own real-food journey, and since Carrie already has a foolproof recipe of her own, I thought, why mess with success?*

Carrie has since switched to a completely Paleo diet (no grains at all!) to help control her autoimmune disorder, Hashimoto's. Be sure to check out her blog for all the details!

1. Melt the butter, if using, over low heat in a small saucepan. In a large bowl, stir together the melted butter, warm water, honey, yeast, and 3 cups of the flour. Cover the bowl with a dish towel and set in a warm, draft-free area for 30 minutes.

2. Line a baking sheet with parchment paper. Uncover the bowl and add the remaining 4 cups flour and the salt. Stir until just combined and then pour the mixture onto a floured, flat surface.

3. Knead the dough with your hands for 1 minute (if the dough is a bit sticky, add a tablespoon or two of flour). Cut the dough in half. Use a rolling pin to roll the first half into a 12 x 9-inch (approximate) rectangle and then use your hands to roll it up the long way, forming a 12-inch-long loaf. Place the loaf seam side down on the prepared baking sheet. Repeat with the rest of the dough, ensuring the loaves don't touch. Place the dish towel over the loaves and let them rise again in a warm, draft-free area for about 30 minutes, or until they double in size.

4. Preheat the oven to 350°F and adjust the rack into the middle position.

5. After the dough has risen, remove the towel and bake the loaves for 20 to 22 minutes, or until golden brown. Another way to tell if the bread is ready is to thump the bread with your finger. If it makes a hollow sound, the bread is ready. Cool for 5 minutes before serving.

NOTE FROM CARRIE: It's best if this recipe is made with white whole-wheat flour from white wheat berries (King Arthur brand or freshly ground recommended). I've found that Bob's Red Mill whole-wheat flour from red wheat berries, along with other white whole-wheat flours, produces a denser bread.

Berry Sauce

Difficulty: Easy
Prep and Cook Time: Less than 10 minutes
Seasonal Note: Freeze locally grown berries (in a single layer, then transfer to a freezer-proof container) in the spring and summer months for this recipe.
Makes 2/3 cup
Special tools needed: Countertop blender, handheld immersion blender, or food processor

GLUTEN-FREE
DAIRY-FREE
VEGETARIAN

1 cup frozen berries (any variety or a mix)

2 tablespoons pure maple syrup

This is a versatile sauce that can be mixed into plain yogurt, poured over homemade ice cream (see page 290), or used to flavor a plain glass of milk (my nine-year-old's favorite!). Use whatever frozen berries you have on hand or feel free to experiment with a different fruit altogether, such as peaches!

1. Combine the berries and syrup with 3 tablespoons water in small saucepan over medium-low heat. Bring to a low simmer and cook until the berries have softened, 5 to 7 minutes.

2. Puree the mixture using a blender or food processor. Cool and then pour over yogurt or ice cream or, using a sieve, remove the seeds and pour a few teaspoons into a glass of milk. The sauce can be stored in the fridge for 4 to 5 days.

LISA'S TIP: If you don't want to wait for the sauce to cool before using, then omit the water and instead add 1 or 2 ice cubes during the pureeing process.

Pure Vanilla Extract

It's amazing how the food industry can "junk up" something as simple as vanilla extract. If you're buying yours from the store be sure to read the ingredients because you might find some surprising (and unnecessary) extras in there, such as corn syrup. Not only is homemade vanilla extract incredibly simple to make, but it can also make for some really beautiful and unique holiday gifts (in pretty glass jars from the craft store).

You can find vanilla beans in the spice section of the grocery store, but you'll likely find them online for less money. Use this extract as a 1:1 replacement for store-bought extract.

Difficulty: Easy
Prep Time: Less than 5 minutes (plus allow several weeks for the vodka to infuse)
Makes approximately 1½ cups

GLUTEN-FREE
DAIRY-FREE
VEGETARIAN

2 vanilla beans

One 375-milliliter bottle mid-grade vodka

1. Using a sharp knife, split each vanilla bean in half down the middle.

2. Add the sliced beans to the vodka bottle. Secure the lid and store the jar in your pantry for a couple of weeks, until the liquid starts to turn brown; then it's ready to use.

Simple Chocolate Sauce

6 tablespoons pure maple syrup

3 tablespoons unsweetened cocoa (I prefer the "special dark" variety)

Whether you are looking for something to drizzle over homemade ice cream (see page 290) or stir into a cup of warm milk to make hot chocolate, this simple chocolate sauce is your answer! I also use this sauce to make my morning "maple mocha" drink. Recipes don't get much easier than this.

Difficulty: Easy
Prep Time: 5 minutes
Makes (a little more than) ½ cup

GLUTEN-FREE
DAIRY-FREE
VEGETARIAN

Whisk the maple syrup and cocoa together in a small bowl continuously until the sauce appears to be wet and all the lumps are gone; it could take several minutes to come together. Store leftovers in the fridge for up to 1 week and stir before each use.

HOT CHOCOLATE OR MOCHA

Mix 1 to 2 heaping teaspoons of Simple Chocolate Sauce with ¾ cup warm milk to make hot chocolate. To make a "maple mocha" drink, add a shot of espresso to the hot chocolate mixture.

Homemade Whipped Cream

I understand that it's convenient to buy Cool Whip, but it tastes nothing like real whipped cream and it contains quite a few questionable ingredients (such as high-fructose corn syrup, hydrogenated oils, and artificial flavor). Making your own whipped cream may sound daunting, but if you have an electric mixer it's actually very quick and easy. Plus you can control the amount and type of sweetener you add, if you add any at all. I sometimes use whipped cream in place of traditional cupcake frosting and also on top of hot chocolate . . . yum!

Difficulty: Easy
Prep Time: Less than 10 minutes
Makes 2 to 2½ cups
Special tools needed: Electric mixer with whisk attachment

GLUTEN-FREE
VEGETARIAN

1 cup heavy whipping cream

1 to 2 tablespoons pure maple syrup or honey (depending on how sweet you like it)

1 teaspoon Pure Vanilla Extract (page 337) or store-bought vanilla extract

1. In a large bowl, combine the cream, syrup (or honey), and vanilla. Beat on high speed with an electric mixer for 2 to 3 minutes, until soft peaks form.

2. Serve immediately or store in the refrigerator in an airtight container for up to 3 days.

Universal Conversion Chart

Oven temperature equivalents

250°F = 120°C
275°F = 135°C
300°F = 150°C
325°F = 160°C
350°F = 180°C
375°F = 190°C
400°F = 200°C
425°F = 220°C
450°F = 230°C
475°F = 240°C
500°F = 260°C

Measurement equivalents

Measurements should always be level unless directed otherwise

⅛ teaspoon = 0.5 ml
¼ teaspoon = 1 ml
½ teaspoon = 2 ml
1 teaspoon = 5 ml
1 tablespoon = 3 teaspoons = ½ fluid ounce = 15 ml
2 tablespoons = ⅓ cup = 1 fluid ounce = 30 ml
4 tablespoons = ¼ cup = 2 fluid ounces = 60 ml
5⅓ tablespoons = ⅓ cup = 3 fluid ounces = 80 ml
8 tablespoons = ½ cup = 4 fluid ounces = 120 ml
10⅔ tablespoons = ⅔ cup = 5 fluid ounces = 160 ml
12 tablespoons = ¾ cup = 6 fluid ounces = 180 ml
16 tablespoons = 1 cup = 8 fluid ounces = 240 ml

List of Recipes by Dietary Need

GLUTEN-FREE

Apple Sandwich
Asian-Inspired Rice
Asian Lettuce Wraps
BBQ Chicken Quesadillas
Berry Sauce
The Best Pulled Pork in the Slow Cooker
The Best Whole Chicken in the Slow Cooker
Black Bean Tostada
Breakfast Sausage Casserole
Breakfast Tacos
Cajun Alfredo with Shrimp
Carrots with Rosemary
Cinnamon Apple Chips
Cinnamon-Glazed Popcorn
Corn Tortillas
Easy Slow-Cooker Refried Beans
(Extra) Dark Chocolate Peanut Butter Bites
Frozen Yogurt Pops Two Ways
Fruit Kabobs with Yogurt Dip
Fruit Salad with Orange Zest
Goat Cheese, Pear, and Pecan Salad
Grilled Caprese Paninis
Grilled Cheese with Apples and Bacon
Grilled Teriyaki Salmon
Grilled Veggie Kabobs
Guacamole with Bell Pepper "Chips"
Homemade Chicken Noodle Soup
Homemade Dried Onion Soup Mix
Homemade Granola Cereal
Homemade Ice Cream Three Ways
Homemade Tomato Sauce
Homemade Whipped Cream
How to Make the Perfect Juice—Three Ways
Hummus Sandwiches Three Ways
Jason's Grass-Fed Burgers
Mango Sorbet
Mini Chocolate Truffles
Mint Chocolate Chunk Ice Cream
Mustard Vinaigrette
My Dad's (Brown Rice) Risotto
Oatmeal
Onion Dip with Veggie Sticks
Overnight Chicken Stock in the Slow Cooker
PB&J Smoothie
The Perfect Omelet
Pimento Cheese Crackers
Popcorn: Microwave or Stovetop
Potato Hash (for Breakfast or Dinner!)
Pure Vanilla Extract
Quinoa and Sausage-Stuffed Peppers
Shortcut Caesar Salad
Sienna's Purple Potion Smoothie
Simple Chocolate Sauce
Slow-Cooker BBQ Ribs
Slow-Cooker Flank Steak Fajitas
Slow-Cooker Pollo al Disco
Slow-Cooker Potato Soup
Spiced Nut Mix
Spinach Salad with Warm Bacon Dressing
Sunday Brunch: Eggs Benedict with Kale
Sweet and Tangy BBQ Sauce
Sydney's Honey Mustard Sauce
Taco Night!
Tahini Dressing
Teriyaki Flank Steak Salad
Teriyaki Marinade
Vegetable Chili
White Bean Dip
Whole-Wheat Breadcrumbs
Whole-Wheat Pasta with Kale-Pesto Cream Sauce

Zucchini with Almonds and Parmesan

DAIRY-FREE

Apple Sandwich
Asian-Inspired Rice
Asian Lettuce Wraps
Berry Sauce
The Best Pulled Pork in the Slow Cooker
The Best Whole Chicken in the Slow Cooker
Carrots with Rosemary
Cinnamon Apple Chips
Corn Tortillas
Easy Slow-Cooker Refried Beans
Eggs in a Basket
Everyday Whole-Wheat Bread
(Extra) Dark Chocolate Peanut Butter Bites
Goat Cheese, Pear, and Pecan Salad
Grilled Teriyaki Salmon
Grilled Veggie Kabobs
Guacamole with Bell Pepper "Chips"
Homemade Chicken Noodle Soup
Homemade Dried Onion Soup Mix
Homemade Granola Cereal
Homemade Tomato Sauce
How to Make the Perfect Juice—Three Ways
Hummus Sandwiches Three Ways
Mango Sorbet
Mini Chocolate Truffles
Mustard Vinaigrette
Oatmeal
Overnight Chicken Stock in the Slow Cooker
Popcorn: Microwave or Stovetop
Potato Hash (for Breakfast or Dinner!)
Pure Vanilla Extract
Simple Chocolate Sauce
Simple Seafood
Slow-Cooker BBQ Ribs
Slow-Cooker Flank Steak Fajitas
Slow-Cooker Pollo al Disco
Spiced Nut Mix
Spinach Salad with Warm Bacon Dressing
Sweet and Tangy BBQ Sauce
Sydney's Honey Mustard Sauce
Taco Night!
Tahini Dressing
Teriyaki Flank Steak Salad
Teriyaki Marinade
Vegetable Chili
Veggie Pancakes
White Bean Dip
Whole-Wheat Breadcrumbs
Whole-Wheat Tortillas

VEGETARIAN

Apple Sandwich
Asian-Inspired Rice
Basic Cheese Sauce
Berry Sauce
Black Bean Tostada
Breakfast Tacos
Carrot Cake with Whipped Cream-Cheese Frosting
Carrots with Rosemary
Cheesy Broccoli Rice Casserole
Cinnamon Apple Chips
Cinnamon-Glazed Popcorn
Cinnamon-Raisin Quick Bread
Corn Tortillas
Easy Slow-Cooker Refried Beans
Eggs in a Basket
Everyday Whole-Wheat Bread
(Extra) Dark Chocolate Peanut Butter Bites
Frozen Yogurt Pops Two Ways
Fruit Kabobs with Yogurt Dip
Fruit Salad with Orange Zest
Goat Cheese, Pear, and Pecan Salad
Grandma Esther's (Whole-Wheat) Crepes
Greek Stuffed Pitas
Grilled Caprese Paninis
Grilled Cheese with Apples and Bacon
Grilled Veggie Kabobs
Guacamole with Bell Pepper "Chips"
Homemade Cream of Mushroom Soup
Homemade Dried Onion Soup Mix
Homemade Granola Cereal
Homemade Ice Cream Three Ways
Homemade Tomato Sauce
Homemade Whipped Cream
How to Make the Perfect Juice—Three Ways
Hummus Sandwiches Three Ways
Macaroni Casserole
Mango Sorbet
Mini Chocolate Truffles
Mini Lunch Box Quiches
Mint Chocolate Chunk Ice Cream
Mustard Vinaigrette
My Dad's (Brown Rice) Risotto
Oatmeal
Onion Dip with Veggie Sticks
PB&J Smoothie
Peanut Butter Cookies

The Perfect Omelet
Pimento Cheese Crackers
Pizza Bites
Polenta with Mushroom Bordelaise Sauce
Popcorn: Microwave or Stovetop
Potato Hash (for Breakfast or Dinner!)
Pure Vanilla Extract
Quinoa Veggie "Burgers"
Shortcut Caesar Salad
Shortcut Eggplant Parmesan
Sienna's Purple Potion Smoothie
Simple Chocolate Sauce
Slow Cooker Potato Soup
Spiced Nut Mix
Sunday Brunch: Eggs Benedict with Kale
Super-Easy Whole-Wheat Biscuits
Sweet and Tangy BBQ Sauce
Sydney's Honey Mustard Sauce
Tahini Dressing
Teriyaki Marinade
Tomato Bisque
Vegetable Chili
Veggie Corn Chowder
Veggie Pancakes
White Bean Dip
Whole-Grain Pumpkin Muffins
Whole-Wheat Banana Pancakes (or Waffles!)
Whole-Wheat Breadcrumbs
Whole-Wheat Bread Pudding
Whole-Wheat Pasta with Kale-Pesto Cream Sauce
Whole-Wheat Pizza
Whole-Wheat Tortillas
Zucchini with Almonds and Parmesan

FREEZER FRIENDLY

Asian Lettuce Wraps
The Best Pulled Pork in the Slow Cooker
The Best Whole Chicken in the Slow Cooker
Breakfast Tacos
Carrot Cake with Whipped Cream-Cheese Frosting
Cinnamon-Raisin Quick Bread
Corn Tortillas
Easy Slow-Cooker Refried Beans
Everyday Whole-Wheat Bread
(Extra) Dark Chocolate Peanut Butter Bites
Frozen Yogurt Pops Two Ways
Grandma Esther's (Whole-Wheat) Crepes
Homemade Chicken Noodle Soup
Homemade Chicken Nuggets
Homemade Cream of Mushroom Soup
Homemade Granola Cereal
Homemade Ice Cream Three Ways
Homemade Tomato Sauce
Jason's Grass-Fed Burgers
Mango Sorbet
Mini Lunch Box Quiches
Mint Chocolate Chunk Ice Cream
Overnight Chicken Stock in the Slow Cooker
PB&J Smoothie
Peanut Butter Cookies
Pizza Bites
Quinoa Veggie "Burgers"
Sienna's Purple Potion Smoothie
Slow-Cooker Pollo al Disco
Slow-Cooker Potato Soup
Super-Easy Whole-Wheat Biscuits
Taco Night!
Tomato Bisque
Vegetable Chili
Veggie Corn Chowder
Veggie Pancakes
Whole-Grain Pumpkin Muffins
Whole-Wheat Banana Pancakes (or Waffles!)
Whole-Wheat Breadcrumbs
Whole-Wheat Pizza
Whole-Wheat Spaghetti and Meatballs
Whole-Wheat Tortillas

Notes

CHAPTER 1: WHAT IS REAL FOOD?

1. *product of industry:* Michael Pollan, *In Defense of Food*, 143.
2. *has more than tripled:* Centers for Disease Control and Prevention, http://www.cdc.gov/healthyyouth/obesity/facts.htm
3. *our children have:* Jamie Oliver, TED Talk, http://www.ted.com/talks/lang/en/jamie_oliver.html
4. *can be traced directly:* Michael Pollan, *In Defense of Food,* 10.
5. *90 percent of processed foods: Food, Inc.*
6. *product ingredient list:* naturesownbread.com
7. *most of the grain's: American Journal of Clinical Nutrition,* http://www.ajcn.org/content/78/3/508S.full
8. *Less than a hundred years:* Michael Pollan, *In Defense of Food*, 21, 66.
9. *In 2003 the American Journal of Clinical Nutrition:* Michael Pollan, *In Defense of Food,* 110.
10. *the big packet of:* Michael Pollan, *In Defense of Food,* 108.
11. *The Whole Grain Stamp:* Whole Grains Council http://www.wholegrainscouncil.org/whole-grain-stamp
12. *Gluten-free whole grains:* Whole Grains Council, http://www.wholegrainscouncil.org/whole-grains-101/gluten-free-whole-grains
13. *nearly 130 pounds: 60 Minutes*, http://www.cbsnews.com/8301-18560_162-57407294/is-sugar-toxic/?tag=-contentMain;contentBody
14. *recommended daily amount:* American Heart Association, http://www.heart.org/HEARTORG/GettingHealthy/NutritionCenter/HealthyDietGoals/Sugars-and-Carbohydrates_UCM_303296_Article.jsp and http://circ.ahajournals.org/content/120/11/1011.full.pdf
15. *Added sugar . . is:* Mark Bittman, http://opinionator.blogs.nytimes.com/2012/06/05/what-is-food/?smid=tw-bittman&seid=auto
16. *The recommended daily allowance:* The Sugar Association, http://www.sugar.org/nutritional-advocacy/artificial-sweetener-labeling-initiative.html
17. *Thirty years ago:* Ibid.
18. *Some examples of added sugar:* Ibid.
19. *right amount of fiber: 60 Minutes*, http://www.cbsnews.com/8301-18560_162-57407294/is-sugar-toxic/?tag=contentMain;contentBody
20. *Naturally occurring sugars:* Ibid.
21. *An 8-ounce serving of Horizon Organic:* http://www.horizondairy.com/products/milk-boxes/lowfat-plain-milk-box/
22. *A 6-ounce serving of:* http://yoplait.com/products/yoplait-original-style
23. *They're made in a lab:* NPR.org, http://www.npr.org/2011/03/30/134962888/fda-probes-link-between-food-dyes-kids-behavior
24. *They've been linked:* CSPINet.org, http://www.cspinet.org/new/201006291.html
25. *Synthetic food dyes:* WashingtonPost.com, http://www.washingtonpost.com/opinions/the-rainbow-of-food-dyes-in-our-grocery-aisles-has-a-dark-side/2011/03/21/AFyIwaYB_story_1.html
26. *a warning label is required:* CBSnews.com, http://www.cbsnews.com/8301-505123_162-44042813/fda-hears-from-critics-on-artificial-food-dyes-next-step-ignore-them/?tag=bnetdomain
27. *They add absolutely no:* CSPINet.org, http://www.cspinet.org/new/201006291.html
28. *They confuse the senses:* Michael Pollan, *In Defense of Food*, 149.
29. *They contribute to:* WashingtonPost.com, http://www.washingtonpost.com/opinions/the-rainbow

-of-food-dyes-in-our-grocery-aisles-has-a-dark -side/2011/03/21/AFyIwaYB_story_1.html

30. *The low-fat craze:* Mark Bittman, *Food Matters*, 88.
31. *a government commission:* 60 Minutes, http://www .cbsnews.com/8301-18560_162-57407294/is-sugar -toxic/?tag=contentMain;contentBody
32. *To make dairy products:* Michael Pollan, *In Defense of Food*, 153–54.
33. *anticaking agent: Wall Street Journal*, http://online.wsj .com/article/SB10001424052748703834804576300991196803916.html
34. *You are what:* Michael Pollan, *In Defense of Food*, 167.
35. *the diet of the:* Michael Pollan, *Food Rules*, 61.
36. *stimulated a fundamental:* Mark Bittman, *Food Matters*, 2–3.
37. *GMOs, or genetically modified organisms:* http://www .nongmoproject.org/learn-more/what-is-gmo/
38. *are currently labeled in more than:* Robyn O'Brien, http:// www.100daysofrealfood.com/2013/02/01/interview-robyn-obrien-the-unhealthy-truth-part-ii/
39. *these refined oils are "cleaned":* Sallie Fallon, *Nourishing Traditions*, 13–14.
40. *"Breaking Down the Different Types of Fats in Your Food"* (chart), Sally Fallon, *Nourishing Traditions*, 8–15.
41. *chemically extracted or:* Melanie Warner, *Pandora's Lunchbox*, 140–41.
42. *when hydrogen is added:* FDA, http://www.fda.gov/ food/ingredientspackaginglabeling/labelingnutrition/ ucm274590.htm#whatis
43. *statistics show:* Ibid.
44. *If a product contains:* FDA.gov, http://www.fda.gov/Food/ ResourcesForYou/Consumers/NFLPM/ucm274590 .htm#after
45. *Pepperidge Farm Goldfish Crackers:* http://www.campbell foodservice.com/details.aspx?code=272
46. *Aunt Jemima Original Pancake & Waffle Mix:* http://www .auntjemima.com/aj_products/pancakeMixes/orginal .cfm
47. *Campbell's Healthy Request Tomato Soup:* http://www .campbellfoodservice.com/details.aspx?code=276
48. *Quaker Instant Oatmeal, Strawberries & Cream:* http:// www.quakeroats.com/products/oatmeal/instant-oat meal/strawberries-and-cream.aspx
49. *Cheerios:* http://www.cheerios.com/Products/Cheerios
50. *Jell-O Sugar-Free Strawberry:* http://www.kraftbrands .com/Jello/products/gelatin/desserts/
51. *Clif Bar Carrot Cake:* http://www.clifbar.com/food/ products_clif_bar/
52. *Oreos:* http://www.nabiscoworld.com/Brands/Product Information.aspx?BrandKey=oreo&Site=1&Product =4400000820
53. *Powerade Mountain Berry Blast:* www.us.powerade.com
54. *Minute Maid Lemonade:* colacompany.com/products/ minute-maid-lemonade#ingredients
55. *Special K Cereal:* http://www.specialk.com/cereals/ original/
56. *Earth Balance Original Buttery Spread:* http://www .earthbalancenatural.com/product/original-buttery -spread/
57. *Trader Joe's Multigrain Crackers:* Trader Joe's store in Charlotte, NC
58. *Yoplait Light Fat Free Strawberry (Yogurt):* http://www .amazon.com/Yoplait-Yogurt-Strawberry-Light-6 -Ounce/dp/B001UHZAN4
59. Snyder's *Eatsmart Naturals Garden Veggie Sticks:* http:// www.eatsmartnaturals.com/
60. *Back to Nature Crispy Wheat Crackers:* http://www .backtonaturefoods.com/product-detail.aspx?category =crackers&productname=Crispy-Wheats&product =5928310004
61. *Jif Natural Creamy Peanut Butter Spread:* http://www.jif .com/Products/Details?categoryId=339&productId =954
62. *Annie's Classic Macaroni and Cheese:* http://www.annies .com/products/Natural-Mac-Cheese
63. *Annie's Cheddar Bunnies:* http://www.annies.com/ products/Cheddar-Bunnies
64. *Pirate's Booty:* http://piratebrands.com/products/pirates booty/agedwhitecheddar
65. *Per USDA guidelines:* USDA.gov, http://www.ams.usda .gov/AMSv1.0/ams.fetchTemplateData.do?template= TemplateC&navID=NationalOrganicProgram&left Nav=NationalOrganicProgram&page=NOPConsumers &description=Consumers&acct=nopgeninfo and http:// blogs.usda.gov/2012/04/26/organic-101-the-lifecycle -of-organic-food-production/
66. *As required by the USDA:* FDA.gov, http://www.fda .gov/Food/ResourcesForYou/Consumers/NFLPM/ ucm274590.htm#after
67. *GMOs (Genetically Modified Organisms) are man-made:* Robyn O'Brien, http://www.100daysofrealfood.com/ 2013/02/01/interview-robyn-obrien-the-unhealthy -truth-part-ii/
68. *if a product contains 0.5g:* FDA.gov, http://www.fda .gov/Food/ResourcesForYou/Consumers/NFLPM/ ucm274590.htm#after

69. *The regulations on these claims:* Center for Science in the Public Interest, http://www.cspinet.org/nah/05_06/grains.pdf
70. *This claim identifies products:* Whole Grains Council, http://wholegrainscouncil.org/whole-grains-101/gluten-free-whole-grains
71. *This is a process in which:* International Dairy Foods Association, http://www.idfa.org/news--views/media-kits/milk/pasteurization
72. *The product is termed:* Ibid.
73. *The fat particles of cream:* Sally Fallon, *Nourishing Traditions*, 15.
74. *rBGH and rBST are genetically engineered:* Grist.org, http://grist.org/article/food-2010-10-06-court-rules-on-rbgh-free-milk/
75. *the USDA has not developed a federal definition:* FDA.gov, http://www.fda.gov/Food/ResourcesForYou/Consumers/NFLPM/ucm274590.htm#after
76. *As of this writing (2014):* http://www.ams.usda.gov/AMSv1.0/getfile?dDocName=STELPRDC5063842
77. *Federal regulations have never:* Ibid.
78. *Nitrate and nitrite have: New York Times*, http://www.nytimes.com/2011/07/02/business/02hotdog.html
79. *This label indicates that:* Ibid.
80. *This label indicates that:* Ibid.
81. *this label does not indicate*: Humane Society, http://www.humanesociety.org/issues/confinement_farm/facts/guide_egg_labels.html
82. *"Wild-Caught" fish have:* Michael Pollan, *In Defense of Food*, 167.
83. *These fish are raised in controlled:* Food & Water Watch, https://www.foodandwaterwatch.org/fish/fish-farming/
84. *For example, the only "fruit":* Food Navigator-USA, http://www.foodnavigator-usa.com/Regulation/General-Mills-must-defend-made-with-real-fruit-claim-for-Fruit-Roll-Ups-court-rules
85. *have been linked to:* National Center for Biotechnology Information, www.ncbi.nlm.nih.gov/pubmed/17805418
86. *Regulated by the American Heart Association:* http://www.heart.org/HEARTORG/GettingHealthy/NutritionCenter/HeartSmartShopping/Heart-Check-Mark-Nutritional-Guidelines_UCM_300914_Article.jsp
87. *Robyn O'Brien explains:* http://www.100daysofrealfood.com/2013/01/25/interview-robyn-obrien-the-unhealthy-truth/
88. *Gluten-free whole grains:* Whole Grains Council, http://wholegrainscouncil.org/whole-grains-101/gluten-free-whole-grains

CHAPTER 2: SHOPPING FOR REAL FOOD

1. *Freezing does not:* Michael Pollan, *Food Rules*, 63.
2. *Dirty Dozen List:* Environmental Working Group, http://www.ewg.org/foodnews/summary/
3. *avoid food products:* Michael Pollan, *Food Rules*, 19.
4. *Fifteen hundred miles:* Michael Pollan, *In Defense of Food*, 157–58.
5. *According to Indian crop ecologist:* Barbara Kingsolver, *Animal, Vegetable, Miracle*, 49.

CHAPTER 3: MAKING CHANGES: DON'T OVERTHINK, JUST START!

1. *in one scientific study*: Karen Le Billon, *French Kids Eat Everything*, 162.
2. *the size of a hamburger has tripled*: CDC http://shine.yahoo.com/healthy-living/cdc-infographic-shows-super-sized-portions-normal-185000601.html
3. *instead of using our internal cues:* Michael Pollan, *In Defense of Food*, 193.
4. *As soon as they got home:* Melanie Warner, *Pandora's Lunchbox*, 208–14.
5. *powerful quote from Dr. Kenneth A. Bock:* Robyn O'Brien, *The Unhealthy Truth*, ix–x.

CHAPTER 4: GETTING YOUR FAMILY ON BOARD

1. *Advice from the French:* Karen Le Billon, *French Kids Eat Everything*, back cover.
2. *Where's the Protein*: http://www.cdc.gov/nutrition/everyone/basics/protein.html

CHAPTER 5: FOOD BUDGET TIPS AND MEAL PLANS

1. *In 1960 Americans:* Michael Pollan, *In Defense of Food*, 187–88.
2. full *food stamp (SNAP) benefits:* USDA, http://www.fns.usda.gov/snap/applicant_recipients/eligibility.htm

Real-Food References

BOOKS

Bittman, Mark. *Food Matters: A Guide to Conscious Eating.* New York: Simon & Schuster, 2009.

Fallon, Sally. *Nourishing Traditions*. Washington, D.C.: NewTrends Publishing, Inc., 1999.

Kingsolver, Barbara, Stevel L. Hopp, and Camille Kingsolver. *Animal, Vegetable, Miracle: A Year of Food Life.* New York: HarperCollins Publishers, 2007.

Le Billon, Karen. *French Kids Eat Everything.* New York: William Morrow, 2012.

O'Brien, Robyn. *The Unhealthy Truth. New York*: Harmony, 2010.

Pollan, Michael. *Food Rules: An Eater's Manual.* New York: Penguin Books, 2009.

Pollan, Michael. *In Defense of Food: An Eater's Manifesto.* New York: Penguin Books, 2008.

Warner, Melanie. *Pandora's Lunchbox: How Processed Food Took Over the American Meal.* New York: Scribner, 2014.

DOCUMENTARY FILM

Fed Up, Katie Couric and Laurie David (producers), 2014.

Food, Inc., Robert Kenner (director), 2008.

WEB SITES AND BLOGS

cspinet.org
deliciouslyorganic.net
eatingrules.com
eatwild.com
ewg.org/foodnews/summary.php (Dirty Dozen List)
foodbabe.com
localharvest.org
100daysofrealfood.com
superhealthykids.com
takepart.com
thefresh20.com

Acknowledgments

Writing a book truly takes a village, and I would be remiss if I didn't (attempt) to thank everyone who played a part in making this "third baby" of mine come to fruition.

To Jason, I love you so much and can't thank you enough for being an amazing partner in all aspects of my life, including this book (and the blog that helped make it a reality). I most certainly lucked out in the husband department. To my daughters, Sydney and Sienna, who I love unconditionally and who also happen to be the best taste-testers on the planet!

To my parents, who provide me with the kind of support any daughter would hope for. I can always count on them to read every article, watch every news clip, and provide encouragement (and advice!) whenever needed. To other family members whose support I've greatly appreciated along the way, including Mark, Cindi, Maggie, Jessica, Richard, Robin, Karen, Grandma Esther, Grace, Wyatt, and my aunts and uncles and cousins, including Diane, for her help early on, and Adam and Rupel, for taking the 10 Days of Real Food Pledge!

To my wonderful BFF, Jenn, for dropping everything in order to support me (on more than one occasion!) and for often being my biggest cheerleader. To my dear friend Valerie and the whole Sappenfield clan, for never getting tired of blog talk or recipe testing. To my talented friend Heidi, for helping with the pictures and for putting me in touch with my rock star literary agent (who was also recommended to me by Harriet Bell—it was a sign!).

To my agent, Meg Thompson, for giving me the exact push I needed early on, and to Cassie Jones, for holding my hand through this first book; I would have been completely lost without you and your talented team, including Kara Zauberman, Megan Swartz, Liate Stehlik, Lynn Grady, Tavia Kowalchuk, Joyce Wong, Lorie Pagnozzi, and Anna Brower. And to my lovely and super-organized freelance publicist, Jill Dykes.

To my other lovely girlfriends, who are always there for me. I am such a lucky girl to have Holly, Cori, Lauren, Natalie, Emily, Trang, Elizabeth, Myrtle-love, Amy B, Jamie S, Erin, Linda, Dawn, and Vani (aka Food Babe!) all on my side.

To my dinner club members (including Dan, Erik, and Alan), for allowing me to subject them to multiple photographers. And to my other adorable "models," including Kate, Sam, Sierra, and Leah.

To all my cul-de-sac neighbors, for always being willing to provide missing ingredients (which happens much more than I'd like to admit), and of course to my old neighbor Amy, for willingly taking all my processed food off my hands at the very beginning! I'll never forget.

To Kiran Dodeja Smith, Shawn Keller, and Amy Taylor for helping me keep my sanity on a daily basis. I'd add some emojicons here if I could. To Andrew Wilder for being the tech guru that showed up at the right place at the right time. To Meg Pattison Brown, for suggesting I start a blog in the first place!

To Jennifer Rothacker, for being the first member of the media to give me a chance. To Erin Chase, for always being a phone call (or message!) away from offering your expert advice, and to Bonnie Bauman for those pep talks early on. And to the rest of my blog allies—you most definitely make this world that I now call "my job" a lot more fun.

To my friend and talented food photographer, Carrie Vitt, who provided me with much more than beautiful pictures throughout this mysterious process called cookbook writing. To my other talented photographer, Kelly Trimble for capturing our family so perfectly. To so many others who helped me pull off the intense weeklong cookbook photo shoot, including Erin Rutherford (again), Erica Bloomquist, Cole Rosenbaum, Poole Shop, Luxe Home Couture, Sloan, Laura James Jewelry, Ivy Robinson Wedding and Events, Matthews Community Farmers' Market, Earth Fare, Poplar Ridge Farm, and my littlest helpers, Hannah and Abby, of course.

And above all, a big *thank you* to you for reading my blog and for buying this book. The support and positive feedback from my wonderful readers is exactly what keeps me going every single day!

RECIPE TESTERS

I cannot forget my amazing army of volunteer recipe testers! Thank you for helping make this book what it is: Mia Albano, Meghan Alpern, Kimberly Bass, Lauren Bassford, Allie Batt, Allison Baxley, Alexis Beare, Jennifer Beeman, Laura Bouchard, Kacey Bryant, Renee Carrano, Mandy Cecil, Jenni Chillstrom, Ashley Collins, Ashley Connelly, Cori Davenport, Kristy David, Natalie Demby, Erin Earp, Heidijo Elyea, Leslie Farrar, Debbie Fehr, Amy Ferezan, Jamie Flaherty, Amanda Francis, Jennifer Frechmann, Cassidy Gleaton, Sara Greene, Darby Grimmett, Cheryl Hardman, Anna Harker, Adrienne Harris, Sara Hatch, Kristin Hathaway, Lisa Haveman, Karen Hipson, Elizabeth Hutchens, Beth Jensen, Heidi Jette, Carrie Johnsen, Shawn Keller, Kristy Knipple, Beth Landis, Jessica Lawter, Carolyn Leiberher, Kate Luxon, Angela Martinez, Lindsey Miller, Jennifer Miller, Virginia Miner, Jamie Moore, Denise Mullaney, KC O'Connor, Jessica Pachler, Erika Paradis, Kathy Pinzon, Marisa Ramsey, Alison Rigsby, Audrey Rixford, Corrie Rowe, Megan Schmidt, Jodi Schweikhardt, Jessica Shortall, Hannah Siburt, Jennifer Smeth, Kiran D. Smith, Leah Stegmaier, Janet Stephan, Melody Stephens, Jamielynn Storch, Amanda Trafton, Jennifer Ward, Chris Williams, Lisa Wilson, and Donna Zittel.

Index

C

D

N

O

P

S

T

Z